The Civil Rights Movement and the Logic of Social Change

Social movements have wrought dramatic changes upon American society. This observation necessarily raises the question: Why do some movements succeed in their endeavors while others fail? This book answers this question by introducing an analytical framework that begins with a shift in emphasis away from the characteristics of movements or general political circumstances, and toward the targets of protests and affected bystanders, their interests, and why they respond as they do. Such a shift brings into focus how targets and other interests assess both their exposure to movement disruptions and the costs of conceding to movement demands. From this vantage point, diverse outcomes stem not only from a movement's capabilities for protest but also from differences among targets and others in their vulnerability to disruption and the substance of movement goals. Applied to the civil rights movement, this approach recasts conventional accounts of the movement's outcome in local struggles and national politics, and also clarifies the broader logic of social change.

Joseph E. Luders is the Gottesman Associate Professor of Political Science at Yeshiva University. His research focuses on social movements, civil rights politics and policy, and American political development.

Cambridge Studies in Contentious Politics

Editors

Other Books in the Series

Ronald Aminzade et al., *Silence and Voice in the Study of Contentious Politics*

Javier Auyero, *Routine Politics and Violence in Argentina: The Gray Zone of State Power*

Clifford Bob, *The Marketing of Rebellion: Insurgents, Media, and International Activism*

Charles Brockett, *Political Movements and Violence in Central America*

Gerald F. Davis, Doug McAdam, W. Richard Scott, and Mayer N. Zald, *Social Movements and Organization Theory*

Jack A. Goldstone, editor, *States, Parties, and Social Movements*

Doug McAdam, Sidney Tarrow, and Charles Tilly, *Dynamics of Contention*

Sharon Nepstad, *War Resistance and the Plowshares Movement*

Kevin J. O'Brien and Lianjiang Li, *Rightful Resistance in Rural China*

Silvia Pedraza, *Political Disaffection in Cuba's Revolution and Exodus*

Sidney Tarrow, *The New Transnational Activism*

Ralph Thaxton, Jr., *Catastrophe and Contention in Rural China: Mao's Great Leap Forward Famine and the Origins of Righteous Resistance in Da Fo Village*

Charles Tilly, *Contention and Democracy in Europe, 1650–2000*

Charles Tilly, *Contentious Performances*

Charles Tilly, *The Politics of Collective Violence*

Stuart A. Wright, *Patriots, Politics, and the Oklahoma City Bombing*

Deborah Yashar, *Contesting Citizenship in Latin America: The Rise of Indigenous Movements and the Postliberal Challenge*

The Civil Rights Movement and the Logic of Social Change

JOSEPH E. LUDERS

Yeshiva University

CAMBRIDGE
UNIVERSITY PRESS

CAMBRIDGE UNIVERSITY PRESS
Cambridge, New York, Melbourne, Madrid, Cape Town, Singapore,
São Paulo, Delhi, Dubai, Tokyo

Cambridge University Press
32 Avenue of the Americas, New York, NY 10013-2473, USA

www.cambridge.org
Information on this title: www.cambridge.org/9780521133395

First published 2010

Printed in the United States of America

A catalog record for this publication is available from the British Library.

Library of Congress Cataloging in Publication data
Luders, Joseph E.
The civil rights movement and the logic of social change / Joseph E. Luders.
    p.   cm. – (Cambridge studies in contentious politics)
Includes bibliographical references and index.
ISBN 978-0-521-11651-0 (hardback) – ISBN 978-0-521-13339-5 (pbk.)
1. Civil rights movements – United States.   2. African Americans – Civil rights.
3. Protest movements – United States.   4. Social change – United States.   5. United
States – Race relations.   6. United States – Social conditions – 1960–1980.   7. United
States – Politics and government – 1963–1969.   I. Title.   II. Series.
E185.61.L82   2009
323.0973–dc22   2009014706

ISBN 978-0-521-11651-0 Hardback
ISBN 978-0-521-13339-5 Paperback

To my mother and father

Sometimes we didn't know who controls this, who controls the other.

So we stomp and stomp, and see whose feet we get. And then somebody's going to holler, "Oh, you got me." So then, when he hollers, that's the direction we go in.

And that was the general strategy.

Charles Sherrod, SNCC activist

Contents

Preface

Three basic purposes motivate this book. First, I seek to refine theories of social movement outcomes. I begin with the simple proposition that, to explain movement success or failure, more attention must be devoted to explaining the behavior of movement targets and bystanders (third parties). The core argument is simple: the target of any social movement, interest organization, or other benefit-seeker must discern the threat posed to its interests and the cost of capitulating to demands, and then respond accordingly. A mugger's declaration, "Your money or your life," succinctly depicts a similar cost calculation. The transaction is coercive, but it is a transaction nevertheless. Factored into these considerations is the actual or anticipated behavior of third parties. Will anyone come to the victim's assistance? As E. E. Schattschneider (1960) famously declared, the audience to a struggle often determines the outcome. There is much truth to this axiom; however, most studies do not account for why some bystanders watch from the sidelines while others get involved, nor why they choose the side that they do. In the case of the mugging, a bystander to this crime must likewise weigh the relative importance of aiding the victim against the personal risk of intervening. Third parties, then, perform a similar computation to direct targets in which they consider how much the mugging affects them as well as the dangers of interceding. Much more will be said about this theoretical argument in the next chapter, and how this approach builds upon, and revises, what others have argued previously. The explication of these cost calculations and the concomitant behaviors is ambitious because it amounts to a general theory of the influence of social movements and interest organizations upon their targets, from economic actors to elected officials. Too, this analysis promises to bridge the chasm that unnecessarily separates political science and sociological research on movement outcomes, interest group influence, and policymaking. Along the way I set forth theoretical propositions to suggest a research agenda that goes beyond the scope of this single volume. As such, this analysis is meant to be provocative, not exhaustive.

Next, I hope to contribute to studies of the American civil rights movement, but from a different perspective – from the vantage point of movement targets and third parties. The civil rights struggle changed American democracy in fundamental ways, pushed gross racial inequalities into the national spotlight, and triggered bold federal action. The well-known struggles in Birmingham and Selma as well as the countless lesser-known efforts to achieve basic human dignity and fundamental rights are heroic and inspirational. Perhaps for this reason, the civil rights movement has received an enormous amount of popular and scholarly attention, from the biographies of towering leaders to histories of local struggles and accounts of the various civil rights organizations. However understandable the emphasis on the courage and tactical ingenuity of movement activists, this has meant that the targets and opponents of the movement are often dealt with in a cursory or caricatured fashion. For those of us who want to understand this movement's historical triumphs, it is necessary to account for the behavior of the movement's targets, opponents, and others, even if they lack admirable qualities. In this case, explaining the success of the civil rights movement requires an analysis of the variation in white responses to protests, from grudging accommodation to fierce resistance.

Finally, I recast conventional accounts of certain key local struggles. The defeat of Martin Luther King's ambitious campaign in Albany, Georgia, for instance, is often attributed to the cleverness of police chief Laurie Pritchett, who responded to nonviolent direct action with nonviolent legalistic repression. Overlooked in this explanation are the peculiar *political* circumstances that made Pritchett's strategy a possibility, and the movement's own tactical mistakes. In retelling the civil rights era with attention to the costs that movements impose upon targets, and to white responses, new insights into the dynamics of this well-researched movement can be offered. From enhancing general theory to elucidating specific episodes of the civil rights movement, this analysis traverses an enormous expanse of terrain and, I hope, offers the reader a useful set of analytical tools as well as provokes further research to better understand the dynamics of social change.

Acknowledgments

In the completion of this book I acquired more debts than I can properly acknowledge. First, I thank Chuck Tilly for inspiring me to ask difficult questions and do my best to provide better answers. Although I hesitated to intrude into his office, Chuck always made time for questions, to read drafts, and to provide thoughtful (and uncannily rapid) feedback. Though I was just a lowly graduate student, Chuck always treated me, and indeed everyone, as a colleague and an equal. Not content to merely point out the flaws, he always sought to bring out the strengths in the research of his students. His work ethic and prodigious output were nothing less than superhuman. I have sought to emulate him in many ways, but he remains unmatched, and he is sorely missed. I am grateful as well to Richard Bensel, Jack Goldstone, Ira Katznelson, Doug McAdam, David Plotke, Andy Polsky, and Elizabeth Sanders for their steadfast encouragement and support. At various stages, many others have shared with me their valuable suggestions. In particular, I thank Beth Buschman-Kelly, David Card, Bryan Daves, Michael Donnelly, Alan Draper, Adam Fairclough, Jeff Frieden, Shamira Gelbman, Jennifer Hochschild, Phil Klinkner, Dan Kryder, Joe Lowndes, Stephen Pimpare, Kim Lacy Rogers, Joseph Sinsheimer, Ann-Marie Szymanski, Brad Usher, and, especially, the anonymous reviewers from Cambridge University Press for their detailed and useful suggestions. All have helped make this a better book. I benefited too from research assistance or comments from the following students: Amanda Altman, Sara Bordan, Schlomit Cohen, Maytal Fligelman, Tova Glatter, Daniel Goldmintz, Gil Landau, Beth Meshel, and Sarah Willig. I thank the helpful staffs from the following institutions: the Alabama Department of Archives and History, the Louisiana State

Archives, the McCain Library and Archives of the University of Southern Mississippi, the McComb Public Library, the Mississippi Department of Archives and History, the North Carolina State Archives, the South Carolina Department of Archives and History, the Hedi Steinberg Library of Yeshiva University, and the Virginia State Archives and Libraries. I am indebted to Yeshiva University, and especially to Dean Karen Bacon of Stern College, for providing me with an invaluable research leave to complete this project. At Cambridge University Press, I very much appreciated Lew Bateman's quiet confidence in the manuscript and his superb management of the review process. Thanks too to Emily Spangler of Cambridge for her able administrative assistance, Regina Paleski for her production editing assistance, and Dan Mausner for his careful editing. Finally, most of all, I thank my beloved wife, Johanna, for tirelessly reading draft after draft, and always believing in me.

I

The Logic of Social Movement Outcomes

Behind some of the most momentous changes in American politics and history lie the struggles of ordinary people. The actions of farmers and workers spurred the expansion of national economic regulation to protect against the predations of big business. The political mobilization of seniors during the Great Depression fostered the development of the welfare state. Civil rights activists won landmark legislation to ban racial employment discrimination and integrate American society. Feminist agitation achieved a host of legislative victories to challenge gender inequalities; and environmental activists brought greater oversight to bear on industries throughout the private sector. Few doubt that social movements matter; indeed, it is difficult to contemplate either the pattern of national political and economic development or changes to inegalitarian social practices without them.[1] This investigation thus begins with a simple question: How were these victories achieved or, more precisely, why do social movement targets give in to demands? Although considerable research has been dedicated to the explanation of movement emergence and development, only more recently has attention been devoted to movement outcomes. Such studies highlight movement characteristics, including differences between violent and nonviolent tactics, while others concentrate on external circumstances and support from third parties. Yet

---

[1] Piven (2006). Numerous sources concern the movements mentioned above. For a sampling, see Sanders (1999) on the activism of farmers and workers; on the mobilization of seniors, Amenta (2006); for the civil rights movement, McAdam (1982); Burstein (1979, 1985); and Morris (1984); on the women's movement, Costain and Majstorovic (1994); Freeman (1975), and Klein (1985); and on the environmental movement, Agnone (2007); Kraft (2000); Rochon and Mazmanian (1993); and Sale (1993).

this research has often produced contradictory or inconclusive findings.[2] To resolve these puzzles, I suggest that it is useful to start with the most elementary propositions about movement outcomes and then, piece by piece, assemble a general theoretical explanation.

Costs and Target Responsiveness

Many studies begin with the assumption that targets respond to movement demands based on their exposure to the *costs* that movements or third parties impose upon them.[3] A target's responsiveness follows from the perceived costliness of disruptions to routine political and economic transactions. As McAdam observes, "In essence, what insurgents are seeking . . . is the ability to disrupt their opponent's interests to such an extent that the cessation of the offending tactic becomes a sufficient inducement to grant concessions."[4] These costly disruptions can take many forms, such as the threat to vote an elected official out of office, or protests that hinder normal business operations. Yet, even as previous studies have assumed that costs matter, they suffer from various weaknesses. First, they do not provide a sufficient description of the *different* costs that movements impose upon their targets and, in particular, how the convergence of varied costs affects target behavior. Next, studies of movement impact often lack a theoretical analysis of the differences among targets, in particular their *vulnerability* to movement-imposed disruptions. And, finally, despite the acknowledged importance of third parties, studies often overlook them and do not provide an explanation for their behavior as they shape movement-target interactions. While it is possible to treat audience interventions as exogenous, to a considerable extent doing so leaves a theory of movement outcomes at the mercy of unexplained interventions. Their inclusion within a general theory makes

---

[2] Statham and Koopmans (1999); Giugni (1999).

[3] Burstein and Linton (2002); Gamson (1975); Lipsky (1968); McAdam (1982). Wilson 1961. I adopt Wilson's assumption that individuals and enterprises are "threat-oriented" in that they are "more sensitive to . . . circumstances that make costs seem likely to go up or benefits to go down than they are when they foresee a chance to reduce costs or enhance benefits." See also Hansen (1985); on cost aversion, Tversky and Kahneman (1991). In most cases, costs and benefits are two sides of the same coin, and therefore do not need to be independently theorized. For instance, the response of an elected official to an interest organization can be viewed both as a move to win votes (a benefit) or as a preemptive response to the prospective transfer of those votes to a political opponent (a cost). Although this analysis concentrates upon costs, this approach does not rule out the possibility that benefits will motivate the behavior of targets or third parties.

[4] 1982, 30.

possible a fuller account of the interactions that determine movement outcomes.

I propose here a theory of movement outcomes based on an analysis of the costs that shape the behavior of both targets and third parties. Such a theory begins with a simple distinction between the two general costs that movements can impose: disruption and concession costs. "Disruption costs" are those losses stemming directly or indirectly from movement actions.[5] By conducting protests, demonstrations, picketing, litigating, and so on, social movements can disrupt the target's ability to obtain political or economic values. Movements may affect electoral calculations of office-seekers by changing public opinion, raising the salience of the issue, or transferring electoral resources to an opponent. Under these circumstances, acting against movement demands or doing nothing can become politically dangerous. The Anti-Saloon League, for instance, developed a reputation for wielding a political cudgel against politicians who refused to support prohibition.[6] For economic actors, movements can interfere with regular business activities, attract negative publicity, or impose financial penalties upon recalcitrant firms. Such actual or threatened costs have prompted targeted firms to, among other things, divest from Burma, adopt stronger codes of corporate conduct, and abandon the construction of nuclear power plants.[7] Movements may also enlist the assistance of third parties, including state actors, to impose additional disruption costs upon targets. These supportive third parties can, for instance, withdraw investments, support boycotts, reduce funding, or impose fines. From animal rights to women's suffrage, movements adopt tactics for the purpose of generating potent disruption costs. Insofar as costs have been addressed in studies of movement outcomes, they have largely focused upon such disruption of a target's interests.

Yet, in addition to the impact of disruption, targets also weigh the actual or anticipated losses resulting from acceding to movement demands, which I designate "concession costs." Voters might punish a politician for offering unpopular concessions; likewise, accepting

---

[5] Costs as described here are analogous to what Gamson (1975) described as "constraints" imposed upon movement targets. For Wilson (1961), they are "negative inducements." As Burstein, Einwohner, and Hollander (1995) suggest, the more dependent a target is upon a movement and its supporters (be they voters or consumers), the greater the target's exposure to disruption costs will be.

[6] Odegard (1928), but see Szymanski (2003) on the reality of this perception.

[7] Respectively, Spar and Le Mure (2003); Elliott and Freeman (2004); Ross and Shaw (1993).

movement demands might reduce the profits of certain firms or entire economic sectors. Included in the assessment of concession costs must be a consideration of opposition to capitulation from other parties upon whom the target is dependent for profits, votes, and so on. For instance, before elected officials concede to pro-life activists, they must anticipate contending with the ire of their organized opponents. I argue that the specific configuration of these disruption and concession costs fundamentally defines target responses to movement mobilization.

The Convergence of Disruption and Concession Costs

While disruption and concession costs affect some actors more than others, prior analyses have not satisfactorily addressed how their relative magnitude affects the behavior of economic and political targets. Depending on the specific combination of disruption and concession costs, targets can be expected to respond differently to social protest. From the convergence of aggregate disruption and concession costs, I derive a set of predictions for the responses of targets to social movement demands, as well as the general prospects of movement success.[8] The constellation of costs can be depicted in a schematic fashion by scaling the magnitude of disruption and concession costs into low and high, and overlapping the two dimensions (see Figure 1.1).[9] Doing so generates four ideal

---

[8] Some have suggested that utility theory and its variants are tautologous and nonfalsifiable, in that post facto explanations can be found for any observed behavior. As such, they have no predictive value. For instance, if a target is shown to capitulate to the civil rights demands, it is possible to suggest that she behaved in this manner because her exposure to disruption costs was high and her concession costs were low. In other words, it is possible to impute the "correct" relevant preferences or interests after observing the behavior to be explained. Several features of my argument resolve this problem. First, specific interests are distinguished a priori according to their predicted exposure to movement disruption and concession costs. Political and economic actors are predicted to be more or less resistant to movement demands based on a set of objective interests to which they must adhere if they are going to stay in business or win reelection. To the extent that targets and others respond to these interests, the theory is falsifiable. Second, instead of imputing preferences to a target based on their behavior, evidence for target and third party calculations of their specific disruption and concession costs is provided. Targeted economic actors, for instance, often made clear in interviews that they capitulated only because they were compelled to do so (or go out of business). Evidence of this sort obviates the problem of post facto rationalization.

[9] Economic and political actors calculate profits and votes, respectively. For economic actors, costs are high insofar as they reduce profits sufficiently to endanger the future of the firm with which they are associated. Political actors deem costs to be high if their reelection is credibly threatened. Also, although depicted as ideal types for the sake of

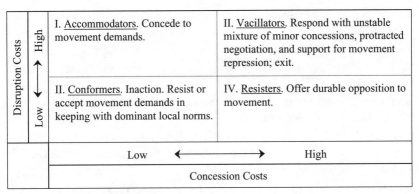

FIGURE I.I. Predicted responses to movement demands.

types from which I infer the likely responses of economic and political actors, including movement targets, to their circumstances.

With a convergence of the low cost of movement acceptance and high exposure to losses due to movement-initiated disruptions, movement targets in Cell I will prefer to make concessions and act on behalf of accommodation.[10] It is expected that these "accommodators" will act before others to advocate concessions, sway community sentiment in favor of reform, or serve as brokers of agreements. For targets capable of responding unilaterally to protest demands, this situation is the most conducive to movement success. However, unless additional gains might be expected, vulnerable actors will bargain for the smallest concession necessary to bring about a halt to protests and a resumption of normal activities.

Vulnerability to both the costs of movement success and movement-initiated disruptions (Cell II) places these targets in an untenable situation. Without the choice of low-cost compromise, but desiring a means to end disruptions, these "vacillators" lack an optimal response. Depending on the formidability of the movement, they will waver between repression, perhaps in alliance with other opponents of change, engage in dilatory

highlighting general patterns, it is useful to remember that these costs are continuous variables, and therefore there is slippage along the frontiers of the cells, particularly if the magnitudes of disruption and concession costs are very uneven. It is therefore possible, for example, for a nominal conformer exposed to moderate disruption costs and minuscule concession costs to behave more like an accommodator. In depicting these broad combinations of disruption and concession costs as distinct types, it is important not to reify the categories themselves.

[10] A benefit-seeker capable of generating high disruption costs has a strong bargaining position, which increases the likelihood of winning concessions.

tactics (such as conducting protracted negotiations), and make nominal concessions to halt protest activities. To escape their situation, more mobile vacillators may pursue exit as an option by closing and relocating their business operation. Or, to the extent that their concession costs are high due to fears of third party reprisals, it is possible that vacillators will seek to outmaneuver or overcome these opponents of capitulation.

Next, unaffected by either movement success or disruptions, the relatively comfortable position of actors in Cell III allows them to respond in a manner consistent with dominant values; they will thus be "conformers" to local or prevailing sentiments.[11] Generally speaking, however, regardless of their personal preferences, it is assumed that these actors will likely free ride rather than organize or participate in collective action.[12] For legislators, such a convergence allows them to vote their own ideological views, or what they regard as better public policy.

Finally, the high cost of social movement success and the relative insulation of the targets in Cell IV will encourage them to offer durable opposition to change; hence, they are dubbed "resisters." Like other opponents to movement ambitions, resisters are predicted to attempt to suppress movements, encourage others to do the same (including state authorities), and thwart the actions of accommodators. Against these adversaries, a movement's success is improbable.

Target Cost Calculations

If target cost calculations fundamentally shape movement outcomes, the elucidation of how targets tally these costs is crucial. Most studies address these cost calculations indirectly and imperfectly. Since they focus on movements, not targets, greater emphasis has been placed upon movement features that are presumed to coincide with overall leverage, such as size, durability, and tactics.[13] Movements that are larger, more tenacious, and tactically clever are presumed to possess greater disruptive leverage than those without such characteristics. Similarly, much research predicts movement clout based on counts of protest events reported in major

---

[11] Although the default response for these insulated actors is conformity, it is possible that some might favor change. Indeed, my approach predicts that conscience constituents are likely to be clustered in this cell. The term conscience constituents, which refers to movement participants who are not members of the beneficiary population, comes from McCarthy and Zald (1977).

[12] See Olson (1965) for the classic explication of the free rider problem.

[13] Gamson (1975); Tilly (1978).

newspapers or figures on membership and budgets for the relevant social movement organizations. In estimating disruption costs, such measures no doubt matter in that they define a movement's general capabilities to disrupt their target's interests. However, they are often insufficient to predict movement outcomes because they do not capture variation in the vulnerability of targets' interests to disruption. It is perhaps no wonder that studies of the relationship between discrete movement characteristics and outcomes have produced inconsistent findings.[14] In other words, a consideration of these characteristics goes only so far since targets are unevenly exposed to movement interference. It is quite possible, for instance, for the same movement or different movements possessing the same objective disruptive capabilities to win concessions from certain targets, but not others. An analysis of movement outcomes must consider not only movement attributes and actions, but also the interaction with the characteristics of targets that make them more or less vulnerable to movement action.

Targets consider not only their exposure to disruption; they also tally the cost of conceding to movement demands. With few exceptions, movement studies overlook the differences in how targets weigh the cost of capitulation.[15] Neglecting concession costs is problematic, however, because it flattens out the different costs associated with specific movement goals. For obvious reasons, targets may accede to demands that are deemed trivial, but resist those that are onerous. Without an appreciation of these differences, such varied target responses may be incorrectly attributed to movement characteristics or political opportunities. Further, inattention to the implications of a movement's goals renders invisible, for instance, the dramatic differences in the costs associated with the demands of the environmental movement and those of Mothers Against Drunk Driving (MADD). To estimate target perceptions of their concession costs, specific movement demands must be differentiated and their implications unpacked.[16] Although it is common to regard "the civil rights movement" as a unified challenge to southern racial inequalities, it is more accurate to view it as an ensemble of distinct struggles involving,

---

[14] Giugni (1999).

[15] In his sample of 53 social movements, Gamson (1975) provides a rare exception with his distinction between radical movements with displacement goals and those with reformist agendas.

[16] This point is analogous to Lowi's (1964) argument that policy type (distributive, regulatory, and redistributive) determines the general patterns of political conflict. See also Wilson (1980).

among other things, the desegregation of public schools and accommodations, voting rights, and an end to employment discrimination. While
the movement challenged Jim Crow in general, whites differed in their
commitment to the defense of the various aspects of southern racial hierarchies. Particular demands, then, may be associated with different cost
configurations.

A target's calculation of concession costs will be affected as well by a
movement's organized opposition.[17] Since the disruptions threatened by
an energetic movement may be more than overmatched by a far stronger
adversary, it is surprising how few studies of movement outcomes include
measures for the capabilities of organized opposition. With a one-sided
emphasis on movement disruptions, such studies not only miss the impact
of variation in concession costs on target behavior, but also the interactions between the two kinds of costs. What is needed, then, is greater
theoretical insight into target exposure to both costs. Such an account
of target cost perceptions begins with a clearer specification of discrete
targets, their interests, and their vulnerabilities.

Perhaps the most basic distinction among targets lies in the difference
between economic and political actors. Economic interests calculate their
exposure based on threats to current or anticipated profits.[18] The operators of segregated lunch counters, for instance, were compelled to weigh
the impact of serving African-Americans against the losses due to disruptive sit-ins, picketing, white violence, and reduced local consumption. By
contrast, political targets in democratic polities are assumed to be keenly
interested in the electoral consequences associated with both resisting and
responding to movement demands.[19] A set of propositions follows from
this basic distinction.

For economic actors I propose a sectoral analysis to account for the
variation in their cost exposure. An expanding body of research demonstrates that sectoral differences affect the behavior of economic actors.
Often used to explain the reactions of certain types of firms to economic
or political changes, this perspective applies as well to how economic targets respond to social movement activism. Accordingly, certain sectors
are predicted to be more vulnerable to movement disruptions than others. Operators dependent upon local consumption, growth, or attracting

---

[17] Meyer and Staggenborg (1996).
[18] For instance, see King and Soule (2007); Luders (2006); Smith (1990); Spar and Le Mure (2003).
[19] Burstein (1999); Kingdon (1973) [1989]; Mayhew (1974); Miller and Stokes (1963).

new investment will be far more exposed to disruption costs than those enterprises engaged in manufacture for distant undifferentiated markets. A comparable analysis clarifies different vulnerabilities of economic targets to concession costs. For instance, firms in less-competitive markets may conceal small concession costs within the price of their products, and pass them along invisibly to their customers. Others in highly competitive markets with no means to conceal unwanted changes will be exposed to greater concession costs. Since targets insulated from disruption or faced with costly concessions are unlikely to concede, sectoral variation in the target vulnerability affects a movement's overall prospects for success against economic targets.

I suggest a more robust political explanation to account for the responses of public officials to organized benefit-seekers.[20] Most accounts begin with the assumption that political actors are preoccupied with their own reelection and that they therefore calculate their cost exposure based on the electoral implications of their activities. This conventional assumption, as Burstein (1999) has effectively argued, suggests that the outcomes of political movements depend upon the combination of public opinion and mass attentiveness, or degree of focus on the issue.[21] Movements with the backing of attentive, mass publics are capable of threatening elected officials with punishing disruption costs and therefore are highly likely to be successful. For the same reason, movements with the latent support of inattentive mass publics often pursue actions that are meant to attract the media spotlight, boost the salience of movement demands, and thereby maximize their disruptive capabilities. Conversely, the high concession costs associated with hostile public opinion almost certainly doom a movement to defeat.[22] An analysis that focuses only on public

[20] In studies of social movements, it is conventional to refer to movements as challengers or claim-makers (Gamson 1975; Tilly 1995). In this analysis, I borrow Harvey's (1997) more generic term "benefit-seeker" to convey that this approach is meant to be applicable more broadly to interest organizations, in which case an antagonistic relationship is not necessarily to be presumed.

[21] Similarly, Giugni's (2004) "joint effects" approach depicts movement impact as stemming from differing combinations of movement mobilization, public opinion, and political alliances.

[22] These points are uncontroversial, but they suggest that the determinants of movement impact on political targets are the same as for conventional interest organizations and therefore, at least concerning explanations for movement outcome, a sharp separation between the two is unnecessary. Put differently, the approach sketched here to delineate the responsiveness of political actors to social movements may be used to account for the influence of interest groups on public policy.

opinion may be helpful if mass attentiveness is high, but it is much less useful in those cases, perhaps the vast majority, in which attentiveness is low.[23]

Therefore the incorporation of another consideration is necessary: the aggregate electoral leverage of the benefit-seekers (the movement and their allies) within a target's reelection coalition relative to that of their opponents.[24] Insofar as constituents are inattentive and likely to remain so, the concession costs for responding to movement demands may be low and a movement with ample electoral resources and minimal opposition can obtain policy concessions. Contrary to the assumption that public opinion necessarily rules, this outcome is possible even if mass preferences are indifferent or nominally opposed.[25] Conversely, a movement that has the support of inattentive publics may be defeated if the movement is too feeble to arouse broader interest and organized opponents possess far greater electoral capabilities. As these examples suggest, amid mass inattention or indifference, officials must calculate the net electoral implications of their actions based on the relative electoral leverage of competing benefit-seekers.[26] Instead of attempting to isolate a relationship between, say, public opinion and movement outcomes, the political explanation sketched here suggests that policy outcomes depend upon the convergence of all three factors: public opinion, attentiveness, and the electoral wherewithal of the movement and its allies weighed against the corresponding sway of countermovement opposition. Despite the presumed significance of each of these factors, it is striking that studies of movement outcomes (as well as much research on interest organizations) seldom include all of them, even though it is their convergence that shapes movement outcome in most cases.[27] Specific propositions and their implications are

---

[23] Burstein (2006).

[24] Previous studies have proposed variables that directly or indirectly measure a benefit-seeker's electoral leverage, such as the total membership of social movement or advocacy organizations (Soule and Olzak 2004). However, these variables are generally treated as indicators of "organizational capacity" (to lobby or litigate, for instance) rather than measures of electoral significance. This perspective explicitly highlights the relationship between electoral clout (relative to opponents) and the prospects for extracting benefits from targets. Despite this difference, Soule and Olzak's (2004) argument for an approach that emphasizes the convergence of multiple factors is compelling. See also Costain and Majstorovic (1994).

[25] The position of the two major political parties on abortion is a good example of how organized benefit-seekers motivate office-seekers to deviate from median voter preferences. See Fiorina (2005). More generally, see Jacobs and Shapiro (2000).

[26] Hansen (1991).

[27] For a similar critique of conventional approaches, see Burstein and Sausner (2005).

spelled out more fully in subsequent chapters. Together, a more nuanced specification of target interests and vulnerabilities promises to elucidate their reactions to the diverse activities of movements, their allies, and their opponents.

Third Party Responses

Social movements seldom tackle their targets in isolation from a multitude of interested parties, and their intervention shapes how targets calculate both disruption and concession costs. Supportive third parties can augment the movement's disruptive impact on targeted officials or businesses, eliciting greater responsiveness to movement demands.[28] Conversely, antagonistic third parties threaten these same interests with countervailing punishments for accommodation, and struggle to discourage accommodation. Movement-target interactions are thus thickly embedded within a larger ensemble of relationships. Although prior research points to the actions of third parties as often crucial to movement outcome, most accounts do not attempt to explain their intervention, often instead subsuming their actions under the rubric of political opportunity. Approaches that explain movement success with references to favorable political opportunities shift a considerable portion of the causal story onto external factors and limit the analytical reach of a theory of movement outcome. Also, there is an ever-present risk of triviality or circularity in the arguments in which a movement wins new benefits simply because the broader political opportunities were favorable.[29] Rather than treating the reactions of third parties in this manner, I suggest that the same

---

[28] Lipsky (1968); Rucht (2004); Schattschneider (1960).

[29] Goodwin and Jasper (1999); Piven (2006). On the political opportunity debate, see also Gamson and Meyer (1996); Goldstone and Tilly (2001); and Jenkins, Jacobs, and Agnone (2003). As with movement theory generally, more attention has been paid to the impact of political opportunities on movement emergence or the level of protest activity, and less to movement outcome. But, for a particularly astute analysis, see Meyer and Minkoff (2004). The argument here is not that exogenous political opportunities do not matter; it is rather that the concept often serves as shorthand for assumptions about target receptivity to movement demands. It suggests, then, that "opportunities" should be disaggregated and more clearly specified to identify more precisely why certain circumstances might be more or less advantageous. Put differently, political opportunities are favorable insofar as the relevant movement targets are vulnerable to the disruptions of specific movements. This is consistent with research that has shown that the dominance of a center-left Democratic coalition is favorable for liberal reformist movements and Republican political control can be conducive to center-right movements; see Amenta (2006).

cost considerations constraining target behavior (depicted in Figure 1.1) account for the responses of many third parties as well.

First, a definition: Third parties refers to all individuals or organizations not directly targeted for disruption by social movement activists.[30] Although this conception of third parties is unbounded, the expectation for nearly all third parties is that they will be inactive bystanders because they are neither affected by movement disruptions nor exposed to the costs of capitulating to movement demands. Indeed, those that are not proximate to movement agitation may be wholly unaware of the movement's existence. Third parties that are aware of a movement's activities and demands are generally predicted to conform to dominant local customs and free ride on the efforts of others to maintain the status quo. If all third parties conform, then a target's cost structure is unchanged. Of course, these unconstrained actors are free to adopt whatever response they prefer, and some may be sympathetic to movement demands. They may behave as conscience constituents such that they take supportive action, as did those white northerners who traveled south to join in civil rights marches.[31] Other similarly situated interests may support movement activities for self-interested reasons, such as organized labor's political interest in expanding the southern black electorate.[32]

Yet, interested third parties can and often do intervene in movement-target interactions. Those third parties that suffer high costs from movement protests and other activities, but are unlikely to be harmed by the target's acquiescence to movement demands, will be disposed to support accommodation. The intervention of these accommodating third parties in movement-target interactions may increase the disruption costs for

---

[30] On "bystander publics," see Turner (1970). Although it is conventional to refer to such actors as bystanders, I generally identify them as third parties since the term is ambiguous regarding their behavior, whereas "bystander" connotes nonparticipation and inaction.

[31] Although public-spirited collective action might appear to be beyond the reach of rational choice explanations, Chong (1991) offers a self-interest explanation for precisely this behavior. His analysis finds support for the importance of *social* costs, such as shame, embedded in face-to-face interactions. Nevertheless, he posits altruism and expressive normative benefits to motivate what he refers to as "unconditional cooperators." His observation that altruistic conduct is rare in any case is consistent with Olson (1965) as well as Burstein and Sausner (2005) on the infrequency of collective action in general.

[32] Such propositions are complicated because union support often derived from pressure within the labor movement by African-Americans for greater commitment to the civil rights cause. Some of the deep racial tensions within the labor movement as well as the mobilization of the Negro American Labor Council (NALC), which lobbied the labor movement for greater support of black civil and voting rights, are described in Foner (1974).

movement targets. For example, in many communities hit with civil rights demonstrations, local economic actors not directly targeted for protests nevertheless urged concessions because of the larger economic implications of movement contention, and they sometimes applied pressure to officeholders to negotiate a settlement.

In contrast, third parties that are unharmed by movement operations but are severely threatened by movement victory are predicted to engage in countermobilization to resist the movement and use their leverage to discourage targets from capitulating. This countermobilization can be decisive for movement outcome.[33] In particular, the actions of counter-movement resisters may boost the concession costs for vulnerable targets, which may, in turn, shift them toward vacillation. Finally, third parties caught between both high disruption and concession costs face contra-dictory incentives in which they may be tempted to urge a cooling off period, enter lengthy negotiations, or align with resisters to crush move-ment agitation. In determining their aggregate disruption and concession costs, targets weigh the implications of movement agitation and demands as well as the behavior of third parties. Their incorporation into the nar-rative enriches the predictions for target calculations of overall disruption or concession costs and thereby expands the overall scope of social move-ment theory.

Defining Movement Impact

This investigation is meant to explain target responses to movement mobi-lization. From these responses, a general account of movement impact can then be assembled. Much more will be said about how to do so in the following chapters. Before proceeding further, it is necessary to clear away some definitional underbrush. While it might appear a straight-forward endeavor to point to movement outcomes, debate surrounds what exactly should be explained. Some argue in favor of a focus upon success, referring to a movement achieving its formally stated goals as they appear in public communications.[34] The advantage of this approach is that formal goals likely represent a broadly accepted statement of objectives within the movement.[35] Others argue that a simple success

---

[33] Andrews (2001); Meyer and Staggenborg (1996); Mottl (1980); Soule and Olzak (2004).
[34] Burstein et al. (1995).
[35] Burstein et al. (1995) offers several other justifications for this understanding of success including ease of measurement, reduction in researcher subjectivity, and greater compa-rability across movements. Some have suggested that a focus on success is flawed because

and failure dichotomy is too restrictive, preferring instead to concentrate more broadly on movement outcomes, impacts, or consequences. Amenta (2006) notes that, even though the Townsend Movement failed to secure the enactment of their preferred program to provide seniors with a retirement income, the Social Security Act and later amendments were adopted in no small measure due to movement activities. Amenta therefore suggests that it is preferable to concentrate on consequences and the extent to which movements deliver "collective goods" to their beneficiary populations.

Despite this definitional disagreement, it nonetheless seems possible to find some middle ground in this dispute. Drawing from Amenta, I use "impact" to refer generally to the degree to which a benefit-seeker obtains new advantages on behalf of ostensible beneficiaries. At the same time, I suggest that a movement impact that achieves formally stated goals may be considered a success, as defined above. In this view, it is thus possible to speak of a movement having an impact with or without formal success. The term "outcome" refers generically to any of these scenarios. This approach reconciles the contrasting definitions described above to permit the identification of a broader range of outcomes.[36]

Theoretical Contribution and Limitations

Although the preceding hypotheses rest upon a set of rudimentary assumptions, they differ from conventional approaches and offer considerable promise to enhance theories of movement impact. This perspective begins with a modest shift in emphasis toward movement targets and the

---

movement factions might have contrasting formal demands. Yet, this defect may be more apparent than real. From the perspective presented in this analysis, movement factions should be treated as separate benefit-seekers with each imposing a different combination of disruption and concession costs upon their shared targets. In this view, speaking of a social movement in the singular (for instance, the environmental movement) fosters an impression of a unified entity, even though the movement is internally highly variegated. In assessing social movement success, it is necessary to treat these diverse benefit-seekers as distinct. It is possible then for the moderate wing of a movement to strike a bargain with a target to win concessions, while a radical wing obtains nothing. As McAdam (1982) has suggested in his notion of a "radical flank effect," the agitation of the radical element might boost the target's aggregate disruption costs and provide the moderate elements with greater bargaining leverage.

[36] Burstein et al. (1995), drawing from Schumaker, propose a typology of various outcomes based on the stages of the policymaking process that provides another means of resolving some of these issues. They propose, for instance, that movements might have agenda responsiveness but not policy responsiveness.

costs that movements impose on them, and reveals a host of new hypotheses and possible directions for research, only some of which are pursued in this book. Attention to disruption costs reveals new ways to think about target vulnerabilities. In particular, a close inspection of target vulnerabilities suggests that a fixation upon movement tactics is misguided; rather, tactics must be evaluated in light of target susceptibility to them. For example, even as certain protest tactics might be effective against vulnerable economic actors, the same actions used to wring concessions from an elected official might be utterly deficient. Second, most studies focus on a movement's disruptions to the neglect of a target's estimation of the results of offering concessions. As such, analytical narratives are commonly one-sided and the *convergence* of both costs, critically shaping target responses, is routinely overlooked. Thus this approach necessitates more self-consciousness about the differences in the costs associated with movement demands and, as will be shown, those aspects of the demands themselves that cause them to be regarded as more or less costly. Finally, such a tack holds promise in explaining the behavior of third parties, which are routinely identified as decisive players in movement struggles but whose conduct is left unexplained. The analysis presented here is not meant to be exhaustive, but instead to offer a suggestive sketch of the value of this conceptual vocabulary and the research agenda that it helps to define.

This volume considers the merits of the hypotheses set forth above in an analysis of the responses of targets and third parties to civil rights mobilization in the American South, from the 1954 *Brown v. Board of Education* decision through the heyday of movement activism, and beyond into the 1970s. Over the course of many years encompassing many victories and defeats, this social movement culminated in the enactment of landmark legislation that profoundly expanded the national commitment to racial egalitarianism.[37] At the same time, the diversity in tactics, demands, and targets across numerous localities allows for research on the interactions among multiple factors. Furthermore, the combination of ample primary sources and rich histories of the movement offers an invaluable treasure trove for research. This combination of historical

---

[37] I do not mean to suggest the movement emerged in the 1950s. The excellent research of Morris (1984) and McAdam (1982) clearly places the movement in a deeper historical context. Since this analysis concentrates not on the movement's origins but rather its impact, the focus is shifted toward the period of greatest movement agitation and immediately beyond.

significance, empirical variation, and evidentiary abundance makes the civil rights movement a compelling case for investigation.

The scope of this work is ambitious, but there are several limitations that should be acknowledged at the outset. First, although this analysis suggests that the magnitude of movement mobilization can be a significant factor shaping outcome, it does not purport to explain variation in movement activity. Research on this topic is already ample. Rather, the existence of an organized benefit-seeker making demands upon targets is assumed. The extent of movement mobilization is incorporated into the assessment of aggregate disruption costs. Second, this investigation does not account for cultural changes that might plausibly be traced back to social movement agitation. While greater acceptance of interracial marriage or same-sex unions may be attributable to movement actions, tracing these diffuse processes is beyond the purview of this study. Nor does this approach explain indirect, unintended outcomes, even though these sometimes have significant implications.[38] Finally, movements might affect different stages in the policymaking process from agenda setting through implementation. This analysis emphasizes agenda setting and enactment, but devotes far less attention to the details of policy formulation and implementation. Nevertheless, this approach might usefully clarify movement outcomes in the implementation phase as well.

Chapter Overview

I articulate the arguments sketched above more fully in six additional chapters, each adding further theoretical refinements and empirical support. In Chapter 2 I begin with an analysis of the third parties opposed to the civil rights movement and their behavior. The intervention of opponents as well as supporters affects how targets calculate their overall cost exposure, in particular the costs of acceding to movement demands. A survey of the cost structures of these third parties offers partial confirmation for the association between cost exposure and responsiveness. The chapter reviews the prediction for resisters as those who are vulnerable to movement concessions but insulated from the costs of movement disruptions, and then surveys the organized opponents of the civil rights movement. In addition to discussing their activities to quash civil rights organizations and threaten individual activists, I detail in particular how

---

[38] See, for instance, Andrews (2004) on this point.

they sought to discourage targets from engaging in negotiation and compromise.

Chapter 3 shifts the focus to those southern actors most willing to make concessions, either as targets or third parties. It is predicted that these interests suffer from movement disruptions and, at the same time, can concede to movement demands without great sacrifice. Many of these vulnerable actors can be found among economic concerns. However, instead of treating the "business community" as a monolithic entity, I elaborate upon a sectoral analysis that differentiates elements within the business community based on the variation in their exposure to movement disruption. I document these patterns of support for compromise based on a survey of a range of primary and secondary sources, including a biographical analysis of the signers of three published petitions in support of concessions.

In Chapter 4 I assemble the components of this analysis in a survey of movement outcomes in seven local case studies of significant movement struggles – Greensboro, Albany, Atlanta, New Orleans, Birmingham, Selma, and Greenwood. For each, I examine the responses of targets and third parties to movement mobilization and document the interaction among them to provide a more nuanced account of these local struggles and revise aspects of the conventional historical accounts. For instance, although the movement's defeat in Albany is often attributed to the strategic cleverness of the chief of police – who met nonviolent protests with nonviolent repression – my perspective concentrates on the movement's tactical mistakes. In particular, the movement attempted to extract concessions from insulated public officials rather than concentrating their disruptions upon vulnerable economic actors.

To bolster the conclusions of the case studies, I broaden the scope of the analysis in Chapter 5 to consider three general domains of civil rights mobilization across the South: voting registration, desegregation of public schools, and desegregation of public accommodations (such as lunch counters, theaters, hotels, and so on).[39] These struggles brought together different combinations of disruptions and concession costs in different locations. Using the perspective proposed here I explain the variation in local outcomes following civil rights mobilization, both prior to stepped-up federal intervention, and after. In brief, I suggest that concentrated

---

[39] By contrast, public facilities refers generally to government-run recreational facilities, such as parks, golf courses, swimming pools, etc. At times, such public facilities were targeted for demonstrations, along with private and public accommodations.

movement imposition of disruption costs upon economic targets was broadly effective at compelling the vulnerable operators of public accommodations to desegregate. By contrast, due to the absence of electoral leverage, the unwillingness of the federal government to compel southern school districts to implement the *Brown* desegregation ruling, and the visibility of large-scale school integration, the struggle for school integration was unable to accomplish more than token results across the South. Depending upon the political risks for white officeholders associated with the enlargement of the African-American electorate, the outcome of voter registration drives ranged widely from substantial enrollment gains achieved in many districts to trivial inroads made elsewhere. Revealing the different combinations of disruption and concession costs associated with these domains, this chapter clarifies local variation in movement outcome.

Chapter 6 explores the responses of the federal government to demands for racial egalitarianism in the period from Reconstruction to the early 1970s. I argue that, for nearly one hundred years, from the close of Reconstruction to the 1950s, the high concession costs associated with support for black civil rights encouraged national public officials to conform to southern racial customs. By the fifties, the rising significance of the black vote and escalation in Cold War national security concerns augmented the disruption cost of inaction. This combination of high disruption and concession costs fostered a politics of vacillation in which national political authorities sought to appease both sides. Finally, movement agitation that provoked dramatic events – violent white reprisals against nonviolent demonstrators – attracted media interest and heightened national attentiveness to civil rights. With rising public attentiveness, supportive public opinion, and the mounting political clout of civil rights supporters, the political calculus shifted in favor of the enactment of comprehensive civil and voting rights legislation. This chapter also explores the political actuation of movement allies, the weakness of nonsouthern countermobilization, and congressional Republican support for civil rights legislation. Whereas most studies concentrate on the electoral incentives used to produce legislative action, this account points to congressional bargaining processes and the manner in which Republican-sponsored amendments to civil rights bills strategically shifted the concession costs away from their constituents and placed them more fully upon southern whites. A consideration of the compromises made to win the support of these pivotal legislators, then, helps to explain the content of the movement's ultimate legislative accomplishments.

The final chapter sums up the principal findings of my analysis to discuss their implications for studies of the civil rights movement and social movement theory more generally. I then define a research agenda to extend this analytical approach further to elucidate the impact of other social movements, as well as other benefit-seeking organizations. In drawing together disparate academic literatures on social movements, interest organizations, and public policy, this perspective helps to resolve previous puzzles in movement studies while defining a fresh research agenda for further investigation. I conclude with some final thoughts on civil rights struggles and the larger prospects for egalitarian social change.

2

Civil Rights and Reactive Countermobilization

Why did southern whites resist the civil rights movement? In retrospect, it might seem that ferocious opposition was preordained given that racial division and white dominance had long been defining features of southern politics.[1] Crucial differences among white southerners fade away in the popular historical imagination as all are cast as a uniform mass of intemperate racists supporting flamboyant, fire-breathing politicians, brutal sheriffs, and shadowy extremist organizations. Such caricatures, however, are unsatisfactory if we wish to account for the outcomes of the civil rights movement.[2] In contrast to the portrait of strident and cohesive opposition, some argue that the southern white countermobilization to civil rights was actually weaker and declined sooner than what might have been expected. It should be remembered as well that organized segregationists calling for massive resistance against civil rights mobilization and federal intervention into southern racial politics often bemoaned the unwillingness of their white brethren to rally in defense of Jim Crow. I therefore suggest that an explanation for the triumphs of the civil rights movement begins with an account of white resistance and countermobilization. Obviously, an analysis of reactive countermobilization highlights how much opposition the civil rights movement had to overcome while, at the same time, reveals considerable weaknesses in the southern defenses of Jim Crow institutions.

This chapter begins with the proposition that the same costs that motivate targets to respond to movement demands in particular ways likewise

[1] Key (1949).
[2] Chappell (1994); Lewis (2006); Sokol (2006).

define how third parties behave. Thus, instead of treating the activities of antagonistic third parties as exogenous, the theoretical approach presented here offers an encompassing explanation for their behavior. As such, this approach suggests certain consistent patterns should be evident. From this perspective, organized opposition is neither automatic nor universal; instead, resisters have the most compelling interests to engage in sustained countermobilization.[3] Such actors combined two defining characteristics: the vulnerability of their interests to civil rights gains and insulation from the disruption costs associated with movement activities. Although conformers (those largely lacking exposure to either cost) are assumed to prefer others to rally in defense of the status quo, some of these actors may opt to participate in organized opposition. Also in an erratic fashion, vacillators too may support countermobilization in hopes of smashing the movement that is interfering with their interests. I predict, then, that the memberships of organizations such as the Citizens' Council, the Ku Klux Klan (KKK), and other smaller white supremacist organizations represented no random cross-section of southern society; instead, resisters can be expected to disproportionately populate their ranks.

Next, I confirm these patterns of vulnerability and responsiveness based on a survey of studies of southern racial politics. Consistent with my predictions, these accounts point to civil rights countermobilization as drawn overwhelmingly from three distinct segments of southern society: plantation interests, elected officials representing localities in which African-Americans constituted a large plurality or outright majority of the population (the so-called "black belt"), and vulnerable white workers.[4] Before mechanization, planters engaged in labor-intensive agriculture and their allies depended upon keeping labor costs down. Jim Crow institutions made this possible; indeed the southern racial order was constructed in no small measure to maintain precisely these labor patterns.[5] The entrance of African-American voters into the electorate threatened those elected officials with large yet disfranchised black constituencies, a commonplace circumstance in plantation districts. Too, white workers exposed to greater competition with African-Americans for scarce

---

[3] Zald and Useem (1987).

[4] Originally a reference to the rich soil of the cotton plantation regions, the term "black belt" changed to refer to those sections in which the African-American population was most heavily concentrated. The black belt arcs from eastern Virginia down through the Deep South, across to Louisiana.

[5] Greenberg (1980); Schwartz (1976); Wright (1986).

resources had advantages to lose if the civil rights movement were successful. Each of these elements potentially regarded civil rights demands as threatening and therefore possessed strong incentives to oppose the movement. At the same time, these interests were generally insulated from the disruption costs from protests that might have induced bargaining and compromise. In addition to those with material interests in racial hierarchy, those whites with the most intense preferences in favor of defending the color line, the most fervent racists, regarded civil rights demands as unduly costly and might be expected to participate in countermobilization based solely on ideological zeal.[6] Most other southern whites, while opposed to integration, seldom participated in organized opposition and engaged in relatively undemanding forms of support, such as voting for segregationist candidates.

Finally, I discuss how the activities of movement antagonists shape target responses and, ultimately, movement outcome. As E. E. Schattschneider asserted in his classic *The Semisovereign People* (1960), the intervention of bystanders to a fight can determine the outcome of the struggle. So it was with the civil rights movement. In addition to the impact of white countermobilization diminishing movement participation, the organized backlash amplified the concession costs for movement targets and others.[7] Merchants suffering from protracted sit-ins and tempted to capitulate might be deterred from doing so by credible Klan threats of reprisal, or southern white moderates might hesitate to support racial integration out of fear of social ostracism and the loss of their livelihoods. In modulating the interactions between movement and targets, segregationist organizations influenced the outcomes of local and national movement struggles and, ultimately, the prospects for movement success. To evaluate these propositions, in this chapter I survey the patterns of white countermobilization and describe their impact upon the civil rights struggle.

[6] Scientific racists (those who purported to have a scientific basis for their white supremacist views) in academia, for instance, fit this description. These actors, formally positioned as conformers, threw their support behind the racial order due to their ardent ideological preferences. To some extent, certain agitators might be viewed as "racial entrepreneurs" who derived economic benefits from their leadership of racist organizations. Even scientific racists might derive exclusive personal benefits (selective incentives) and notoriety in their own market niche in southern society. For instance, these individuals often spoke before audiences to legitimate Jim Crow institutions, published opinion articles, and so on. The general assumption here is that actors without a clear interest in resisting the civil rights movement nor otherwise rewarded for doing so will constitute a relatively small bloc of organized opponents.

[7] Terchek (1974).

The Civil Rights Challenge to Southern Racial Inequalities

Accounting for the local patterns of response to civil rights mobilization begins by specifying the disruption and concession costs that the movement produced for southern whites. Disruption costs stemmed from the movement's capabilities to engage in persistent and significant interference with the interests of targets and third parties. To impose these disruption costs, movement activists used a wide array of institutional and unconventional tactics including litigation, lobbying, petitions, voter registration, political campaigns, marches, rallies, direct-action protests (such as sit-ins), economic boycotts, and on rare occasions violent actions, the last often in response to segregationist brutality. Several indicators suggest that the civil rights movement at times possessed the means to generate extensive disruption. The *New York Times*, a standard source for social movement event data, reported nearly thirteen hundred movement-initiated actions across the South from 1955 to 1965.[8] Estimates for total participation in the movement vary, but many estimates convey high levels of involvement. In contemporaneous interviews of southern African-American college students, 16 percent said that they had taken part in a sit-in during the first year of these protests.[9] Fully 24 percent indicated that they had participated in the student protest movement in some manner. After two years of sit-ins, an estimated one hundred thousand blacks and whites had actively participated in these activities. Over two hundred thousand spectators cheered at the March 28, 1963, March on Washington. During the surge in mass protests in 1963, the Southern Regional Council (SRC) estimated 930 individual protest demonstrations in 115 cities throughout the South, and more than twenty thousand arrests. In addition to these scattered campaigns, movement elements launched major sustained community-wide protests in Albany (1961–1962), Birmingham (1963), and Selma (1965). The many economic boycotts against downtown merchants, which were often effective at depressing profits, depended on the broader support of the black community. And, despite intimidation and violent repression by state authorities and private citizens, the movement demonstrated a fierce tenacity. With the escalation in protest activities and heightened media attention, the combined annual income of the top civil rights organizations rose sharply to total over

---

[8] McAdam (1982, 152). The South here does not include the Border South, but only the eleven states of the former Confederacy.

[9] Matthews and Prothro (1966, 412).

five million dollars in 1965.[10] Against vulnerable interests, coordinated community-wide protests and boycotts produced sizeable and durable disruptions. Although all too rare from the perspective of civil rights supporters, Justice Department lawsuits, court orders, and direct federal coercion at times added to the movement's capacities to impose costs upon intransigent public officials and private citizens.

Southern whites differed in their exposure to the disruptions that the movement generated. Local commerce, in particular, might be reduced with the onset of coordinated agitation. Lunch counters were blocked and downtown retail purchases plummeted. Too, segregationist violence against civil rights proponents drove customers away and tarnished the images of localities eager to attract external investment. The tumult that accompanied the 1957 integration of Central High School in Little Rock, Arkansas, in which President Eisenhower called in soldiers from the 101st Airborne Division to restore order, brought a sudden halt to that city's success in attracting new industry. At the same time, the movement's electoral leverage in southern politics was sorely limited. The localities in which African-Americans were most heavily concentrated were also those that discriminated the most aggressively in voter registration. In national politics, the migration of African-American voters to northern states that were crucial in presidential elections made office-seekers hesitant to invite their disaffection, at least until the latter 1960s. The disruptive capabilities of the civil rights movement, then, interfered more with certain economic interests and the political aspirations of national office-seekers than with black belt elected officials. Too, insofar as the movement successfully enlisted support of the national government, federal intervention vastly augmented the movement's disruptive capabilities.

Along with these disruption costs, the demands of the civil rights movement defined a constellation of concession costs for their targets and third parties. Despite the division of the movement into a few main organizations, as well as differences in tactics and demands, the disparate elements that constituted the civil rights movement focused during the years of peak activism on three principal goals: the desegregation of southern public schools, the integration of other public accommodations, and political inclusion (in particular, equitable voter registration).[11] Transformative

---

[10] McAdam (1982, 253).

[11] The "big four" organizations were the National Association for the Advancement of Colored People (NAACP), the Student Nonviolent Coordinating Committee (SNCC), the Southern Christian Leadership Conference (SCLC), and the Congress of Racial Equality

as they may have been for the pattern of racial interactions in the South, they threatened no fundamental redistribution of resources for the vast majority of southern whites. Although whites overwhelmingly preferred segregation, few whites actually derived tangible material benefits from the color line. If African-Americans went to white schools, the schools continued to educate all of the children. Black access to lunch counters or restaurants made a minimal difference in the availability of service for whites. In other words, civil rights demands were not zero-sum such that African-American gains amounted to equivalent white losses. Yet, to suggest that few whites gained material benefits from Jim Crow is not to suggest that none did. Certain actors did derive considerable benefit from white political dominance and economic disadvantage, and thus had a far greater interest in resisting the civil rights movement. And resist they did.

The Political Economy of the Plantation South

It is a fundamental axiom of southern politics that the most strident defense of the color line historically came from whites living along-side a greater concentration of African-Americans. As V. O. Key (1949) observed in his magisterial *Southern Politics*: "The hard core of the political South – and the backbone of southern political unity – is made up of those counties and sections of the southern states in which Negroes constitute a substantial proportion of the population."[12] From secessionist sentiment to Dixiecrat support in the 1948 presidential election, southern black belt counties were the foundation of southern political unity and the most tenaciously committed to white supremacy. As suggested above, this proposition rests upon the convergence of three overlapping but distinct interests. Specifically, civil rights threatened the economic imperatives of labor-intensive plantation agriculture. Although often overlooked,

(CORE). Some campaigns included other demands as well, including the desegregation of government-run public facilities, such as swimming pools or golf courses; equal employment opportunities; and the provision of public goods (including paved streets, lighting, enhanced fire protection services, and so on). In practice, the main civil rights organizations developed a division of labor, with the venerable NAACP often concentrating upon litigation to integrate public schools and accommodations, and to some extent voter registration. Church organizations, often affiliated with SCLC, participated in marches, protests, and boycotts to integrate public accommodations and promote voter registration. SNCC and other student organizations embraced direct action protests to bring about the integration of public accommodations and voter registration.
[12] 1949, 5; Heard (1952); Heer (1959).

embedded in Key's analysis was a keen appreciation for the economic interests in opposition to racial egalitarianism. The localities with large black populations crucially were also those in which "large-scale plantation or multiple-unit agriculture" prevailed.[13] The importance of maintaining a cheap, docile, and immobile labor force for plantation agriculture united these elites around the preservation of white supremacy. Elements of Key's analysis resonate with studies of democratic transitions from authoritarianism. These studies point to the reactionary impulses of agricultural elites engaged in labor-intensive production.[14]

Not only did the civil rights movement challenge an ensemble of economic interests tied to plantation agriculture, black enfranchisement represented a political threat to the electoral fortunes of black belt public officials as well.[15] The magnitude of the threat increased with the relative size of the potential African-American electorate. In those localities in which African-Americans made up an outright majority or a significant plurality, and had been barred from political participation, their sudden entrance into a political order premised on this exclusion represented a tremendous political threat. In Sunflower County, Mississippi, the birthplace of the Citizens' Council, African-Americans made up nearly 70 percent of the population, but only a handful were eligible to vote.[16] As the sheriff of Terrell County, Georgia, told a reporter: "I tell you, cap'n, we're a little fed up with this registration business... We want our colored people to go on living like they have for the last hundred years."[17]

Finally, at the most general level, aggregate white preferences in favor of racial segregation were often strongest in localities with large black populations.[18] Among less-educated whites, larger African-American population represented a greater competitive threat for various resources, particularly employment opportunities. Along with their economic interests, public opinion data suggest that black belt whites harbored the most negative beliefs about African-Americans and were strongly opposed to the prospect of racial integration. While hostile opinion might not be

[13] Key (1949, 5).
[14] Rueschemeyer, Stephens, and Stephens (1992).
[15] Although this chapter primarily addresses the conduct of third parties, the movement at times directly targeted black belt officials. As argued in the previous chapter, this analysis predicts the same behavior for both targets and third parties with the same cost configuration.
[16] McMillen 1971.
[17] *New York Times*, October 25, 1964.
[18] Heer 1959; Black 1976.

sufficient to elicit active countermovement participation, these intransigent whites often provided crucial electoral support for the most ardent segregationists. Collectively, this convergence of interests constitutes the foundation of Key's argument that the black belt whites cohered on racial matters – a hypothesis that has been the central analytical device for countless studies of southern racial politics.[19]

At the same time, southern planters, their allies, and black belt officials were insulated from movement disruption costs. Although many civil rights advocates believed that the southern racial order was vulnerable at the ballot box, absent white defection or supportive federal action to transform the structure of local political rewards, marches to city hall to demand evenhanded voter registration represented no real electoral threat to white officeholders. For African-Americans residing in the plantation belt, economic dependence upon whites made them especially vulnerable to repression. As Harold Fleming of the SRC pointed out: "The livelihood of Negroes in this agricultural area, except for an occasional professional man, has traditionally depended on the good will of white landlords, bankers, merchants and local officials. This economic dependence has always been a major instrument of social control."[20] NAACP field reports document numerous cases of Delta sharecroppers and farmers suffering economic reprisals because of their civil rights activities.[21] To the extent that civil rights organizers sought to unite African-American day laborers under the banner of the Mississippi Freedom Labor Union, their efforts met with crushing failure.[22] Coupled with extreme dependence on plantation elites, the reduction in demand for farm labor resulting from agricultural mechanization further discouraged protest and weakened the ability of African-American insurgents to disrupt agricultural interests. Civil rights activities threatened plantation interests in the fifties but, by the time African-Americans were capable of organizing agricultural labor, these workers lacked the bargaining leverage to exact concessions from planters. Instead, they could be casually discarded. The waning of the economic interest in defending labor-repressive agriculture that

---

[19] For instance, Black and Black (1987); Button (1989); Corzine, Creech, and Corzine (1983); Glaser (1994); Matthews and Prothro (1966).

[20] Fleming (1956, 48).

[21] Field Report from Medgar Evers and Mildred Bond, NAACP Papers, Part 20, Reel 3, Frames 408–11. On the fears of economic or violent reprisals even after the enactment of the Voting Rights Act of 1965, see Salamon and Van Evera (1973).

[22] Cobb 1994.

accompanied mechanization also lessened the imperatives for elite countermobilization – a point discussed further later in the chapter.

The serious threat that black enfranchisement posed to political targets and the movement's inability to directly impose disruption costs upon the targets' electoral prospects placed these interests decisively against accommodation. Under these circumstances, lingering on the sidelines of this struggle was not a satisfactory option; instead, these political targets had a compelling interest in entering the fray to resist the movement.

As the shock from the 1954 *Brown v. Board of Education* decision settled in across the region, it was overwhelmingly the political and economic elites from each state's black belt section that stepped forward to call for "massive resistance."[23] In his classic study, Numan Bartley (1969) found that the rural "neobourbons" – a coalition of labor-intensive producers of cotton and tobacco, their allies in banking and commerce, and local elected officials – provided the decisive impetus for reactionary countermobilization against *Brown*.[24] After scattered murmurs in support of rule of law, appeals for moderation were drowned out as the clamor against the decision swelled. The countermobilization of black belt elites manifested in three overlapping ways: they provided electoral support to the office-seekers espousing the most segregationist views, they provided political leadership in the construction of new legal fortifications to defend Jim Crow institutions, and they sought to unite southern whites into an interest organization capable of compelling racial orthodoxy throughout the region.

Rural black belt whites from all classes voted disproportionately for ardent segregationists. Updating Key's analysis for the post-*Brown* period, Earl Black found that counties where higher percentages of the

[23] *Brown v. Board of Education of Topeka, Kansas* 347 U.S. 483 (1954). The phrase was coined in 1956 by Governor Harry Flood Byrd of Virginia.

[24] Next to research on the civil rights movement, scholarship on southern resistance to civil rights gains is surprisingly limited. Bartley's *The Rise of Massive Resistance* (1969) remains a classic as does McMillen's *The Citizens' Council: Organized Resistance to the Second Reconstruction* (1971). Others include Wilhoit, *The Politics of Massive Resistance* (1973). There are additional studies concerning specific states and localities, such as Gates, *The Making of Massive Resistance* (1964) on Virginia, or Moye, *Let the People Decide* (2004) on Sunflower County, Mississippi. Recently, however, there has been more attention devoted to southern countermobilization. See Lewis, *Massive Resistance: The White Response to the Civil Rights Movement* (2006); Webb, *Massive Resistance: Southern Opposition to the Second Reconstruction* (2005). On the broader political dynamic that the *Brown* decision unleashed, see Klarman, *Brown v. Board of Education and the Civil Rights Movement* (2006).

population were African-American (greater than 30 percent) offered militant segregationists far more support in gubernatorial elections than counties with lower concentrations. "In the South after 1954 as well as in the pre-*Brown* South that Key analyzed, consistent support for the more outspoken advocates of racial segregation centered demographically in rural counties with large black populations."[25] To the extent that the black belt amounted to a significant share of the total statewide vote, this electoral leverage no doubt pushed the political field toward more extreme positions on racial integration and black enfranchisement.

From state capitols to county courthouses, black belt representatives advocated for the construction of legal barricades against encroachments from the federal courts and NAACP. In the years following the *Brown* decision, southern state legislatures enacted over 450 new laws to protest and evade the ruling with a range of devices from resolutions of defiance and pupil placement plans that limited desegregation to the barest tokenism to the more audacious, including nullification, interposition, and the closure of integrated public schools.[26] In many states, these representatives pushed for the formation of legislative committees to propose legal strategies of resistance, investigate "subversives," and roll back the threat to segregation and white supremacy.[27] In South Carolina, L. Marion Gressette, a representative from a cotton county, chaired the first legislative committee devoted specifically to orchestrating state anti-integration activities. In Louisiana, William Rainach, state senator

[25] 1973, 76. Black defines a "militant segregationist" as a candidate whose campaign rhetoric fulfils any of three criteria: statements of emphatic support for segregation without a counterbalancing qualifier (such as respect for the federal judiciary), segregation is a major campaign theme, or appeals to racial prejudice are used against political opponents (68). For a more detailed analysis, see also Black (1976).

[26] Murphy (1959); Roche (1998). Moye (2004) likewise reports the enactment of "nearly five hundred" such laws. Cook (1964, 133) reports 250 such laws in the first four years after *Brown*.

[27] During this struggle for civil rights legislation, southern congressional representatives – active in both the House Un-American Activities Committee (HUAC) and the Senate Internal Security Subcommittee (SISC) – charged that civil rights activists and organizations were Communists and a threat to American democracy. From their southern-controlled bastions in the federal government, the representatives of Dixie waged a propaganda war on integrationists. At the same time, these representatives had close ties to segregationist organizations and to the investigative committees created by most southern state legislatures after *Brown*. In turn, these state investigative committees cited HUAC and SISC hearings and reports to demonstrate the sinister Communist conspiracy lurking behind the struggle for civil rights. For a brief description of these connections, see "Reporter Gets Anti-Civil Rights Info from Segregationists Sources," *Atlanta Inquirer* (May 30, 1964).

from a cotton parish, led the Joint Legislative Committee to Maintain Segregation. Other leading segregationists came from the same parish, including Louisiana House Representative John S. Garrett, who served as vice chairman of Rainach's Segregation Committee, and William M. Shaw, who acted as the committee's chief legal counsel. Following the onset of widespread sit-in demonstrations and boycotts in 1960 in Virginia, committee chairman State Senator Joseph C. Hutcheson, from the black belt town of Lawrenceville, spearheaded investigations of Virginia chapters of the Southern Christian Leadership Conference (SCLC) and the Congress of Racial Equality (CORE). Similarly, governors and congressional representatives whose political bases resided in their state's black belt sections encouraged mobilization against federal encroachment upon "states' rights."

In addition, these legislators fashioned, in many states, new state sovereignty commissions to bolster the defense of Jim Crow. During the peak years of the massive resistance movement against the implementation of *Brown*, the Mississippi legislature created the Sovereignty Commission to oppose federal government "encroachment."[28] At the time, Walter Sillers, the speaker of the Mississippi House, called the Commission "the greatest forces [sic] we have in this battle to save the white race from amalgamation, mongrelization, and destruction."[29] Often with substantial appropriations, sovereignty commissions churned out a torrent of segregationist propaganda, conducted surveillance, infiltrated civil rights organizations with paid informers, helped local law enforcement identify potential "trouble-makers," and orchestrated various forms of economic intimidation and reprisals against movement participants and supporters. Almost without exception, the instigators and chief organizers for the political defense of white supremacy followed this pattern. In addition to the mobilization within state and local politics, black belt elites sought to extend their reach beyond their plantation strongholds under the auspices of the most formidable interest organization to emerge to defend segregation: the Citizens' Council.

The Citizens' Council

In the months immediately after *Brown*, new Citizens' Council chapters spread rapidly from the cotton plantation counties of the Mississippi

[28] *General Laws of the State of Mississippi*, Chapter 365. Similar agencies were established in most other southern states in this period as well; see McMillen (1971).

[29] Quoted in Carter (1959, 63). On the Mississippi State Sovereignty Commission, see Katagiri (2001).

Delta to establish a large membership base. Invoking the motto "States' rights and racial integrity," the organization attracted thousands of enthusiastic supporters. Council chapters spread across most Deep South states and into the Peripheral South as well.[30] Estimates of the total membership of the many local Council chapters vary widely. According to Neil McMillen, perhaps the most informed source on the southern resistance movement, the combined membership of all southern resistance organizations probably never exceeded three hundred thousand with the Council achieving a peak membership of perhaps two hundred fifty thousand.[31] Comparable organizations, though not under Council auspices, emerged as well. These included the Virginia Defenders of State Sovereignty and Individual Liberties, the Tennessee Federation of Constitution Government, and the Georgia States' Rights Council.[32] In April 1956, the leadership of various associations founded the Citizens' Council of America to form a loose confederation among the various state segregation organizations.

From the start, the Citizens' Councils core leadership and supporters were overwhelmingly drawn from plantation belt political and economic elites.[33] The Councils' organizational strength lay in states with the lingering strongholds of plantation agriculture: Alabama, Louisiana, Mississippi, and South Carolina. Robert B. Patterson, a principal founder of the White Citizens' Council in Mississippi, managed a Delta plantation. William J. Simmons, the son of a wealthy planter, organized the Council in Jackson and emerged as a major figure in the Council organization.[34] Indeed, six of the fourteen charter members of the first Citizens' Council, formed in Indianola, Mississippi, were farmers and closely tied to the plantation interests.[35] In Alabama, State Senator Engelhardt, "a planter whose feudal domain spread over 6,500 acres of Macon County," served as executive secretary of the state organization.[36] So too did State Senator Givhan of Dallas County, Alabama, who was "widely considered the

---

[30] The Deep South includes Alabama, Georgia, Louisiana, Mississippi, and South Carolina. The Peripheral South encompasses Arkansas, Florida, North Carolina, Tennessee, Texas, and Virginia.

[31] McMillen (1971, 153); Routh and Anthony (1957).

[32] There are exceptions to this general pattern. Unlike other states, the segregationist Patriots of North Carolina emerged in the Piedmont section of the state.

[33] McMillen (1971). As with black churches and colleges, Council organizers often turned to preexisting civic and fraternal organizations as mobilizing structures for membership recruitment.

[34] Muse (1964, 47).

[35] Moye (2004, 64–5).

[36] Bartley (1969, 88).

spokesman for the State Farm Bureau Federation" – the voice of the state's planters. U.S. Senator James O. Eastland of Mississippi, an ardent Council supporter, owned a large Delta plantation. Farley Smith, a Lynchburg planter and son of Senator "Cotton Ed" Smith, provided leadership in South Carolina.[37] In Louisiana, the Council derived core support in "the upland cotton districts along the Arkansas border and the fertile lowlands of the Red River and upper Mississippi River deltas, [where] the Councils formed a solid bloc of twenty-two parishes in the large-plantation area of the state, [and] where Negro concentration was heaviest and resistance to social change greatest."[38] State Farm Bureaus, the principal organization of plantation interests, "overwhelmingly aligned themselves with a vigorous defense of white supremacy."[39] Malcolm Dougherty, the president of the Louisiana Farm Bureau Federation, served in his state's Council leadership.[40] Many other examples might be cited. In sum, "the impetus, the organization, the leadership, and the control of this movement rested in the hands of the traditional black-belt ruling class that had emerged after Reconstruction."[41]

In 1954, before the mechanization of the cotton harvest, the civil rights movement continued to be a threat to these interests. As a Council member explained, "The NAACP's motto is, 'The Negro shall be free by 1963'– and shall we accept that? We can't have it, for if we do, it would ruin the economic system of the South. The men of the South are either for our council or against it. There can be no fence straddling."[42] Of course, as planters and their allies attempted to build a membership base, others joined to conform to local racist norms and to escape sanctions for deviation. "Many a Southerner," explained James Graham Cook in his analysis of organized segregationism, "has joined the 'socially acceptable' Council in his home town simply as a gesture of half-hearted willingness to drift along with the segregationist mood of the community."[43] Many lawyers, doctors, professors, and journalists thus went along with the current of local public opinion. In other words, exposed neither to disruption nor concession costs, they behaved as conformers. Others with passionate views about their own racial superiority, the perils of integration,

---

[37] McMillen (1971, 79).
[38] Ibid., 63.
[39] Bartley (1969, 314).
[40] Ibid., 91; McMillen (1971, 61–2).
[41] Bloom (1987, 101).
[42] Quoted in Vander Zanden (1965, 28).
[43] Cook (1964, 117).

and states' rights signed up as well. Nevertheless, it is difficult to imagine the mobilization of the Council without the backing of the political and economic elite of the plantation regions.

Organizational Activities

With the support of these black belt elites, the Council eschewed violence and instead meted out severe economic and legal reprisals against civil rights activists, supporters, and those whites who expressed less than full-throated support for white supremacy. From the beginning, Council spokesmen asserted their willingness to use black economic dependence upon whites to punish those who transgressed the color line or challenged white supremacist politics. The Citizens' Council in Yazoo City, Mississippi, published in a full-page newspaper advertisement "an authentic list of the purported signers to an NAACP communication to our school board."[44] Many signers lost their jobs and subsequently asked that their names be removed from the petition. A Council organizer in Dallas County, Alabama, candidly commented: "The white population in this county controls the money, and this is an advantage that the council will use in a fight to legally maintain complete segregation of the races. We intend to make it difficult, if not impossible, for any Negro who advocates desegregation to find and hold a job, get credit or renew a mortgage."[45] After harsh criticism in the press of this oft-quoted statement, the Council retreated from overt statements regarding the use of economic intimidation and reprisals. Nevertheless, subsequent reports of cases of economic reprisal indicate that this weapon remained in the Council arsenal. Allegations of economic reprisals persisted in Alabama, South Carolina, and Mississippi.[46]

The Council, whose membership included many black belt public officials, pushed for the enactment of a host of new legalistic devices for rolling back the civil rights movement. The Council supported new laws designed to harass civil rights organizations, expose their membership lists, and shut down their legal operations. Further, the Council argued for a myriad of legislative subterfuges and evasions to preserve segregated

---

[44] Bolton (2005, 240).
[45] Quoted in Fleming (1956, 48).
[46] Various reports in the *New York Times* describe these allegations, for instance April 9, 1955; November 27, 1955; February 13, 1955; July 31, 1956; September 19, 1956; November 14, 1957; September 13, 1958. Between 1954 and 1965, the *New York Times* reported over 80 instances of economic reprisals against individuals, mostly blacks, for support of civil rights activities.

public schools or, if necessary, shut them down and transfer their property, equipment, and funding to private academies. Councilors also advocated the maintenance of a white electorate. With the assistance of state representatives, they sponsored purges of black voters from the registration rolls. Between 1954 and 1959, north Louisiana parishes purged some thirty-one thousand registered African-Americans voters from the rolls.[47] In plantation counties, black exclusion had long been the pattern. In addition to substantial historical evidence, quantitative research likewise documents a strong association between indicators of labor-intensive agriculture and lower rates of black voter registration.[48]

As the rising tide of civil rights agitation disrupted movement targets, segregationists sought to defend Jim Crow through the imposition of even greater costs for capitulation upon public officials and private citizens. To do this, these movement antagonists, like all benefit-seekers, had various strategic options to affect the behavior of public officials.[49] They can attempt to shape public opinion to coincide with the organization's goals or activate latent public support by stimulating attentiveness to their cause. They may provide office-seekers with electorally valuable resources. Since obtaining information about constituent preferences can be costly, organizations can collect and communicate this information to office-seekers to encourage their conformity to local preferences. Similarly, organizations provide the electoral resources in the form of voter mobilization and campaign contributions, in addition to information about constituent preferences. Office-seekers weigh these electoral benefits against those provided by the organization's competitors. The greater the organization's capabilities in these strategic channels and the more likely that the organization's central issue will recur, the more formidable the benefit-seeker will be.[50] To this strategic list should be added the following: benefit-seekers will seek to undercut and outmaneuver their competitors in order to deprive office-seekers of electoral options. As Numan Bartley explains, "The Councils strove to counter political pressure activities of moderate and integrationist groups and to ally support behind segregationist public officials."[51]

---

[47] Bartley and Graham (1975, 58).

[48] James (1988). "All of the thirty-one counties in which the early voting rights suits," explains Aiken (1998, 189), "[were] brought by the Civil Rights Division were in the Deep South, and most were nonmetropolitan ones in the plantation regions."

[49] On these strategic options, see Burstein (1999).

[50] Hansen (1991).

[51] 1969, 199.

With elite support, Council leaders pursued all of these strategies. In particular, the Councils sought to shape southern public opinion, foster attentiveness among white voters, and punish moderates. As a Council publication declared: "The only reliable prophet for the future is the past, and history proves that the Supreme Power in the government of men has always been Public Sentiment. The Citizens' Council simply provides the machinery for mobilizing, concerting and expressing public opinion."[52] Across the South, Council speakers fanned out to rally white citizens to the cause. Council organizations produced and distributed vast quantities of anti-integration books and pamphlets extolling the virtues of southern traditions and states' rights, and exposing the sinister Communist machinations behind the movement for integration. In some states these activities included radio and television broadcasts to spread their interpretation of current events. In the early sixties the Mississippi State Sovereignty Commission channeled approximately $200,000 to the state Citizens' Council to promote the organization's campaign to trumpet the virtues of segregated institutions and to combat the alleged anti-southern bias of northern news coverage.[53] Many of these activities were aimed expressly at southern audiences to mold public opinion and heighten the white commitment to defense of segregation. As Lubell observed, "What these white-supremacy councils are trying to do is to kill off any hopes of gradual, evolutionary change by hammering Southern opinion into an embattled, unified state of feeling which will brook no compromise."[54]

The Council in particular sought to narrow the range of legitimate political debate about the South's racial situation. "The ways and means whereby moderate voices in the white community could be suppressed," wrote Council historian Neil McMillen, "were among the organization's first concerns."[55] Councils tolerated no other position than absolute support for Jim Crow, and deviation invited charges of traitorous betrayal of cherished southern values. A Council leader declared at the outset that, in addition to economic reprisals against unruly blacks, deviant whites

[52] Quoted in Carter (1959, 43).
[53] McMillen (1971, 337). Beginning in 1960, the director of the Sovereignty Commission announced the donation of a lump sum of $20,000 and a monthly contribution of about $5,000 a month to the Council to support the Council Forum – a radio and television program to broadcast themes of racial reaction.
[54] Quoted in Cook (1964, 136). On the more general point of movements seeking to shape "the universe of political discourse," see Jensen (1987).
[55] 1971, 251.

would be subjected to "social and political pressure."[56] The Council argued in particular in favor of ostracism for southern moderates, a disastrous prospect for an individual's business or political prospects. White moderates, including journalists, academics, and ministers, who strayed from or dared to challenge the Council position, were smeared with charges of Communist sympathies, and efforts were made to bring about their ouster.[57] And, as was often the case, individuals lost their jobs, newspapers lost advertisers, and businesses lost customers.

In *Mississippi: The Closed Society* (1964), James Silver, a historian at the University of Mississippi, describes how the Councilors challenged academic freedom and open discussion. After James Meredith integrated the University of Mississippi in 1962, the Council demanded that university faculty members either take an oath to support segregation or leave the university.[58] Faculty members who offered anything less than a wholehearted endorsement of segregation were singled out for a postcard campaign sent to the university authorities demanding that specific professors "and all other integrationists be removed immediately from the pay roll of Ole Miss."[59] The Council also instigated a challenge to the university's accreditation and threatened to seek the closure of the newly integrated university. Taking the defense of segregation into the classrooms involved as well a review of textbooks and library materials. Erle Johnston, the director of the Mississippi State Sovereignty Commission and a self-described "practical segregationist," declared in retrospect that "the Citizens Council was just stirring up hate *among* whites."[60]

Along with keeping southern white opinion in line, the Council actively participated in electoral politics and threatened white politicians with the tag of weakness on segregation. As Cook pointed out at the time, the Councils "screen, endorse, support, oppose and denounce candidates and public officials... to preserve segregation."[61] As suggested above, information is assumed to be costly for both voters and office-seekers. For voters, it is costly to learn about the actions of public officials, and public officials need accurate information about the priorities of actual

[56] The speaker was former Mississippi state senator Fred Jones, quoted in Fleming (1956, 48).
[57] Routh and Anthony (1957, 55).
[58] McMillen (1971, 246).
[59] Quoted in McMillen (1971, 247).
[60] Emphasis added. Available at: http://www.usm.edu/crdp/html/cd/citizens.htm (accessed March 15, 2006).
[61] 1964, 137.

or prospective majorities.[62] Benefit-seekers often attempt to reduce the information costs for voters so that political targets will conform to mass preferences, as well as provide office-seekers with information about constituent interests. The Council provided both types of information. To make certain that candidates espoused the "right" position on segregation – unbending resistance even if this meant closing the public schools – the Council in several cases sent out political questionnaires to candidates for public office. These questionnaires were meant to encourage them to profess their heartfelt devotion to segregation or risk denunciation.[63] Their effectiveness is unclear. Yet, in Alabama, the incumbent Governor James Folsom and allies were devastated in the 1958 election after they had not completed the questionnaires, whereas their opponents had affirmed their commitment to massive resistance in theirs. In that election, fervent segregationist challengers had derided Folsom and his associates as weak on the race issue. Fear of electoral reprisals doubtless impelled many legislators to adhere to the Council's orthodoxy, despite their own misgivings. As a Mississippi legislator explained, when the "hot eyes of Bill Simmons [the head of the state Council] were watching," he would vote in favor of a bill that "didn't make sense."[64] Regarding a bill to allow cities and counties to donate to the Council, another Mississippi legislator stated, "When the bill came up in the House...I thought it was unconstitutional. But I voted for it because if I had voted against the Councils, Bill Simmons would brand me as an integrationist."[65] In the states and localities of greater Council strength, the organization threatened to behave as an instigator capable of elevating voter attentiveness to punish wayward lawmakers for deviating from the Council's preferred position.

With elected officials in need of information about constituent preferences and their intensity, the Council eagerly obliged. In New Orleans, after fewer than two hundred moderates had signed a petition in favor of open schools and compliance with *Brown*, the local Council circulated a counterpetition that, in two weeks, attracted "almost 15,000 signatures demanding a continuation of segregation."[66] In Alabama, Louisiana, and Mississippi, Council affiliates surveyed white residents

[62] Arnold (1990); Hansen (1991).
[63] McMillen (1971, 306–8).
[64] Silver (1964, 42).
[65] Ibid.
[66] Bartley (1969, 199).

to determine their views on segregation and conveyed their findings (of virtually unanimous support) to elected officials. The electoral activities of the Council discouraged office-seekers, irrespective of their own views about the best responses to the *Brown* decision and the broader civil rights challenge, from deviating from intransigence. As Bartley explains, they "hoped to make the politicians dependent on the Councils."[67] So long as the Council had the capacity to punish moderate lawmakers or until other organizations were emboldened to mobilize against the Council, the political incentives were decisively weighted in favor of defiance.

Insofar as most southern whites believed in segregation and suffered no harm from civil rights protests, Councilors generally assumed that there would be adherence to local racial customs. However, for those business interests hit with protests that interfered with their normal operations (see Chapter 3), the Council applied threats of social ostracism and economic reprisals to discourage white defections. Roy Harris, president of the Citizens' Councils of America, called for "a boycott of merchants who fail to join and actively support racial segregation."[68] As with political actors, these prospective costs were more serious in those places with greater Council support. In the months immediately after the enactment of the 1964 Civil Rights Act, a Council boycott put out of business a movie theater that had integrated in Greenwood, a town in the heart of the Mississippi Delta. Similarly, the Jackson Citizens' Council threatened white businesses with boycotts if they complied with the new law. "Businessmen," cautioned the Jackson Citizens' Council, "cannot play both sides of the street; they must ultimately choose whether to serve white or Negro customers."[69] However, outside their black belt strongholds, the threat proved empty. Indeed, despite numerous reports of economic retaliation against insurgent blacks and the occasional white liberal, there are surprisingly few accounts of the same tactics being used by the Council against white businesses in cities outside the black belt. The Council's inability to impose severe concession costs in such cases reveals a fundamental weakness in their defense of Jim Crow – a defect that the civil rights movement effectively exploited. Further, in the states of the Peripheral South, such as Florida, North Carolina, Tennessee, and Texas, the Council or

---

[67] Ibid., Note 36.

[68] Southern Regional Council, "Intimidation, Reprisal, and Violence in the South's Racial Crisis" (1960, 9). The Council encouraged merchants to post Council membership stickers in their store windows to demonstrate their fealty to the organization.

[69] Quoted in McMillen (1971, 262).

analogous organizations were generally unable to extract policy concessions from lawmakers. Yet within their organizational strongholds, the
Council effectively wielded the threat of economic, political, and social
reprisals against movement targets and others who might dare articulate
support for anything less than absolute fealty to white supremacy.

Resource Competition and the White Countermobilization

Along with mobilization among black belt elites, the civil rights movement threatened other whites with significant concession costs. Specifically, the color line furnished lower-income and less-educated whites
with advantages in various spheres, including the labor market. Those
at the bottom rungs of the southern socioeconomic hierarchy derived
advantages due to the confinement of blacks to more menial occupational sectors and the privileging of whites in others. This view appears in
Gunnar Myrdal's classic *An American Dilemma* in which he observes that
lower-class whites "feel actual economic competition or fear of potential
competition from the Negroes. They need the caste line for much more
substantial reasons than do the middle and upper classes."[70] Bonacich
(1972), Cummings (1980), and Olzak and Nagel (1986) likewise posit
a theory of ethnic antagonism based on racially split labor markets in
which African-Americans threatened the relatively advantaged position
of certain blue-collar whites.[71] This competition perspective is consistent
with countless other studies on racial identity, attitudes, and politics.[72]
Popular news accounts of the period present similar analyses. Describing

---

[70] 1944, 199. See also Blalock (1967); Blumer (1958); Bobo (1983); Bobo and Hutchings
(1996). This general perspective is referred to variously as a competition theory, group
competition theory, or realistic group conflict theory, but, in important ways, the main
assumptions are the same.

[71] Based on occupational differences, Cummings (1980) distinguishes whites based on their
vulnerability to competition with African-Americans for jobs. He finds that those exposed
to greater economic competition generally hold more racially intolerant attitudes. At
times, research has collapsed the distinction between the black belt hypothesis, which
often rests on elite opposition to civil rights, and competition theory under the rubric
of a general "group threat" explanation; see Giles (1975). Group threat approaches
presume that ethnic or racial animus rises with the relative size of a minority population
and thereby blurs the main instigators of interracial strife. Despite some overlapping
hypotheses, I suggest that the black belt and competition approaches generate distinct
propositions and should be distinguished.

[72] Bobo (1983); Glaser (1994); Huckfeldt and Kohfeld (1989). The long history of working-
class white mobilization in Birmingham, Alabama, for protection against competition
with blacks in the labor market is richly described in McKiven (1995). Nor is this
competition confined to the South. Man (1951) offers a labor competition explanation
for the New York draft riots of 1963.

the racial strife in Birmingham, for instance, *Time* magazine observed that local whites "view desegregation less as an abstract threat to be fended off by lawyers than as a specific, bread-and-butter threat to jobs, promotions, and family security."[73] Likewise, as the editor of the McComb *Enterprise-Journal* explained, "A large part of the conflict in the area of race is economic."[74]

Although historical studies of reactionary movements have often pointed to status anxieties, more recent research treats countermobilization as an instrumental response to the intensification of competition over resources.[75] Again, economic competition drives variation in ethnic mobilization and conflict. Supplemental to these economic advantages, Roediger (1999) suggests that marginal whites gained other social and psychological "wages" associated with their whiteness. Not coincidentally, in opinion surveys, whites in more vulnerable occupations and those with less education often harbored the most negative views of African-Americans and hostile attitudes toward integration.[76] Finally, the working-class neighborhoods often had less residential segregation and therefore found the prospect of school desegregation relatively more threatening (or were selected by local school boards for desegregation before middle- or upper-income districts). This exposure to the concession costs associated with the egalitarian thrust of the civil rights movement fostered opposition among vulnerable whites and stimulated reactive countermobilization.

Coupled with their greater exposure to concession costs, these threatened lower-income whites had weak incentives to bargain or compromise with movement activists due to a corresponding insulation from disruption costs. They were not generally vulnerable to civil rights disruptions,

---

[73] December 15, 1958; quoted in Eskew (1997).

[74] Oliver Emmerich, McComb *Enterprise Journal*, October 23, 1964.

[75] McVeigh (1999); Olzak (1992). In addition to economic competition, civil rights gains threatened lower-class whites with additional specific concession costs as well. In Little Rock and New Orleans, the public schools attended by the children of these whites were singled out for integration while segregation was allowed to continue in schools of upper-income families. In both cases, large crowds formed to resist integration. In sum, multiple sources support the contention that certain lower-income whites favored defending their relatively advantaged position under Jim Crow. On reactionary militia mobilization during the 1990s as a response to structural social changes, see Van Dyke and Soule (2002).

[76] Sheatsley (1966). Those employed in unskilled, semi-skilled, and skilled occupations reported far less racial liberalism than other categories such as professionals.

particularly because the principal targets of civil rights protests were public officials and the operators of downtown retail establishments. Mostly, the impact of civil rights protests would have been felt as an inconvenience as crowds of onlookers and police interfered with shopping in the downtown center. Damage to a locality's reputation in the national media or the indefinite losses in external investment too seem unlikely to have been felt as a significant cost. A local business slowdown due to reduced economic activity might have taken months to be felt by working-class whites. Thus, in general, these whites were shielded from movement disruption costs but vulnerable to those associated with certain tangible, immediate civil rights gains. These marginal whites, then, might be deemed conformers insofar as they dealt only with concession costs in the abstract, but as resisters if they were confronted by prospective losses from immediate concessions to movement demands.[77]

The threat of heightened racial competition and insulation from disruption costs encouraged certain lower socioeconomic status whites to support the most vehement segregationists for elective office. In their careful analysis of voting behavior, Bartley and Graham (1975) found strong support for militant segregationists in working-class precincts during the heyday of the civil rights movement. In the 1960 Democratic gubernatorial primary election in North Carolina, for instance, the fierce segregationist I. Beverly Lake attracted 44 percent of the runoff vote, despite the opposition of most Democratic party regulars. In that election, he swept the rural black belt section and attracted considerable support among lower-income whites.[78] Although lower-income whites previously supported populist reformers and New Dealers, the sudden entrance of race into southern politics drew this element of the electorate into alliance with their traditional opponents – black belt elites. "Voting patterns varied, of course, but in state after state the populist–New Deal alignments of the early postwar years broke apart, as rural and low-income whites shifted from support of economic reform to defense of social conservatism."[79] This pattern nevertheless coincides with the expectation that those whites with the most to lose from civil rights gains formed a bulwark of political support for segregation. Of these whites, some went beyond voting

---

[77] Soule and Van Dyke (1999) find support for competition theory in their analysis of black church burnings, which were widely reported in the 1990s.

[78] Bartley and Graham (1975, 76).

[79] Ibid., 80.

for militant segregationists and random scuffles with civil rights demonstrators to enter the ranks of the most infamous foe of the civil rights movement – the Ku Klux Klan.

The Ku Klux Klan

The Klan that emerged after the *Brown* decision was actually the third incarnation of that organization.[80] Unlike the prior waves of mobilization during Reconstruction and then again in the 1920s, the Klan that arose to oppose the civil rights movement was far smaller, divided into multiple organizational units with diverse and competing leaders, and perhaps more importantly, it lacked respectability or elite endorsement. Nevertheless, along with Council mobilization, the various Klans gained new recruits after the *Brown* decision. Eldon Edwards, an Atlanta autoworker, organized a new ensemble of "klaverns" under the aegis of U.S. Klans, Knights of the Ku Klux Klan, Inc. In a founding ceremony in 1956, this new organization drew a crowd of more than three thousand from across the South to Stone Mountain, Georgia, which had been the birthplace of the Second Klan. A 1958 survey by the Anti-Defamation League placed the membership of Edwards's U.S. Klans between twelve and fifteen thousand; the North Carolina Klan between two and five thousand; and estimated that another fifteen hundred belonged to the seven other Klan organizations.[81] By the end of the decade these organizations had weakened, but the acceleration of civil rights protests in the 1960s stimulated further Klan countermobilization. By the 1960s the United Klans of America (UKA), headed by Robert Shelton, became the largest of the Klan organizations. Headquartered in Tuscaloosa, Alabama, the UKA had an estimated membership between twenty-six and thirty-three thousand. The UKA had numerous affiliates in other southern states with the strongest branch located in North Carolina, where more than half the total membership resided. Overall, the Klan was not a mass organization; across the South, Alabama, Georgia, Mississippi, North Carolina, and Virginia were the only states with local memberships in excess of one thousand.[82] The many Klan leaders and organizations competed for membership and never offered a unified defense of white supremacy. By 1967, after stepped

[80] Some commentators, counting the resurgence in the immediate postwar period, might argue that the Klan of the 1960s was the fourth incarnation.
[81] Given the organization's secretiveness, studies of the Klan suffer from many uncertainties regarding total membership over time. Researchers commonly rely upon data from the Anti-Defamation League.
[82] Aiken (1998, 176).

up federal and state repression had been used to check the organizations, the estimated membership had fallen below seventeen thousand. While these figures suggest an organization capable of doing significant harm, they do not depict an organization composed of more than a small minority of southern whites.[83] Several other smaller organizations, lacking the Klan appellation, were essentially variants of the same organizational type, such as Americans for the Preservation of the White Race (APWR).

Whereas the Citizens' Council represented the elites of the plantation regions, the various factions of the Klan served as the principal segregationist organizations for the white lower and lower-middle classes of the cities and towns. Both the patterns of participation in the KKK and ostensible motivations in this organization coincide with the predictions of competition theory. Virtually every journalistic account describes the Klan leadership and rank-and-file membership as less educated and economically marginal. Based on a limited sample of 153 Klan members and leaders (of unknown representativeness), Vander Zanden found a mix of skilled and semi-skilled workers as well as marginal white-collar workers (store clerks, service station attendants, etc.).[84] Bartley suggests that the Klan's membership "was drawn almost exclusively from the lower socioeconomic groups in Southern society."[85] A "former officer of the United Klans of America described the 'rank and file members' as persons 'drawn from uneducated elements of the population who never attained the social status they would [have liked] to achieve.'"[86] Whereas

---

[83] In accounting for the weakness of southern countermobilization, Chappell (2004) provides a somewhat different explanation. He argues that, unlike the civil rights movement, southern religious figures and institutions refused to provide a compelling moral defense of the segregated South. Without this philosophical and infrastructural foundation upon which to construct an effective countermovement, organized opposition was inherently weak. Since countless studies document the centrality of the black church to the civil rights struggle (see McAdam [1982]; Morris [1984]), the unwillingness of white churches to operate as a counterweight certainly seems relevant. The lack of this preexisting set of social ties and organizational infrastructure denied the white backlash an essential mobilizing structure and no doubt hindered collective action. From the perspective presented here, in addition to a cultural aversion to expounding a religious argument for white supremacy, the southern white clergy could behave as conformers in large measure because civil rights demands were threatening to neither their fundamental interests nor those of their congregants. It is suggestive that, in the antebellum period, when there was a more direct threat to a larger share of their parishioners, these institutions were capable of finding a moral justification for racial subordination. Ultimately, antislavery activism produced sectional rifts in the Baptist, Methodist, and Presbyterian dominations.

[84] 1965, 43.

[85] 1969, 204.

[86] Aiken (1998, 177).

the Citizens' Councils were strongest in small towns of the black belt, it is telling that those found in urban, non–black belt settings relied on rhetoric much like the Klan's and were "usually composed of individuals from lower and lower-middle class stations." The North Alabama Citizens' Council, for example, drew support from "the industrial suburbs of Birmingham... [and the membership] was comprised almost entirely of laborers, many of whom were union men."[87] Recent research based on a representative sample of Alabama Klansmen (in 1963–64) confirms the portrait of Klan membership as drawing heavily from lower-income whites.[88]

While the threat to the political economy of plantation agriculture actuated black belt elites, racial egalitarianism provoked certain marginal whites in the Klan to defend the competitive advantages that they derived from their skin color. Although fierce racism, preexisting social ties to Klan members, and permissive state authorities no doubt facilitated the entrance of certain whites into the hooded order, multiple accounts of working-class hostility to racial equality and countermobilization corroborate the competition explanation. For example, a civil rights activist in Natchez, Mississippi, noted that "the whites there feel definitely threatened by Negro labor (terrorism and brutality are believed to be the work of white industrial workers in the area)."[89] Regarding membership of the Klan and the motivations of members, Cook writes:

> The Ku Klux Klan... is made up mainly of people of low income – people who cannot afford to send their children to private segregated schools, who cannot afford to flee to racially pure suburbs to escape Negro neighbors, and whose jobs might seem to them to be most immediately threatened by the institution of "fair-employment" laws.[90]

In his analysis of Birmingham, Alabama, Eskew (1997) argues that the civil rights movement "threatened white jobs and family security" and that "massive resistance protected white workers during the transition into a service-consumer economy." Fairclough, in his exhaustive investigation of the civil rights movement in Louisiana, sketches how resource competition shaped racial contention in the Klan-ridden town of Bogalusa. "The Bogalusa crisis... exposed the economic dimension of the racial conflict: the struggle for desegregation was fought against the

[87] McMillen (1971, 47).
[88] Cunningham (2007A).
[89] Sutherland (1965, 67).
[90] 1962, 118.

backdrop of the giant Crown-Zellerbach plant, where black and white workers competed for a shrinking number of jobs and promotions."[91] In Bogalusa, Fairclough demonstrates, the civil rights struggle was cast as a direct challenge to white economic privileges.[92] Northrup and Rowan (1970) found in their investigation of southern pulp and paper mills that "Negro jobs and Negro employment were especially hard hit in the South, but this first heavy taste of job insecurity since World War II [in the early 1960s] tended to harden opposition of white workers to improved job opportunities for Negroes, while at the same time strengthening the demands of Negroes for a change in the racial-occupational pattern."[93] In Laurel, Mississippi, Klansmen kidnapped and flogged a leader in a Mississippi woodworkers' union because "the union had approved a Federal order giving Negroes equal treatment in the Masonite plant."[94] Comparing data on the occupations of Alabama Klansmen with the larger local population, Cunningham (2007A) found additional support for the competition explanation of reactive countermobilization. Specifically, he found that, whereas whites in higher-skill and professional sectors exposed to less competition from nonwhite workers were significantly underrepresented in the Klan, whites in sectors with higher proportions of African-American workers were overrepresented. Cunningham concludes that the evidence "support[s] the view that the Klan's appeal was strong within sectors where workers' status would be most vulnerable to looming changes posed by desegregation policies."[95] Thus, as indicated above, a growing body of research finds reactive mobilization to be an instrumental response to heightened resource competition.[96]

Organizational Activities

To protect their advantaged position within the Jim Crow racial order, whites in the many Klan units and comparable supremacist organizations engaged in various actions to heighten the concession costs for movement targets and frighten civil rights sympathizers. Rallies were

[91] Fairclough (1995, 346).
[92] Labor organizations, feeble though they were in the South, typically reinforced the color line to protect the advantaged position of white workers. Although national and some local union leaders affirmed their commitment to biracial labor organizations, rank-and-file whites resisted these moves time and again.
[93] Northrup and Rowan (1970, 55).
[94] Forster and Epstein (1965, 26).
[95] 2007A, 303.
[96] See also Beck (2000).

widespread and, despite the relatively small formal membership, it was not uncommon for these to attract more than a thousand spectators.[97] Klan orators regaled listeners with stories of the grave dangers of Communism and "race mixing," and they called on the white "Anglo-Saxon South" to defend Christianity, white womanhood, and "the Southern way of life." These events culminated in a parade of uniformed Klansmen setting aflame a large wooden cross. Despite the absence of open calls for violence, contemporary observers regarded these occasions not only as recruitment devices but as a means to intimidate conciliatory whites, local politicians, and civil rights activists.

Aware of the organization's unpopularity among white southerners, the Klan purported to be a conventional political organization with the purpose of swaying the behavior of movement targets. They argued for registering more whites to vote to overwhelm any increase in black voter registration and maintain the political rewards tilted toward strict segregation. Like the Citizens' Council, the Klan and comparable organizations staged counterprotests and pickets of stores, restaurants, theaters, and other public facilities that had desegregated. As sit-ins began in Atlanta in late 1960, nearly one hundred Klansmen in Atlanta counterpicketed those department stores that were the target of civil rights activities.[98] They urged whites "not to patronize firms that desegregate, but buy from those that don't."[99] Segregationist countermobilization indeed fostered concerns among business interests that they might suffer from concessions. The *Atlanta Constitution* summed up the worries of many members of the business community: "Even the most moderate is likely to contemplate desegregation with real uneasiness. The fears, sound or baseless, of segregationist reprisal and economic failure run strong."[100] In Charleston, as the merchants brokered an agreement with demonstrators to integrate, five men from the National Association for the Preservation of the White Race circulated a flyer reading: "Attention. If you are in favor of preserving our way of life won't you please boycott any store who favor integration. Thank you." Segregationists in Savannah likewise began a boycott against stores that had desegregated.[101]

---

[97] Bartley (1969, 20).
[98] *New York Times*, November 7, 1960.
[99] *New York Times*, August 11, 1963.
[100] Quoted in Tuck (2001, 136).
[101] *New York Times*, July 11, 1961.

Yet, unlike the elite backers of the Council movement, Klansmen had relatively fewer options at their disposal to deter insurgent blacks, and to intimidate white supporters and those willing to capitulate to movement demands. Along with public rallies and occasional picketing, the Klan therefore resurrected the historical use of harassment, violence, and fear. The SRC reported: "Gunpowder and dynamite, parades and cross burnings, anonymous telephone calls, beatings, and threats have been the marks of their trade. These attacks have been directed not only at Negroes, but at some white persons who have strayed from local customs."[102] In an extensive report of four years of southern resistance immediately after *Brown*, the SRC tabulated some 530 instances of "intimidation, reprisal, and violence" against African-American civil rights advocates and white moderates. Although all of these events cannot necessarily be attributed to the Klan, the statistics of the lengthy summary section on violence are striking:

6 Negroes killed; 29 individuals, 11 of them white, shot and wounded in racial incidents; 44 persons beaten; 5 stabbed; 30 homes bombed; in one instance (at Clinton, Tenn.) an additional 30 houses were damaged by a single blast; attempted blasting of five other homes; 8 homes burned; 15 struck by gunfire, and 7 homes stoned; 4 schools bombed, in Jacksonville, Nashville, and Chattanooga, and Clinton, Tenn.; 2 bombing attempts on schools, in Charlotte and Clinton; 7 churches bombed, one of which was for whites; an attempt made to bomb another Negro church; 1 church in Memphis burned; another church stoned; 4 Jewish temples or centers bombed, in Miami, Nashville, Jacksonville, and Atlanta; and 3 bombing attempts on Jewish buildings, in Gastonia, N.C., Birmingham, and Charlotte.[103]

The SRC acknowledges that the tally, drawn from press reports, is doubtless incomplete. Further, the more notorious events, particularly those that appeared in the media, had broader significance in that they signaled to others the risks of supporting racial change.

Already fierce, intimidation and violent resistance against civil rights advocates grew stronger as the sit-in movement gathered momentum. According to an Anti-Defamation League report, in March 1960, "more than a thousand crosses were burned in Alabama, Florida, Georgia, and the Carolinas and other southern states [as a] show of strength by the then newly formed National Knights of the KKK."[104] Although the Klan

---

[102] Southern Regional Council, "Intimidation, Reprisal, and Violence in the South's Racial Crisis" (1960).
[103] Ibid.
[104] Forster and Epstein (1965, 26).

leadership insisted that the organization was nonviolent, it was presumed to have conducted numerous terrorist incidents.[105] Using arson and bombings, the Klan sought to silence civil rights activists, frighten white moderates, and foster a climate of fear in which few wished to question the racial order. During a CORE-sponsored Freedom Ride in 1961, in which participants rode on interstate buses into the South to test federal willingness to enforce a Supreme Court ruling banning segregation in interstate transportation facilities, riders sometimes met with severe violence. In Birmingham, local law enforcement allowed Klansmen fifteen minutes in which to assault riders with baseball bats, chains, and metal pipes. At times, Klansmen resorted to murder, including the notorious killing of four girls in the 1963 bombing of the Sixteenth Street Baptist Church in Birmingham as well as the slayings of Lemuel Penn, James Chaney, Andrew Goodman, and Michael Schwerner, Viola Liuzzo, and Vernon Dahmer.[106] Although Klan responsibility for these events was sometimes uncertain, a tally of incidents against civil rights activists from the annual *New York Times Index* from 1954 to 1965 includes over fifteen hundred events instigated by white citizens. Among them were over three hundred incidents of harassment, one hundred bombings and arsons, over one hundred racial clashes, and in excess of five hundred acts

---

[105] Schaefer (1971, 55).

[106] I briefly summarize these episodes here for readers unfamiliar with them. After the climax of the Birmingham campaign in 1963, Klansmen bombed the local movement headquarters at the Sixteenth Street Baptist Church. Four girls, Addie Mae Collins, Denise McNair, Carole Robertson, and Cynthia Wesley, died in the blast as they prepared for Sunday school. Next, traveling through Georgia as he returned home to Washington, D.C., Lemuel Penn, a Lieutenant Colonel in the U.S. Army Reserve and a decorated World War II veteran, died after local Klansmen fired into his automobile. Acting nine days after President Johnson signed the Civil Rights Act of 1964, the murderers evidently believed, due to his license plates, that Penn was affiliated with the Johnson administration. Also in 1964, at the outset of the Freedom Summer, Mississippi Klansmen, including members of the local police, abducted three civil rights workers, murdered them, and buried their bodies in an earthen dam. Unlike previous murders in which African-Americans were the victims, this case attracted national attention because two of the victims (Goodman and Schwerner) were white. President Johnson pushed the FBI to pursue an extensive search for the civil rights workers. During this massive search operation, the bodies of two missing African-Americans (Henry Dee and Charles Moore) were also found. Liuzzo, a civil rights supporter from Michigan who had traveled to Alabama for the 1965 Selma to Montgomery march, died after Klansmen fired into her car while she was returning demonstrators to their homes. In 1966 Klansmen firebombed the home of Vernon Dahmer, a local NAACP leader in Hattiesburg, Mississippi. Although his family escaped the flames, Dahmer suffered fatal burns as he returned gunfire coming into his house.

of violence.[107] These actions resulted in more than one thousand injuries and at least twenty-nine murders.[108] Again, countless other incidents of harassment and threats were likely never reported.

For some whites willing to concede to movement demands, attempted violence and actual assaults no doubt affected the perceptions about the cost of doing so. Various examples demonstrate this point. For instance, two school board members in Baton Rouge who had opposed the governor's school board "packing" measure to resist integration had nighttime visits at their homes from hooded figures who left notes simply stating, "No integration – KKK," and a third received death threats over the telephone.[109] In St. Augustine, after a protracted struggle and the reaching of an agreement to integrate certain public accommodations, picketers carried inflammatory signs outside the newly integrated facilities. An exasperated businessman declared: "We have been caught in a dilemma . . . we are forced to serve Negroes although it hurts our business. If we serve them, then white pickets run the rest of the business away."[110] Threatening phone calls began for the operators of integrated restaurants and motels. Then, after arson damaged the motel restaurant of a racial moderate, the businesses that had integrated reversed themselves. Similarly, in Bogalusa, Louisiana, following the enactment of the Civil Rights Act of 1964, six whites invited Brook Hays, a former congressman and racial moderate, to speak about the challenges of integration. Immediately, the Klan began a terrorist campaign against the six, in particular, Ralph Blumberg, the operator and co-owner of a local radio station. Callers harassed them constantly with threats of violence. "He's signed his death warrant," declared an anonymous caller to Blumberg's wife.[111] Station sponsors were intimidated until most canceled their commercials. In a leaflet distributed around the town, whites were warned against attending the prospective meeting with Hays. "Those who do attend . . . will be tagged an integrationist and will be dealt with accordingly by the Knights of Ku Klux Klan." Despite the cancellation of the meeting, Blumberg editorialized on the radio about freedom of speech

---

[107] Data collected by the author.
[108] These figures do not include incidents of ostensibly racially motivated violence but with no apparent connection to the civil rights movement. Maya Lin's civil rights southern memorial includes the names of forty fatalities of the civil rights struggle.
[109] *New York Times*, February 25, 1961
[110] Quoted in Colburn (1982, 229).
[111] Forster and Epstein (1965, 28).

and respect for law. The threats and harassment continued unabated. His car windows were smashed, his tires flattened, and shots were fired at the station's transmitter. Eventually, Blumberg went out of the business and moved his family out of the state.

A similar fate befell Albert W. "Red" Heffner, Jr., of McComb, Mississippi. Though he was a respected and popular member of the community, everything changed after Heffner invited two civil rights workers to his house for dinner in 1964 to discuss how to reduce community tensions stemming from an ongoing voter registration drive. After months of continuous harassment, threats, ostracism, reprisals against his business, and the mysterious death of the family dog, Heffner and his family left the state.[112] As Bartley suggests regarding the Klan, the "everpresent threat of physical retribution was a significant factor in encouraging those who would dissent to hold their peace."[113] Even in the absence of great numbers, anonymous intimidation and threats of violence might substantially affect target perceptions of the costs of conceding to movement demands.

In politics, the Klan was less formidable. Except in Alabama, the Klan lacked political clout to shape the electoral calculations of office-seekers. In Alabama politics, the Klan pushed for more aggressive policies to defend segregation. Gubernatorial candidate John Patterson openly sought support from the Council and leaders of the Klan in the 1958 election and made his commitment to segregation the centerpiece of his campaign. With his successful election into the governor's office, Patterson met with Council leaders and state policy tilted toward massive resistance to the implementation of *Brown*. In the same election, George Wallace had resisted courting the Klan's support but, stung by his defeat, promised never to be outdone in racist appeals and sought Klan backing in

[112] These events are recounted in newspaper stories, Mississippi State Sovereignty Commission Papers, and secondary sources. See Mississippi State Sovereignty Commission Papers (MSSCP) online, Folder Red Heffner, SCR ID # 2-36-2-37-1-3-2 (accessed July 11, 2008). See also Dittmer (1994). The Klan and similar organizations, such as Americans for the Preservation of the White Race, engaged in other operations that targeted local businesses. At times, a business owner might be notified by these organizations that certain African-American employees were "trouble-makers" and must be fired. If they refused to comply, trouble began. After a merchant in Liberty, Mississippi, refused to terminate a long-time employee, "within 24 hours a strangling boycott had been set up against his business." After a few weeks, the abandonment of his white customers left his business in a shambles and he capitulated to the organization's demands. Kenneth Tolliver, "New Racist Organization Terrorizes Several South Mississippi Counties," *Delta Democrat-Times*, undated, MSSCP, SCR ID # 6-36-0-19-1-1-1 (accessed July 11, 2008).

[113] 1969, 201.

his successful 1962 bid for the governorship. His inaugural vow of "segregation now, segregation tomorrow, segregation forever," foreshadowed Wallace's own fervent defense of Jim Crow throughout his administration. However, beyond Alabama and a few scattered localities, the Klan's numbers were too few to offer credible threats of electoral reprisal.

Overall, the general pattern of Klan mobilization coincides with the vulnerabilities of certain whites to the concession costs associated with civil rights gains. The various Klans engaged in a wide range of tactics to oppose the civil rights movement and others in favor of racial moderation. These included conventional rallies and political mobilization, but shaded into more sinister acts meant to intimidate, injure, and sometimes kill movement supporters. As movement targets and others contemplated how to respond to civil rights agitation, Klan threats and picketing no doubt discouraged many from deviating from southern racial norms. Irrespective of the preferences of movement targets toward civil rights, fear of organized reprisals and violence discouraged capitulation and fostered instead hesitation and vacillation. Further, Klan intimidation and violence against civil rights activists and supporters might have deterred participation and threatened local movements with collapse. Yet, the willingness of participants in the civil rights movement to brave these fears and to continue their struggle deprived vulnerable targets of the option of indefinite delay.

Council and Klan Mobilization in the 1960s

The divergent life histories of the Citizens' Councils and the Klan further suggests that exposure to concession costs affects the intensity of reactive countermobilization. Although the Citizens' Council mobilized in the immediate wake of the *Brown* decision, it limped into the 1960s, despite the eruption of provocative direct-action civil rights protests across the South. This is all the more surprising because contemporaneous observers in the late fifties pointed out that Council membership generally surged amid challenges upon Jim Crow. Yet, rather than experiencing an organizational resurgence, the Council movement peaked in 1957 and declined steadily thereafter.[114] The attempted revitalization of the moribund Citizens' Council in response to the escalation of civil rights agitation failed miserably, even though the apparent threat to the southern racial order was greater than ever before. By contrast, the escalation of civil rights

[114] McMillen (1971, 152).

protests triggered Klan countermobilization with the membership rising steadily into the middle 1960s. Writing in the mid-sixties, Forster and Epstein declared, "Today, the Klans have replaced the Councils as the symbol and instruments of last-ditch resistance."[115]

While various explanations might be offered for this pattern, such as the Council's failure to halt token integration in the decisive challenges with federal authorities or growing urban elite unease with the Council's extremist policies, some measure of the Council's weakness in the 1960s appears attributable to declining concession costs among plantation interests. Throughout most of the plantation South, the astonishing pace of mechanization of the cotton harvest substantially reduced dependence upon black farm labor and produced a corresponding diminution of the economic threat from civil rights gains. In the year of the *Brown* decision, nearly 90 percent of the Mississippi cotton harvest was still picked by hand, but, by 1965, in the cradle of organized countermobilization, the figure had fallen to less than 25 percent.[116] Thus, despite the escalation of civil rights agitation, it was insufficient to inspire renewed elite countermobilization, even within much of the plantation belt.[117] At the same time that mechanization was weakening the resolve of plantation interests to defend Jim Crow, the threat of economic competition had not abated for vulnerable working-class whites. Accordingly, as elite countermobilization dwindled, segregationist organizations were resurgent in numerous communities across the South as these vulnerable working-class whites joined them to keep blacks "in their place." Thus, what might appear to be a puzzling divergence in the organizational histories of the two principal segregationist organizations can be traced in some measure to changes in the costs associated with movement success.

Summary

This chapter addresses three general propositions. First, the responses of third parties are patterned and based on the same logic that shapes target responses. As most third parties suffer neither from movement disruptions nor the cost of a target's capitulation, they are expected to behave

[115] Forster and Epstein (1965, 7).
[116] Wright (1986, 244). Aiken (1998, 26) reports that "the percentage of cotton harvested by machines [in the Yazoo Delta] jumped from 69% in 1964 to 95 in 1966."
[117] On the declining elite concern over the agricultural labor supply in this period, see Greenberg (1980); Wright (1986).

as conformers in which they take no action and adhere to dominant local customs. By contrast, third parties that intervene in movement-target interactions will be disproportionately interests shielded from movement disruptions but vulnerable to the costs of movement victory. Next, multiple studies of southern racial history and politics document this cost configuration. To delineate these specific concession costs, I have relied mainly upon two approaches applicable to southern race relations: the black belt hypothesis and competition theory. These perspectives clarify the specific patterns of white countermobilization among black belt elites and marginal whites. Thus, members of both the Citizens' Council and the Klan represented elements of the white populations most vulnerable to civil rights gains and relatively insulated from the costs of movement disruptions. Circumstantial evidence appears in the divergent life histories of the Council and the Klan. Finally, countermobilization by third parties affects how movement targets and others respond to movement demands; in particular how they calculate the costs of capitulation. Surveying the activities of black belt officials, Councilors, and Klansmen, it is clear that countermovements do more than simply lash out at movement activists and supporters. Rather, they seek to deter targets from capitulating as well as discourage supportive intervention from other third parties. The intensity of countermobilization conditions a movement's likelihood of success. Greater countermobilization diminishes a movement's prospects for extracting concessions from targets as the magnification of concession costs pushes targets toward either vacillation or resistance. Conversely, weak or absent organized opposition furnishes targets with greater latitude in defining their optimal response to movement demands, and improves the likelihood of movement success. Together, these propositions highlight the fundamental point that any explanation for movement outcomes must incorporate an account of the actions of antagonistic third parties, a point elucidated further in the case studies found in Chapter 4.

3

The Calculus of Compromise

Against organized countermobilization and hostile southern white public opinion, how were local civil rights struggles capable of winning concessions? This perspective draws attention to the relative magnitude of disruption and concession costs for both targets and third parties. As the previous chapter demonstrated, the combination of high concession costs and low disruption costs for certain interests prompted them to react with fierce countermobilization. However, I suggest that, for most southern whites, the economic or political costs associated with acceding to civil rights demands were low, and therefore that Jim Crow institutions were far more vulnerable than might be assumed based on southern public opinion alone, an "imposing but hollow structure" as civil rights stalwart Bayard Rustin averred.[1] Of course, the vast preponderance of southern whites undoubtedly preferred segregation, but relatively few derived significant benefits from segregated public accommodations, public schools, or black disfranchisement. Though intimidation and violence pervaded segregationist strongholds in Alabama, Louisiana, and Mississippi, overall countermobilization against the civil rights movement was often anemic.[2] Although the Citizens' Council and Ku Klux Klan (KKK) beckoned

---

[1] Rustin (1965).

[2] I do not mean to suggest here that non-material interests cannot motivate individuals to engage in collective action. Indeed, a central feature of mobilizing structures is their value in the provision of a sense of belonging or solidary incentives to override tendencies toward free riding. That said, even in cases in which non-material interests appear to be paramount, other factors might be relevant as well. For instance, the political mobilization of evangelical Christians against same-sex marriage might appear to be based solely on the individual perceptions that traditional values are threatened by secular humanism. Yet,

white southerners to rise up in rebellion against the challenge to the southern racial order, few rallied to these clarion calls for resistance. Whites might scuffle with sit-in protesters at a lunch counter, and the imminent integration of a local public school sometimes prompted a flurry of countermobilization; however, in most localities, sustained, broad-based organization against the general civil rights thrust failed to develop.[3] It is no wonder that countermovement activists often expressed frustration that so few of their white brethren felt inspired to enter the fray. The weakness of organized opposition meant that third parties were often unable to augment significantly the concession costs for movement targets. Thus, where countermobilization was weak, lower concession costs enhanced the prospects for victory in local struggles; however, the mere fact that targets could abandon Jim Crow without significant damage to their interests is hardly sufficient to produce a willingness to do so. Despite a general lack of political or economic imperatives to maintain Jim Crow, southern whites lacked inducements to abandon segregation. Enter the civil rights movement. Except for fleeting moments of federal government assertiveness, civil rights gains depended upon the sustained imposition of punishing disruption costs associated with movement agitation and racial tumult. A key challenge for the movement, then, was the identification of vulnerable local targets and the effective application of these disruption costs to coerce change.

Inflicting disruption costs of sufficient magnitude is no simple endeavor, as movements may be incapable of interfering with their targets' interests. Indeed, in the case of the civil rights movement, few southern whites suffered significant losses from civil rights agitation. In local politics, most southern officials lacked exposure to electoral reprisals from liberal whites or African-American voters either because they were too few to matter or they had been effectively disenfranchised. Nor was the federal government inclined to intervene on behalf of racial egalitarianism. This aversion, as well as an explanation for the eventual escalation of federal involvement in the mid-sixties, will be explored in detail in Chapter 6. Without federal coercion to augment the movement's disruptive

even in such cases, ambitious political elites may regard mobilization around certain issues to be politically advantageous. In other words, individuals that appear to be responding to non-material concerns may be self-consciously pulled into politics based on a top-down mobilization for the pursuit of political advantages against their rivals. On elite actuation of citizen political participation, see Rosenstone and Hansen (1993). Also, see Oldfield (1996) on the role of the New Right in the political mobilization of the Christian Right.

[3] Chappell (1994).

capabilities and absent the electoral leverage to compel responsiveness, the political rewards tilted heavily in favor of defiance, and most southern politicians therefore dutifully vowed to thwart the 1954 *Brown v. Board of Education* decision while depicting civil rights agitation as instigated by "outside agitators" and Communists. For others, protests, rallies, demonstrations, and racial contention often amounted to irritating inconveniences that discouraged them from eating, shopping, swimming, and so forth at their accustomed places. Absent the impetus of painful disruption costs, most whites had the option to behave as bystanders on the sidelines of the civil rights struggle, conforming to local customs and allowing others to define the response to movement demands. Insofar as the movement challenged interests that were indifferent to protests and potentially supportive third parties were inactive, defeat and disappointment might be anticipated. Critically for the movement, not all prospective targets were shielded in this manner, and those that were exposed often had considerable sway to promote change.

Specifically, among white southerners, civil rights organizers found, and self-consciously exploited, critical weaknesses within the urban business community. As protesters marched, picketed downtown merchants, and boycotted their establishments, local economic activity was disrupted. To cite the most familiar example, lunch counter operators were unable to serve their customers as long as demonstrators occupied their stools. Patrons might steer clear of downtown commercial centers out of fear of violence or simply to avoid traffic. Heightened and sustained disruption costs associated with civil rights agitation and racial tumult provided these incentives, and civil rights gains depended upon them. Multiple studies attest to the vulnerability of economic interests to protests and boycotts.[4] Yet, paradoxically, despite the conventional prediction that economic development fostered racial moderation in southern politics, others find almost no statistical association between the two.[5] To resolve this puzzle, I suggest that economic actors differed considerably in their exposure to the costs associated with civil rights disruptions, and that only certain interests were exposed sufficiently to elicit support for concessions. Instead of regarding "the business community" as uniformly vulnerable to civil rights disruptions, I propose a sectoral analysis that

[4] Aiken (1998); Bloom (1987); Cramer (1963); Jacoway and Colburn (1982); Luders (2006); Patterson (1966).
[5] Matthews and Prothro (1966); Vanfossen (1968).

disaggregates elements of the business community based on the distinctive exposure of certain interests to disruption costs.[6] An analysis of this sort not only clarifies the circumstances specific to civil rights successes, but promises to elucidate more general patterns of movement efficacy in contests with the business community.

Several patterns might be identified. First, economic interests dependent upon local consumption are especially vulnerable as consumers shy away from the sites of contention. As mentioned above, lunch counter sit-ins blocked white patrons from ordering a meal. Picketing and fears of violence kept shoppers away from downtown stores. Local consumers might change their behavior to honor a boycott, to avoid harassment by picketers or boycotters, or they may have refrained from consumption due to anticipated inconvenience (such as extra traffic, crowds, and so on) or violence. Thus, the interests most vulnerable to the disruption costs of standard protest activities include retail merchants, hoteliers, restaurateurs, and tourist-related businesses. Second, certain interests that depend heavily upon continuous economic growth and infusions of external investment for their profits may be indirectly exposed to disruption costs caused by protests and general disorder. As Black and Black (1987) observe: "Big city banks, power companies, transportation firms, and communications media stood to gain from rapid economic development, from servicing constantly expanding markets."[7] Aligned with these interests were real estate and insurance brokers, developers, and various service sector enterprises. In the developing South, civil rights disruptions – direct action protests, school closures, national media coverage of white lawlessness and violence – chilled the enthusiasm of outside investors

---

[6] No doubt certain movements, in particular those with revolutionary ambitions, threaten so many interests that subtle distinctions are virtually unnecessary. However, reformist movements in democratic polities will generally affect certain interests more negatively than others. Of course, the particularities of movement demands will generate a unique constellation of opponents and other interested parties, but quite apart from the cost of conceding to the movement's specific demands, I suggest that economic actors differ in their exposure to the disruption costs that movements generate in launching protest marches, sit-ins, boycotts, picketing, and so on. Some of these insights have been investigated by labor historians and economists seeking to explicate strike outcomes. See Friedman (1988); Kennan and Wilson (1989); Montgomery (1979). Curiously, the labor movement is conventionally ignored by scholars of social movements. Further, insofar as explicating the bargaining processes between movement and target is crucial, studies of movement outcome might benefit as well from greater attention to research on negotiation; see Pruitt and Carnevale (1993); Zartman (1978).

[7] 1987, 45–6.

and thus threatened the prospective profits of interests reliant on local growth.[8] For those dependent upon the attraction of new industries, racial tumult set back their plans for robust economic development. In general, then, relatively immobile, locally oriented, and consumption- and growth-dependent sectors are more susceptible to interruptions in routine spending and investment behavior, and thus are more vulnerable to disruption costs. More-nuanced historical accounts of the civil rights movement and southern politics often point to precisely these interests as instigators of calls for moderation. For instance, James Cobb describes the "Men of Montgomery," the forty businessmen who sought to quietly resolve the Montgomery bus boycott without publicity, as "mainly merchants, realtors, land developers, bankers, insurance agents, and contractors."[9]

Finally, although not necessarily troubled by local disorder, similarly exposed to boycotts or reputational damage are makers of brand-name consumer goods and national chain stores or franchises. These well-known chains or products might be singled out for national boycotts to punish them for their tacit support of the status quo and to put pressure on them to urge change. For example, after the onset of the sit-ins at Woolworth's in Greensboro, sympathy pickets appeared at their northern stores as well. To the extent that these interests were not dependent upon Jim Crow nor concerned about third party reprisals, mounting disruption costs predicts for accommodation. As targets, they are expected to accede to movement demands; and, as third parties suffering from the damaging ramifications of disruption, they will be drawn into movement-target interactions to urge conciliation.

By contrast, other interests are more insulated from disruption costs. While demonstrations, protests, boycotts, and pickets may be sufficient to dampen ordinary consumption and local growth, they are less effective at interrupting manufacturing processes, unless the employees of the targeted enterprises are rendered unwilling or unable to execute their routine tasks (as with sympathy strikes among industrial workers). Shielded from external disruption as well are those enterprises in uncompetitive, high-demand markets (such as operators of key transportation nodes) and those selling undifferentiated goods and services in high-demand nonlocal markets (petroleum, for instance).[10] Also, economic actors that do

[8] Miller (1960).
[9] 1993, 110.
[10] Movements attempting to boycott enterprises will be more successful against companies selling a differentiated product in a competitive market where substitutions can be easily

not depend on continued local growth or attracting new investment, such as those relying on prior capital investments, including mineral extraction, refining, manufacture, and so on, may be less vulnerable to protest activity.[11] For example, in his analysis of the southern textiles industry, Minchin (1999) observes:

Textile companies were also able to embrace the racial status quo because of their isolation from consumers. Unlike retail stories, textile mills did not have to consider the reaction of their customers and were not influenced by consumer pressure to integrate. One mill owner, for example, told the AFSC [American Friends Service Committee] in 1962 that 'as a manufacturer, he has no reason to consider the attitudes of customers (retail). He said that the situation would be different if he, for example, were operating Woolworths or a supermarket.'[12]

Those interests that suffer neither from disruption nor concession can be expected to conform to dominant local customs. While not exhaustive, this sketch hints at the value of differentiating economic actors based on their uneven exposure to movement disruption costs.

In this chapter I offer a preliminary assessment of these propositions. First, drawing from studies of the civil rights movement and racial politics, I survey a small portion of the evidence that certain business interests stepped forward to urge conciliation, and that economic considerations prompted them to do so. I demonstrate that multiple studies document how the disturbances associated with civil rights agitation caused particular southern businesses to suffer real and anticipated economic pain, and encouraged them to make concessions. In addition, sifting through these historical accounts, I tease out the sectoral patterns in the responsiveness of various elements of the broader business community to civil rights demands. Finally, I assess these sectoral patterns based on an examination of the occupational profiles of the signers of public statements in favor of concessions to civil rights demands published in the newspapers of three cities: Norfolk, Virginia (1959); New Orleans, Louisiana (1961); and McComb, Mississippi (1964). These statements, which were signed by

---

made. Boycotts will be less effective against those selling undifferentiated products or monopolists. Transportation interests might be further differentiated. Those profiting from local growth are far more vulnerable to movement disruption than those serving as a critical node in a regional or national transportation network.

[11] On the other hand, if their own employees are involved in protest activity, especially strikes, these enterprises may be especially vulnerable because they are unable to exit the locality. Thus, as suggested above, the specific characteristics of protest activity affect how particular business enterprises will be affected.

[12] 1999, 22.

local civic and business leaders, variously expressed support for keeping open the public schools, preserving the rule of law, and making concessions to the movement. Since each of these cities experienced disruptions to public order (such as school closures, school boycotts, and violence) amid the challenges to Jim Crow, these public statements arguably identify those interests with the strongest preferences for the restoration of public order. These statements are particularly significant because they often coincided with a retreat from extreme opposition in favor of some measure of accommodation to movement demands. Finally, although these propositions are considered in the specific context of the civil rights struggle, I suggest that the same sectoral logic applies to other movements in which economic interests are directly or indirectly implicated.[13]

Civil Rights Mobilization and Southern Business

For many decades, Jim Crow had not hampered southern economic development; on the contrary, racial segregation and industrial expansion had been fused together without difficulty. Labor-intensive planters, bankers, and merchants and others united behind segregation and white dominance. Manufacturers too welcomed the benefits of the racially split labor market, which was thought to keep wages down.[14] Southern recruiters seeking to attract investment and new industrial facilities pointed to the region's many virtues, including the low-wage labor force, the weakness of organized labor, and the general quality of life. Investments poured into the region in the preceding decades as the South's economy flourished. To take advantage of the favorable business climate, northern industry migrated to the "sunbelt" states. These activities were hugely successful as the region's industrial output rose and economic development proceeded apace.

Starting in the latter fifties, civil rights demonstrations and violent racial strife attracted national media attention and marred the carefully crafted images of racial harmony, imperiling indigenous ambitions for economic development. From the outset, these racial disruptions divided business elites. While plantation belt whites clamored for "massive resistance," others were more reticent about the costs of diehard intransigence. For example, the 1955 bus boycott in Montgomery, Alabama, "caused

---

[13] See Luders (2006) for additional examples of the application of the sectoral analysis to other movements.

[14] Bonacich (1972); Cobb (1988); Wright (1986).

immediate consternation among the city's businessmen, who were already worried about their city's difficulties in attracting new industrial investment."[15] Concerned that they had lost a DuPont plant as well as four other facilities, development-minded business sought to circumvent a crisis that might attract broader attention. Their inability to do so, as Cobb explains, "should not obscure the fact that as early as 1956 many of the city's business leaders made a connection between a community's race relations image and its prospects for economic growth, and took action, however limited, to forestall further confrontation and violence."[16]

Similarly, the integration crisis in Little Rock, Arkansas, in September 1957, provided businesses elsewhere evidence of the economic dangers inherent in the defiance of federal authorities and the breakdown of public order. After Governor Orval Faubus failed to block a federal court order to desegregate Little Rock Central High School, he withdrew the National Guard. To the surprise of none, an unruly mob formed and, ultimately, the disruption compelled President Eisenhower to take decisive action. For local boosters, the effect was cataclysmic, as it became well known that, after having attracted an average of five major plants a year from 1950 to 1957, the city was unable to lure a single new plant for the next four years. Local supporters of orderly integration elsewhere brought speakers from Little Rock to tell "their city's tale of woe and urged business and civic leaders to do everything in their power to keep their schools open and the local populace calm."[17]

Likewise, in Norfolk, Virginia, in 1959, when it appeared that massive resistance meant the closure of the public schools, business leaders stepped forward to avert this eventuality. According to a report for the *New York Times*, "most of the business community agrees with Henry Clay Hofheimer, industrialist and president of the Chamber of Commerce, that abolition of the public school system as threatened by the City Council would force an exodus of Navy personnel, discourage new industry and eventually confront the city with economic ruin."[18] After the Virginia governor closed several schools to block integration, economic elites pushed behind the scenes for a strategic retreat from counterproductive intransigence. Regarding the political response to the *Brown* decision, Benjamin Muse states, "It may be confidently stated that Virginia business

[15] Cobb (1984, 110).
[16] Ibid.
[17] Ibid., 111.
[18] *New York Times*, January 25, 1959.

leaders brought vigorous and effective pressure, of which the public was not aware, to bring massive resistance to an end."[19] Describing public opinion toward school desegregation in Guilford County, North Carolina, Melvin Tumin found that the group most prepared for integration "contains many of those persons whose interests in the economic growth and development of their area are being injured by the restrictive influences of the system of segregation."[20] Even before the period of heightened and sustained civil rights protests, then, economic actors evinced vulnerability to civil rights disruptions and willingness to compromise to maintain or restore public order.

With the onset of the sit-ins, civil rights demonstrators ratcheted upwards the costs of intransigence. This time, disruption costs involved not only the "collateral damage" from public disorder. Rather, civil rights activists deliberately targeted vulnerable businesses to coerce concessions from them. Often, civil rights activists carefully calibrated the imposition of these disruption costs to inflict maximum harm and generate greater bargaining leverage against their targets. Boycotts and demonstrations, for instance, were often timed to coincide with the peak shopping seasons of Easter and Christmas. Along with attracting media attention to the dismal state of local race relations, sit-ins interfered with routine business operations, in part because lunch counter seats were occupied but also, and perhaps more importantly, because downtown shoppers stayed away from trouble spots. Sit-in strategists often selected their targets with great care. Wyatt T. Walker, a Southern Christian Leadership Conference (SCLC) associate of Rev. Martin Luther King, Jr., recalled his planning before the 1963 sit-ins in targeted downtown stores in Birmingham: "Under some subterfuge, I visited all three of these stores and counted the stools, the tables, the chairs, etc., and what the best method of ingress and egress was."[21] The profit margins of the targeted firms and the percentage of the trade with African-American customers were calculated to select those most likely to feel an economic pinch from disruption. These protests cut deeply into merchant profits as local consumption slipped. A Kress department store executive reported that the profits of targeted stores slipped 15 to 17 percent.[22]

---

[19] Muse (1961, 110). As in other cases, statistics of industrial expansion were circulated to demonstrate that massive resistance had reduced the pace of economic growth.

[20] 1958, 201.

[21] PBS, "Eyes on the Prize." Available at: http://www.pbs.org/wgbh/amex/eyesontheprize/about/pt_104.html (accessed July 8, 2007).

[22] *New York Times*, February 19, 1960 reported in Southern Regional Council, "The Student Protest Movement, Winter, 1960." 1191 XVI: 216.

A renewed surge of demonstrations in 1963 triggered another round of civil rights concessions. Downtown merchants on King Street in Charleston, South Carolina, smarted under intense protests with profits down between 20 and 50 percent.[23] The Chamber of Commerce in Savannah, Georgia, called on local firms to integrate their facilities after weeks of civil rights protests produced "a substantial loss of retail sales along Broughton Street and other shopping centers."[24] During the massive protests in Birmingham, Alabama, that targeted downtown merchants, local retailers suffered a $750,000 weekly loss due to civil rights boycotts and a white aversion to shop near trouble spots.[25] Amid turbulent protests in the tourist city of St. Augustine, Florida, the National Park Service reported that visits to a popular local attraction declined by 45 percent compared to the same time during the previous year.[26] The Greensboro Chamber of Commerce reported demonstrations to integrate downtown restaurants from the previous spring had "an adverse effect in attracting new industry."[27] A 1964 boycott in Canton, Mississippi, threatened several local merchants with "financial ruin."[28]

The passage of the 1964 Civil Rights Act prompted various business associations to call for compliance with the new law. Even in Jackson, Mississippi, which had been supportive of the Councils' firm opposition to civil rights, a majority of the board of directors of the Chamber of Commerce produced a public statement in favor of immediate compliance.[29] The *New York Times* reported that "some business leaders here were reported to feel that unless some effort was made to comply with the law and court orders it would become more and more difficult to attract industry to the state and tourists would stay away."[30] Similarly, in Selma, Alabama, another site of fierce resistance to the movement, business interests began to take action to assure public order. In April 1965, both the city council and the Chamber of Commerce ultimately supported a newspaper statement in favor of equal employment opportunities to improve the city's chances of attracting two new industries.[31] Summing up the

---

[23] Southern Regional Council, "The Price We Pay," 5 (citing *The State*, July 21, 1963). See also Cox (1996, 413).

[24] *New York Times*, June 15, 1963, 9; August 4, 1963, 64.

[25] Southern Regional Council, "The Price We Pay" citing *Time*, June 7, 1963.

[26] *New York Times*, June 14, 1964.

[27] Quoted in Southern Regional Council, "The Price We Pay," 2 (citing *Greensboro Daily News*, September 6, 1963).

[28] *New York Times*, March 2, 1964.

[29] *New York Times*, July 13, 1964, 1.

[30] Ibid.

[31] *New York Times*, April 18, 1965, 53.

general pattern in 1966, a researcher for the pro-integration Southern Regional Council (SRC) observed:

The paramount fact is this: Businessmen have everywhere exerted an important, and in some places decisive, influence on the reaction of the white South to Negro protest. Largely, exerting this influence has been a gradual, usually painful process whereby business managers, acting under pressure to defend their economic welfare, have joined other community groups to make concessions to Negro demands, especially as those demands were backed by new federal legislation.[32]

Due to this support for concessions, many have suggested that business interests *in general* represented a decisive force for moderation in local politics. By contrast, I suggest that more refined predictions for the responses of economic actors to social protest are possible.

Profile of Public Statement Signers

As movement mobilization produced racial contention, school closures, or negative publicity, vulnerable interests responded with public statements in favor of negotiation and compromise. The perspective presented here predicts that a preponderance of the signers will be those with clear interests in local economic growth and the maintenance of local consumption behavior, and with no obvious threat from acceding to movement demands. Depending upon the specific demands and disruptions in the community, different constellations of economic actors are expected to express their support for concessions. As suggested above, this faction includes bankers, insurers, real estate interests, developers, construction, and utilities. Lawyers often serve as adjuncts to these concerns and, as such, they are less vulnerable to white reprisals for challenging the status quo. In addition to this pro-growth group, downtown merchants, restaurateurs, hoteliers, and others sensitive to immediate disruptions in the local economy will be responsive to movement disruptions that cut swiftly into their profit margins. As suggested above, manufacturing interests, on the other hand, are expected to vary according to their dependence upon new investment, their brand-name recognition, and whether they operate in primary consumption markets. Ongoing operations, with no interest in attracting new investment and lacking a name brand that might be vulnerable to public relations damage, are expected to be conformers. In general, they are not predicted to be signers on these petitions

---

[32] Patterson (1966, 69–70).

or, to the extent that they appear, the historical record should suggest that they were not instigators but rather latecomers to the agreement. In contrast, enterprises selling readily identified name-brand products that might be risk averse to prospective boycotts and those operating in local consumption markets, such as soft drink makers, will be relatively more inclined to support concessions. Also, manufacturers that might benefit from concessions may be willing to throw their support behind a measure favorable to the civil rights movement.[33] To sort out these patterns, each of the three petitions is described separately and then compared for overall fit with the predictions sketched above. This approach is not meant to suggest that all interests necessarily signed these petitions for economic reasons. Many likely signed the petition because they simply believed in the merits of keeping the public schools open or because of their social ties to other signers.

Norfolk, Virginia

After the Supreme Court handed down *Brown* (1954), Virginia officials led the defensive reaction against the decision under the banner of "massive resistance." It was Virginia elites who crafted the last-ditch constitutional doctrine of "interposition," in which state authorities "interposed" themselves between the federal government and local school boards for the purposes of thwarting federal court orders to integrate.[34] Regarded as a constitutional sham by national authorities, interposition fell by the wayside under federal judicial assault in the late fifties and this outcome compelled massive resistance forces to accept either token integration or to close their public schools. As the prospect of closing the public schools loomed, white middle-class professionals and educators began to argue in favor of the abandonment of interposition and in favor of a local option, which allowed school districts to craft their own response to demands for desegregation. Nevertheless, at the beginning of the 1958 school year, Governor J. Lindsay Almond, Jr., closed six white Norfolk public schools that were under court order to desegregate. During the ensuing Norfolk public school crisis, local economic elites published a petition to the city council in favor of keeping the public schools open

---

[33] For instance, Heckman and Payner (1989) suggest that it was a combination of the tightness of the labor market and federal coercion that facilitated rapid integration in this sector. See also Minchin's (1999) superb research on the further role of black assertiveness and litigation under the provisions of the Civil Rights Act.

[34] On the Virginia massive resistance movement, see Bartley (1969); Ely (1976); Gates (1964); Muse (1961); Muse (1964).

TABLE 3.1. *Occupational Profile of Open Schools Petition Signers, Norfolk, Virginia (January 25, 1959)*

	%	#
Local Pro-Growth Interests	54.1	40
Banking	10.8	8
Insurance	13.5	10
Law	12.1	9
Real estate, development, construction supplies	16.2	12
Chamber of Commerce executive	1.4	1
Downtown Consumption	14.9	11
Retailers and auto sales	12.2	9
Restaurateurs	2.7	2
Other Interests	31.1	23
Transportation	6.8	5
Manufacturing	12.2	9
Medical (doctors and dentists)	12.2	9
TOTAL	100.1*	74

* Total does not equal 100 due to rounding.
Source: Virginian-Pilot and Portsmouth Star.

even if this meant integrating them. The petition depicts a cross-section of the business community (see Table 3.1).

The preponderance of signers are clearly in those sectors that are most keenly attentive to local growth and development: bank presidents, investment and insurance executives, real estate interests, and lawyers. Other signers were associated with local consumption and downtown business interests: owners or operators of automobile dealerships, retail stores, and restaurants. Although transportation interests are generally predicted to be aloof to localized disruptions, school closures threatened the continued presence of Navy personnel, which were closely tied to the health of the port economy. Also, several of the nine manufacturers were specifically affiliated with local growth or consumption, including a local soft drink maker, a brewer, a maker of construction materials, a candy maker, and a dealer in home heating oil. Several signers were white-collar professionals who lacked obvious exposure to concession costs.[35] The support from

[35] Ample research has demonstrated that highly educated professionals were both less exposed to economic competition and harbored less hostile attitudes toward African-Americans. See Cummings (1980). On racial attitudes generally, see Schuman, Steeh, and Bobo (1985). Social ties to signers may have encouraged others to add their names to these petitions. For example, the four signers associated with automobile sales were from the same firm.

TABLE 3.2. *Occupational Profile of Open Schools Petition Signers, New Orleans, Louisiana (August 31, 1961)*

	%	#
Local Pro-Growth Interests	51.3	116
Banking, investment, accounting	9.7	22
Insurance	9.3	21
Law	15.9	36
Real estate, development, construction	7.5	17
Media (newspapers, radio), advertising	8.9	20
Downtown Consumption	12.8	29
Retailers, wholesalers, distributors	9.3	21
Hotel/Restaurants/Theaters	3.5	8
Other Interests	35.8	81
Shipping/Warehousing	.9	2
Manufacture	4.4	10
Petroleum/Chemicals	3.1	7
Medical (doctors and dentists)	9.7	22
Religious/Clergy	2.7	6
Misc.	15	34
TOTAL	99.9*	226

* Total does not equal 100 due to rounding.
Source: New Orleans Times Picayune.

the medical community, for example, is not consistent with obvious economic motivations. Nonetheless, the broad cross-section coincides with predictions.

New Orleans, Louisiana

As in Norfolk, New Orleans elites published a statement in favor of open schools and rule of law at the height of the turbulence that accompanied the desegregation of two schools in the 1960–61 academic year (see also Chapter 4). Raucous white protests, racial clashes, and a school boycott attracted national and international media attention. Press accounts focused in particular on the "cheerleaders," a crowd of white women who jeered and shouted at the black children as they entered the integrated schools. These racial disturbances, coupled with intermittent civil rights protests to desegregate public accommodations, reduced tourism and seriously hampered downtown commercial activities. By the end of this year of turmoil, business interests finally acted to support accommodation. The public statement, published in August 1961 in the *Times Picayune*, declared "public education in Louisiana must be preserved" and denounced "lawlessness, intimidation, and coercion." Pro-growth interests rallied behind this position. Banking, insurance, real estate, lawyers, and elements of the media offered their support for a position in favor of accommodation. Although the petition concentrated on public schools, the "cheerleaders" had damaged the city's reputation and reduced both tourism and local consumption. In many ways, the analysis of the New Orleans petition bolsters the central propositions of the cost assessment approach (see Table 3.2).

Among the 226 identified signers, support for concessions came disproportionately from business leaders dependent upon downtown consumption and local growth as well as ancillary supporters in the legal profession. Among the manufacturers, many were associated with consumer markets and sellers of name-brand products such as Coca Cola bottlers. Officers from International Harvester, which had an interest in supporting the transition away from labor-intensive agriculture toward mechanical pickers, appear on the list of manufacturers. Few signers were associated with chemicals, petroleum, or transportation, despite the importance of these sectors for the local economy.

McComb, Mississippi

In 1961, Student Nonviolent Coordinating Committee (SNCC) organizers, with the support of the local NAACP leadership and local activists, began a voter registration drive in this small city, situated in southwestern Mississippi. These activities provoked regular reprisals from local authorities, the Klan, and Americans for the Preservation of the White Race (APWR), another extreme segregationist organization. In September, a state legislator shot and killed Herbert Lee, an African-American who had participated in voter registration efforts. After the perpetrator was not charged with a crime, the local movement stagnated.[36] Activities escalated in July 1964 when SNCC spearheaded a sustained voter registration drive to crack the most resistant Mississippi communities, which later became known as Freedom Summer. In preparation for the "invasion" by civil rights activists including a host of northern student volunteers, the Klan held a rally of nearly one thousand near McComb at the county fairgrounds. With the onset of voter registration activities, violent retaliation ensued, earning McComb a national reputation for violence and lawlessness. "By rough count," reported *Time* magazine, "at least 13 Negro homes, churches or business places have been bombed,

[36] Payne (1995, 124).

another half-dozen burned."[37] It was also in McComb, as described in the preceding chapter, that Red Heffner and family fled after a relentless barrage of threats and a stony silence from their former friends.

On the editorial page of the McComb *Enterprise-Journal*, the moderate Oliver Emmerich lamented: "Too may of us have been too timid, fearful that any expression of positive opinion might result in boycotts, harassment, and intimidation." The *Enterprise-Journal* published numerous reports of the drastic economic implications of ongoing racial turmoil.

> Fifteen industrial prospects have been interviewed by the Southwest Mississippi Industrial District in recent months. When the name of McComb was suggested to them each asked, 'What about your racial trouble?'...Unless our people take up the suggested crusade for responsibility it can be expected that some of our business houses will close down, more buildings will be vacated, property values will diminish and industry will pass us by.[38]

As racial tensions continued to rise, downtown businesses suffered badly as few shoppers ventured on the streets. "Many Negro people, fearful of the tension or resentful of things which have happened, are avoiding our retail stores."[39] So severe were the disturbances that many feared the imposition of martial law. Based on his interviews of the principals, John Dittmer writes: "New industry would not consider locating in McComb, and several national insurance companies directed their local agents not to write any more coverage. The major McComb manufacturer was now shipping his products from a point across the line in Louisiana to avoid the 'made in McComb' stigma."[40] In October, the local paper warned that civil rights organizations were researching a boycott of Mississippi products in general and goods produced in McComb in particular.[41] Yet, despite mounting economic damage, local interests had vacillated out of fear of white reprisals. Finally, in late November 1964, following several bloody months of reactive mobilization and Klan violence, McComb's civic and business leadership spoke out reluctantly on behalf of rule of law.

A group of concerned business leaders coalesced to draft, circulate, and publish a statement in favor of the preservation of public order.

---

[37] "Do Not Despair," November 27, 1964. The *New York Times* reported on several such incidents.
[38] McComb, *Enterprise-Journal*, October 26, 1964, 2.
[39] Ibid.
[40] Dittmer (1994, 309).
[41] *Enterprise-Journal*, October 27, 1964.

Additionally, the "Statement of Principles," eventually signed by hundreds of McComb residents, called for "equal treatment under the law for all citizens regardless of race, creed, or position of wealth."[42] After much racial turbulence, it was a bold statement from hundreds of citizens against white supremacist violence and intimidation. Following the publication of the statement, Emmerich thanked ten of the 20 organizers in his newspaper column. Based on the city directory, these ten included three bankers, an insurance executive, two downtown merchants, a car dealership operator, a lumber company executive, a certified public accountant, and a lawyer. (See Table 3.3.) Consistent with predictions, these actors are concentrated in sectors that were vulnerable to economic disruption, and not dependent upon Jim Crow. And, while individuals from industrial enterprises eventually signed, the leaders of the petition drive who could be identified lacked representation from manufacturing. As conformers, these interests appear to have followed the broader elite current in favor of a restoration of rule of law.

Again, McComb merchants and pro-growth interests accounted for the overwhelming share of signers. Doctors, clergy, and local school officials made up around 14 percent and manufacturing interests, particularly in oil and wood products industries, made up nearly 13 percent of all signers. Since manufacturing interests are generally expected to be conformers, it is worthwhile to more closely inspect these interests. Unlike some industries in which strict segregation was maintained, the logging and wood products industries of southeastern Mississippi were already thoroughly integrated. Others may have been seeking to shake off the McComb "stigma" or acting to preempt the onset of threatened national boycotts.

Summary: The Petitions

The petitions described above addressed two distinct civil rights demands. The Norfolk and New Orleans cases concentrated primarily upon school desegregation, in which business interests responded as third parties. Some direct-action protests were taking place in New Orleans at downtown stores at the time of the petition, but these were limited in scope and impact. In contrast, the McComb petition dealt with the violence associated with civil rights activities pertaining to voter registration. Despite these differences, the patterns bear out the logic suggested here. In each of these cases, economic disruptions stimulated a range of actors to mobilize for concessions. Over 60 percent of the signers were associated with pro-growth interests, which generally included executives from banking,

---

[42] "Statement of Principles," McComb, *Enterprise-Journal*, November 17, 1964.

TABLE 3.3. *Occupational Profile of "Statement of Principles" Signers, McComb, Mississippi (November 18, 1964)*

	%	#
Local Pro-Growth Interests	27.1	101
Banking/Accounting/Tellers	12.9	48
Insurance	4.0	15
Real estate and construction (includes electricians, plumbers, carpenters)	3.5	13
Media	3.5	13
Utilities	2.7	10
Law	.5	2
Downtown Consumption	38.6	143
Retail sales (drug stores, apparel, furniture, groceries, autos, etc.)	25.9	96
Hotels/Restaurants/Theaters	4.6	17
Service (repairs, service station operators, barbers)	8.1	30
Other Interests	34.3	127
Transportation (railroad engineers, railroad mechanics)	5.4	20
Manufacture/Industrial Production (lumber, milling, textiles, petroleum, etc.)	12.4	46
Medical (doctors, dentists)	9.2	34
Religious/Clergy	2.2	8
Government	2.4	9
Education	2.7	10
TOTAL	100	371

Note: The data in this table do not include signers whose occupations could not be discerned from the 1964 McComb city directory as well as female signers who appeared not to have an occupation independent of their spouse. Many of the women who signed the statement were bank tellers, cashiers, salespersons at downtown stores, secretaries, and nurses. Finally, there are ambiguities in certain categories, such as among oil producers and distributors. While oil production is presumed to be highly insulated from disruption costs, those involved in the distribution and sale of gasoline for local consumption may be vulnerable. Directory listings were sometimes unclear on the specific aspect of the signer's occupation. To be conservative, such cases were generally coded as belonging to the category of "industrial production or manufacture," even though this most likely understates the number involved in wholesale distribution of petroleum products in local settings.
Source: McComb *Enterprise-Journal.*

insurance, utilities, and real estate, and local merchants. While these patterns are suggestive, this argument will be documented more fully in the next chapter.

Across the three cases, manufacturers participated in petition coalitions ranging from four percent of all signers in New Orleans to around 12 percent elsewhere. The key point here is that these manufacturing interests were often already racially integrated, operating in tight labor markets (and therefore more eager to increase their labor supply), producers of name-brand products, or manufacturers of items for either local and regional consumption markets (makers of candy, soft drinks, alcoholic beverages, for example). Thus, even within sectors, further distinctions can be made to refine the analysis. In all of the three cases, the overall composition of petition signers is consistent with predictions.

White Liberals and Racial "Moderates"

Before proceeding, a word should be said about those southerners who supported integration without compulsion. Although the perspective presented here assumes that self-interest shapes behavior, some white southerners offered reliable support of the movement, even though it was decidedly not in their interest to do so.[43] Ministers orated from their pulpits about the brotherhood of man; educators advocated for integration; and some organized into "save our schools" organizations to speak out in favor of open schools, even if this meant some measure of integration. The courage of these white southerners should not be omitted from an account of this period; however, it is consistent with this analysis that these racial moderates amounted to a vanishingly small share of the region's population. Chappell's (1994) analysis of these "inside agitators" describes this population as a "tiny minority." (To the extent that these participated in the civil rights movement, they are not properly regarded as third parties.) In fact, it is easy to overstate the racial liberalism of southern white moderates. Many opposed integration and regarded themselves as "practical segregationists" who argued in favor of token desegregation only because of their opposition to what they regarded as extreme measures, such as closing the public schools to prevent integration. Similarly, some simply found violent, bitter-end defense of Jim Crow both abhorrent and counterproductive. It is telling, however, that those whites who tended to populate "save our schools" organizations were often middle-class professionals (or their spouses) and were far less exposed to the economic competition with African-Americans that incited their lower-income counterparts.[44]

Third Party Intervention – The Federal Government

Along with those economic interests willing to support capitulation to movement demands, some third parties can have a decisive affect upon

[43] Chappell (1994).
[44] See generally, Bartley (1969).

movement outcomes by vastly augmenting the movement's disruptive capabilities against insulated and otherwise recalcitrant targets. The most important of these was the federal government. Ultimately, the enactment of substantive civil and voting rights legislation committed the federal government to the demolition of Jim Crow and African-American disenfranchisement. This greater engagement and the federal government's capacity to mete out overwhelming disruption costs had enormous implications for the achievement of civil rights successes over time. Obviously, the use of federal coercive capabilities strengthened the bargaining position of the movement against its antagonists; however, federal authorities long resisted getting pulled into confrontations with southern authorities and white supremacists. Despite the unpunished lynching of thousands of African-Americans in the South since Reconstruction, the federal government had not enacted anti-lynching legislation. Even after the Supreme Court's 1954 ban on public school segregation, presidential and congressional action in most cases was tentative and limited until the mid-sixties. Federal incursions into southern racial politics were largely reactive. In rare moments, presidents acted with boldness against intransigent southern whites, as with Eisenhower's activation of the 101st Airborne in the 1957 Little Rock crisis and Kennedy's comparable use of the military to implement the mandated integration of Ole Miss in 1962. Deviating from characteristic hesitation, these dramatic clashes stemmed from the executive branch's commitment to the enforcement of federal court orders over the opposition of state officials and white extremists. I explain the variation in the willingness of federal authorities – in particular presidents and Congress – to act in Chapter 6. At this point, it is sufficient to observe that the federal government often resisted direct involvement in the interactions among the movement, southern authorities, and countermovement agitators unless a breakdown of public order compelled its intervention. As such, for those targets for whom movement demands entailed significant concession costs, the federal government's addition to the movement's overall disruptive capabilities could be discounted in most cases.

Patterns of Cost Assessment

In deciding their responses to movement demands, targets and third parties weigh the combination of both disruption and concession costs. As described in the previous chapter, the threat of civil rights gains for certain whites ignited their active opposition and inspired massive resistance countermobilization. Most others, however, regarded the changes

as unwelcome, but insufficient to induce participation in a reactive countermovement. As such, they conformed to local customs and allowed
others to take charge of formulating an appropriate response to the civil
rights challenge. For most southern politicians, the balance tilted against
compromise and in favor of the defense of segregation. Civil rights agitators, without the votes to represent an electoral threat in most cases,
lacked a means to impose significant disruption costs upon them. White
opposition to concessions, regarding public school desegregation in particular, meant that few officeholders had an interest in responding with
moderation in advance of community sentiment or considerable support
from community notables. Along with the fear of reprisals from constituents, elected officials in localities with high concentrations of African-
Americans regarded enfranchisement as an imminent threat to their own
electoral fortunes and therefore they often led the charge for massive
resistance. Only in communities in which African-Americans constituted
a negligible proportion of the local population were the concession costs
sufficiently low that officials might be capable of providing leadership.[45]

Many economic actors, by contrast, often found their interests vulnerable to disruption and were compelled to behave accordingly. Appreciating
the financial implications of racial disorders and absent a corresponding
economic justification to defend segregation, multiple economic actors
came forward, often reluctantly, to support concessions. They did so not
because of their personal support for racial equality, but instead due to
their perception that the costs of continued tumult and resistance were
even higher. Cramer's (1963) interviews of eighty southern white community leaders document precisely this pattern. Even those most committed
to attracting new industries expressed a strong preference for segregation,
but they accepted the compromises as necessary to avert a more dire outcome – crippling economic damage to their economic interests. Against
the fortification of the Jim Crow South, then, civil rights protesters found
a weakness within the urban business community. Without an economic
necessity to bind them to Jim Crow institutions and exposed to severe disruption costs, multiple business interests had ample reason to defect from

---

[45] Interestingly, in these communities, before the enactment of civil and voting rights federal
legislation recast the political incentives, the movement achieved far greater gains in
black voter registration than public school desegregation. In Chapter 5 I argue that the
greater gains in voter registration stemmed from the differences in the politics associated
with these distinct demands. Specifically, constituents were more likely to notice and
react negatively toward school desegregation than voter registration. In both domains,
officials responded to calculations of political expedience.

intransigence even before the enactment of federal legislation. Until the costs of civil rights demonstrations and white violence persuaded these interests that massive resistance involved real economic pain, these elites often hesitated to take decisive action in favor of conciliation, particularly in communities with active countermobilization. However, school closures, demonstrations, tumultuous public disorders, and critical media coverage brought home the economic implications of these events and compelled vulnerable interests to reconsider the prudence of allowing extremists to define the contours of local reaction. Sooner or later, vulnerable targets and third parties either capitulated outright or entered the fray on the side of open schools, public order, and concessions to bring protests to an end and salvage a favorable local image.[46]

Instead of lumping the business community together, a sectoral analysis accounts for variation in the responses of economic actors to protest activities. Certainly, downtown merchants were often the hardest hit as civil rights activists selected their firms for direct action protests and boycotts. When mobilization for the desegregation of public accommodation escalated, these highly vulnerable interests were often among the most vocal proponents of negotiation and compromise. But conciliatory responses were not limited to downtown retailers. As an Atlanta department store executive explained about the relationship between civil rights protests and damage to the local economy: "The effect is not going to be confined to the retail stores. It will hit the bank, the office supply concerns, the insurance firms, the real estate interests, and all the rest."[47] From the foregoing analysis, it is indeed evident that bankers, insurance executives, real estate and construction interests, and often lawyers provided considerable leadership in promoting change. Similarly, the disorders and negative media exposure that accompanied public school desegregation necessitated the intervention of pro-growth interests, even if they were not targeted for protests. According to Harry Kelleher, a respected corporate attorney and a key interlocutor in the New Orleans integration struggle, major local banks lent crucial support.[48] Indeed, he recounted how the local Chamber of Commerce president came to him at the behest of the bankers. Together, fearing the loss of external manufacturing investment

[46] Cobb (1993); Greenberg (1980); Jacoway and Colburn (1982); Luebke (1990); Nicholls (1960); Wright (1986).
[47] *New York Times*, July 28, 1963.
[48] Harry B. Kelleher, interview by Kim Lacy Rogers, 8 May 1979. Kim Lacy Rogers–Glenda B. Stevens Collection, Amistad Research Center, Tulane University.

or sharp declines in local consumption, these economic elites formed ad hoc coalitions to negotiate with civil rights activists and broker compromises with city officials. With strong preferences to protect their city's reputation and to attract external investment, they organized to make concessions to the civil rights movement and push back against the excesses of white extremists. At the same time, it is important not to overstate their support for racial change. Compelled by economic necessity rather than principle, they offered the smallest concessions possible to bring about the cessation of demonstrations and boycotts. Often acting as "practical segregationists," they advocated modest changes to preempt both federal intervention and more far-reaching concessions.[49]

A sectoral analysis further confirms that not all interests responded to the same degree and that insulated interests were often absent or less visible as proponents of moderation. Many national corporations, absentee-owners, and most manufacturers had no particular interest in departing from local racial customs. As such, they seldom stepped forward to broker an agreement or throw their support behind such an agreement. Contrary then to the popular notion that economic development automatically produced racial moderation, the insulation of certain targets and third parties from costly disruption permitted the most advanced methods of production to be combined with deeply illiberal social attitudes and practices. Some manufacturers did support concessions, but these exceptions prove the rule, as many had interests that inclined them against defiance. In some cases they were already racially integrated. In others, they produced name-brand products that might be boycotted, or were involved in the production of goods for local consumption markets.

This variation in the exposure of targets and third parties to disruption highlights a set of key strategic choices in movement mobilization. In particular, movement activists need to select potential accommodators, if at all possible; that is, interests that are vulnerable to disruption and for whom concession costs are relatively low. A focus on insulated targets risks squandering precious movement resources, as was often the case in civil rights struggles against southern elected officials.[50] While such campaigns might produce the dramatic events necessary to bring about national legislative action, a topic I address in Chapter 6, they were

---

[49] See generally Jacoway and Colburn (1982).
[50] Obviously, sometimes target concession costs are not low; in such cases, a movement's bargaining leverage depends upon maintaining robust disruption costs and perhaps attracting the assistance of powerful allies.

virtually doomed to defeat without the assistance of third parties. By contrast, movement strategists found downtown merchants to be ideal targets. As Bayard Rustin explained, "In a highly industrialized twentieth-century civilization, we hit Jim Crow precisely where it was most anachronistic, dispensable, and vulnerable – in hotels, lunch counters, terminals, libraries, swimming pools, and the like. For in these forms, Jim Crow does impede the flow of commerce in the broadest sense; it is a nuisance in a society on the move (and on the make)."[51] The strategic selection of appropriate targets and tactics improved the prospects for winning multiple local victories.

Summary

So far, the analysis has surveyed the behavior of competing elements of the white South. Amid countless individuals conforming to local racial customs, interests vulnerable to movement gains and insulated from disruption instigated reactive countermobilization. They called for relentless defiance against the egalitarian thrust of the Second Reconstruction. Following the preferences of most voters, the organized demands of massive resisters, and sometimes their own political self-interests, elected officials obliged with the enactment of countless forms of legal subterfuge to shore up Jim Crow and swat down black insurgency. On the other side, economic actors vulnerable to movement disruptions and racial turmoil often responded with a willingness to negotiate the compromises necessary to keep the financial damage to a minimum. Rising economic anxieties among vulnerable interests thus sometimes precipitated a clash between those committed to the defense of segregation at all costs and others willing to offer concessions. This analysis suggests that local movement impact depended upon the outcome of this competitive struggle among movement, targets, and diverse third parties. I turn to these interactions in specific localities, and across the entire region more generally, in the following chapters.

[51] Rustin (1965).

4

Local Struggles

While certain whites fiercely opposed civil rights gains, others demonstrated a cautious willingness to support concessions. Thus, as suggested in the previous chapter, an explanation of local movement outcomes must necessarily consider the interaction among these competing elements and movement targets.[1] In this chapter, the disparate pieces, examined separately up to this point, are assembled in a series of case studies of local movement struggles to elucidate how targets tabulate their disruption and concession costs based on their own specific exposure to movement tactics and demands as well as the anticipated action (or inaction) of third parties. Case studies are used here because they can be sufficiently fine-grained to capture these interactions and trace out the imputed causal processes.

In order to tease out these causal mechanisms and explore their robustness, three principal considerations guided case selection. First, the cases depict targets and third parties exposed to disruption and concession costs of differing magnitudes. As such, it is possible to document if targets and others are responding to movement agitation based on their cost perceptions as predicted. Next, the cases incorporate a wide range of actors responding to civil rights contention. This diversity allows for the further exploration of the merits of the sectoral analysis presented in the last chapter. And although my emphasis thus far has been upon the reactions of economic actors to movement disruption costs, the analysis purports to explain the behavior of political actors as well. The inclusion of elected officials permits an examination of the extent to which they respond to the same bargaining logic. Further evidence for the sensitivity of political

[1] Rucht (2004).

actors to electoral costs as well as additional theoretical refinements concerning their behavior are presented in subsequent chapters. Finally, the cases address different goals of the southern civil rights struggle: the desegregation of public accommodations, public school integration, and voting rights. As these demands often brought together different ensembles of targets, tactics, and interested third parties, they entailed diverse combinations of disruption and concession costs. These differences make possible further evaluation of the merit of this approach beyond any single issue or policy domain.

Combining these considerations, I selected six cases for analysis: Greensboro, North Carolina; New Orleans, Louisiana; Albany, Georgia; Birmingham, Alabama; Greenwood, Mississippi; and Selma, Alabama. For each case, I rely on the many rich studies of the civil rights movement to sketch the interests and vulnerabilities of the key actors. I describe movement activities, demands, and the intensity of countermobilization in these localities to estimate the magnitude of both disruption and concession costs. In their selection of targets, demands, and tactics, movement organizers made a set of key strategic choices affecting both costs and therefore the probabilities of success. Finally, I document the responses of targets to civil rights mobilization and survey the evidence for the proposed relationship between differences in cost exposure and responsiveness to movement demands.

Greensboro, North Carolina

Situated in a bustling center for textile manufacture and insurance, major economic actors in Greensboro, North Carolina, had neither a compelling interest in the defense of Jim Crow nor considerable exposure to the disruption of civil rights protests. Consequently, it is anticipated that these interests will largely conform to dominant local customs, and are unlikely to mobilize against integration. Downtown merchants and other consumption-dependent enterprises are predicted to be vulnerable to protest events. Coupled with the weakness of Greensboro segregationists and their inability to heighten concession costs, these exposed interests should behave as accommodators.[2]

In this context, on February 1, 1960, four African-American college students began a sit-in campaign to desegregate the downtown

---

[2] The weakness of organized segregationism in North Carolina is documented in Neil McMillen's 1971 classic *The Citizens' Council*.

commercial facilities and inaugurated a new wave of direct action that spread across the South. The students carefully chose to limit their targets to the large downtown department stores. They did so to draw attention to those national chains that abetted racial discrimination in their southern operations and to avoid spreading their impact too thinly.[3] Sit-in tactics, later coupled with a boycott, threatened merchants with severe disruption costs. With their occupation of lunch-counter stools, no other customers could be served and concerns about the unruliness of white onlookers interfered with the activities of would-be shoppers. Participation in the sit-ins and pickets soon swelled into the hundreds as support broadened to encompass local black colleges as well as some white students. Thus, the nascent movement was capable of inflicting significant economic harm upon their targets. Sympathy pickets formed at Woolworth stores in northern cities as well. Yet, despite the exposure of these businesses, lacking prior experience with the costs of this form of protest, these Greensboro merchants initially feared that integration "would lead to a major loss of profits and disaffection of white customers."[4] However, out of concern for their national reputation, Woolworth's management resisted the governor's call to use anti-trespass laws to have the protesters arrested.

In reaction to escalating disruptions, though, the merchants vacillated. During a truce in which protests were suspended to permit negotiation, the merchants at first refused the April recommendations of a biracial committee for a trial period of integration.[5] This refusal met with the renewal of protests and the further imposition of an even more crippling economic boycott. Woolworth's manager estimated that protest activities had cost the store some $200,000 and that 1960 profits dropped by 50 percent. Therefore, after only a few months of sit-ins, downtown merchants buckled. In June, the local Woolworth's manager exclaimed to the mayor, "For God's sake do something, my business is going to pot."[6] By

---

[3] Flowers (2005, 58).

[4] Chafe (1980, 93). They further resisted capitulation because they feared that their desegregation would simply cause whites to flee to other facilities that had not been singled out for protests and remained segregated. While the movement benefited from a concentrated focus, the intensity of a target's resistance was likely augmented due to their desire to have all facilities desegregate simultaneously so that they could not be singled out for reprisals.

[5] *New York Times*, April 6, 1960.

[6] Chafe (1980, 97). Consistent with the general predictions of this analysis, Mayor George Roach, who supported negotiations and compromise, was both "a realtor and insurance agent" (Chafe 1980, 89). Likewise, during the resurgence of protests in 1963, Mayor David Schenck was an insurance broker.

late July, because of considerable economic duress, an integration agreement had been reached in which the four main department stores, including Woolworth's, would quietly and simultaneously desegregate their lunch counters. In retrospective interviews, the key actors on both sides agreed that the cause of this success "was the tremendous economic pressure put on the stores by the Negroes' boycott, along with the reticence of whites to trade there because of fear of trouble."[7]

Whereas other cities sometimes desegregated their lunch counters only after protests lasting a year or more, the relative rapidity with which prominent economic actors and public officials in Greensboro accepted the necessity of a brokered settlement is telling. The merchants initially vacillated due to their uncertainty about the concession costs associated with white reaction to integration but soon felt their keen exposure to movement disruption as profits plummeted. Instead of rallying to the defense of the color line, other major economic interests conformed, taking no action to block lunch-counter integration. The weakness of countermobilization meant that the movement's chokehold on the merchants' profits provided them with a compelling motivation to capitulate. With this cost configuration, movement targets in Greensboro reluctantly accepted change and gave the movement an important early victory.

New Orleans, Louisiana

At the junction of the Mississippi River and the Gulf of Mexico, New Orleans served as a major transportation node for the region. Petroleum refining, petrochemical production, natural gas industries, and tourism contributed to the city's economic base. None of these sectors depended on Jim Crow for economic prosperity and all but tourism were insulated from the disruption costs that movements might impose. Not only were industrial and shipping interests shielded from disturbances to production processes, they lacked motivation to act as "boosters" in favor of attracting new investment.[8] This combination of low vulnerability to disruption and ostensibly low concession costs vested key economic actors with the capacity to conform to the dominant Jim Crow heritage and to remain indifferent to racial turmoil. The exposure of the tourism sector, downtown consumption interests, and a few pro-growth boosters provided

---

[7] Wolff (1970, 173).
[8] Cobb (1993).

civil rights activists with a possible weakness, but, unlike in Greensboro, segregationist organizations such as the Greater New Orleans Citizens' Council exerted considerable leverage and had the capacity to push these prospective accommodators toward vacillation. This combination of conformers and vacillators foreshadows a response not so much of intense resistance as indecision, drift, and fecklessness.

The sit-in movement in New Orleans began in March 1960. Local economic interests reacted with indifference, abdicated a leadership role, and ceded control over the local response to organized segregationists. Reactive mobilization emerged primarily from the twenty-two rural parishes (counties) most committed to labor-intensive cotton agriculture.[9] Unlike Greensboro, in which protests escalated rapidly to include hundreds of participants, the small-scale pickets and sit-ins in New Orleans generated enthusiasm, but the activities of this fledgling chapter of the Congress of Racial Equality (CORE) failed to operate at a scale sufficient to harm local merchants. Without any organized demands for moderation, local authorities responded to student protests against segregated seating arrangements and employment discrimination with expulsions, fines, arrest, and imprisonment. At the urging of segregationist organizations and members of the legislature, Governor Jimmie Davis introduced a set of "law and order" bills to further reinforce the legal resources available to punish demonstrators.[10] At the close of 1960, as local merchants in other states desegregated their lunch counters, the sit-in movement in New Orleans ended in failure.[11]

The pace of movement agitation accelerated in the fall of that year. Indeed, before the students in New Orleans began their struggle to desegregate downtown facilities, the NAACP had been prodding the federal courts to implement the 1954 *Brown v. Board of Education* decision. In response, federal court orders compelled local authorities to select two New Orleans schools for integration in November. Events in Little Rock in 1957 had already demonstrated that federal authorities, however unwilling they were to push for desegregation, would not tolerate outright defiance of federal court orders. Federal coercion presented local movement targets with insurmountable disruption costs and, perversely

---

[9] McMillen (1971, 63). Claiborne Parish, where the Louisiana Council originated and whose state legislative representatives provided the political leadership for state segregation policy, combined cotton plantation agriculture with interests from oil and natural gas.

[10] McCarrick (1964).

[11] Oppenheimer (1963) [1989].

perhaps, concession costs could be reduced as the blame might be shifted onto the federal government.

The commencement of this process was fortuitous for the student protest movement because it turned out to be more disruptive to the city economy than sit-ins had been. This supportive federal action, which was not aimed at particular economic actors but instead at the local educational authorities, provoked a severe backlash. The White Citizens' Council promptly held a rally during which segregationists called on the audience of five thousand to boycott the schools and march on the offices of the school board to protest the board's compliance with the order.[12] The next day, thousands of whites walked through the downtown, passing by the state supreme court, city hall, the federal courts, and the board of education building. Later, the demonstration arrived in the business district and there deteriorated into a riot in which whites made unprovoked attacks upon blacks. After African-Americans began to fight back, law enforcement intervened. Taking up the call to boycott the school, a group of white women – known as the "cheerleaders" – gathered daily to scream at and shove all who dared to enter. Verbal intimidation and disorder around the school persisted for the entire academic year without public officials offering any serious attempt to disperse the segregationists despite national and international publicity of this horrific racial hatred.[13] On the contrary, the city's mayor refused to intervene for the

---

[12] Keesing's Research Reports (1970, 74).

[13] Bartley (1969, 337). It is possible that challenges to preferred values or a prospective reduction in social status might be regarded as costs as well. The abandonment of the color line threatened the "southern way of life," which conferred status benefits, however modest, to working-class whites. The behavior of the "cheerleaders" might be regarded as responding to such considerations. Assuming that satisfactory metrics can be identified for these measures, they might be successfully incorporated in a fuller account of reactive countermobilization in a manner consistent with this analysis. To the extent that a target's racial ideology, cultural preferences, or status benefits interferes with the pursuit of their economic or political interests, the relative weight of these different factors for targets might be investigated. However, as I suggest elsewhere (Luders 2006), the decision of the overwhelming majority of southern business operators to desegregate their facilities, rather than go out of business, is suggestive that material interests predominated. Further, although cultural and status considerations may have facilitated the mobilization of certain white women in New Orleans, upon closer inspection, this episode does not deviate from the logic presented here. The two schools that had been targeted for desegregation were located in lower-income neighborhoods, in which interracial resource competition is presumed to be strongest. Also, although it might seem that the preponderance of women in the crowds deviates from a competition explanation, it is quite possible that their presence is attributable to their availability for activism during school hours (McAdam 1986). As representatives of white families threatened with

sake of protecting civil rights or quelling the public disorders wrought by the segregationists.[14]

These events are striking because they deviate from the conventional expectation that disruptions in public order or negative publicity automatically compelled southern economic actors to capitulate to movement demands.[15] Whereas in cities like Greensboro, Atlanta, Dallas, and elsewhere, business fears about the economic consequences of racial disturbances had prompted relatively rapid calls for moderation or even advance preparation for integration, New Orleans business elites refused to accept any such leadership role for over a year. Further, the black vote was too small to punish office-seekers for courting segregationists. This combination of business quiescence, vocal segregationist opposition, and black political weakness meant that local officials had no incentives to take the electoral risks associated with containing organized extremists. Accordingly, Mayor DeLesseps "Chep" Morrisson did "practically nothing to avert the crisis" as he steered a path of "least political resistance."[16]

Explanations for this lack of business leadership in New Orleans typically highlight the greater "traditionalism" of the New Orleans elite. For example, Inger (1968) describes them as closed, insular, and uninterested in recruiting new industry to the city. Likewise, Fairclough claims that, "the city's leaders did not fail to head off the crisis simply through miscalculation or lack of nerve...one can argue that they indeed *were* more prejudiced than their counterparts in more 'progressive' cities."[17] Lacking guidance from moderate business leaders, vehement organized

intensified competition over educational resources, this pattern seems consistent with the perspective presented here. The introduction of additional cultural or status variables into the analysis depends on the extent to which they are actually needed to explicate the behavior and outcomes under consideration. Researchers differ over the extent to which this is necessary. The general supposition here is that such factors will be most analytically useful in those cases in which conventional economic and political costs are deemed smaller, less immediately relevant, or otherwise less identifiable. Gusfield (1966), for example, points to social status as a driving force behind the American temperance movement. A similar analysis is applicable to evangelical Christian mobilization against same-sex unions (Haider-Markel and Meier 1996).

[14] McCarrick (1964, 202).

[15] Ashmore (1957); Bloom (1987).

[16] Fairclough (1995, 251). Privately, Morrison blamed the business community for not taking action to avert the crisis. Fairclough (253) reports that Morrison declared: "Well, if those s.o.b.'s aren't going to do anything, I'll be damned if I'm going to stick my neck out."

[17] Ibid., 261–2.

segregationists were capable of directing the local response toward intransigence and tolerance for anti–civil rights disorders. Yet little evidence is offered to demonstrate that New Orleans elites were more traditional than elsewhere, and since similarly traditional elites capitulated to the civil rights movement in other cities, something more is necessary to explain the distinctiveness of the case.

A cost assessment explanation of this unwillingness to act draws attention to the exposure of economic actors to protests and movement success. As indicated above, from this perspective, the constituent elements of the "New Orleans elite" are perhaps less distinctive for their traditionalism than for their peculiar insulation from both disruption and concession costs of civil rights mobilization. The fundamental importance of the port and shipping in New Orleans economy, the relative insulation of these sectors from the ramifications of racial unrest, and the lack of interest in attracting new investment allowed for disinterest in bids for racial equality. The major industries based on the extraction and processing of natural resources (petroleum and natural gas) were similarly shielded. With a strong market position, local and absentee owners or managers of these firms had less reason to worry about the negative effects of racial contention on routine economic transactions. Cobb identifies both New Orleans and Birmingham as cities "whose well-developed heavy industrial base helped to make its Big Mule leadership less interested in further growth."[18] Finally, the common description of these actors as "old money" implies fortunes less dependent on robust local economic development.

Since this ensemble of interests lacked compelling economic imperatives to organize for the defense of Jim Crow institutions, a cost assessment analysis accounts for conformity to the dominant racial preferences of the community. Economic development, then, does not necessarily prompt local elites to embrace liberal or democratic values; instead, certain forms of development permit continued support of institutions and practices hostile to these currents. The opposition to racial equality among these actors should not be regarded simply as an expression of their traditionalism, but also as evidence of their unusual isolation from the disruption costs that precipitate moderation, as well as the strength of segregationist mobilization.

Other business interests in New Orleans, however, suffered from the costs of public disorders associated with school desegregation. Consistent

[18] 1988, 66.

with predictions, tourism and downtown business activity fell with the escalation in black protest and press coverage of contentious white countermobilization against school integration. By late 1960, these disruptions reportedly reduced sales at the large department stores by as much as 40 percent, hotel and restaurant business was down 20 percent, and other tourist-dependent interests were likewise feeling hardship.[19] Against the backdrop of public school disorders, CORE's 1961 resumption of sit-ins and picketing in the downtown shopping section only intensified the financial pain of resistance.

After the disastrous tumult of the 1960–61 academic year and amid ongoing protests, these vulnerable economic actors in particular began to show greater interest in accommodation. As Rogers notes, "The events of 1960–1961 had made the city's white economic elites extremely sensitive to the costs of racial disruption."[20] As the economic situation worsened in early 1962, a representative of the Chamber of Commerce implored Harry Kelleher, a respected corporate lawyer, to negotiate a compromise with black representatives. Major bankers likewise supported action to head off further disruption. Describing the impetus for this action, Kelleher observed, "The specter of economic pressure certainly tipped the scales in favor of affirmative action."[21] With the new support of these critical elements of the business committee behind orderly integration and the containment of extremists, school desegregation in the fall of 1961 finally proceeded without disturbance. At the same time, fear of economic reprisals instigated by the Citizens' Council produced secrecy, hesitation, and delay, and discouraged the merchants from accommodating. Finally, after a visit from Martin Luther King, Jr., rising concern about strengthened sit-ins, pickets, and a tightened boycott prompted downtown merchants finally, and very quietly, to desegregate their lunch counters, toilets, and water fountains in September – two years after the onset of protests.[22]

---

[19] Inger (1968, 61–2).

[20] 1993, 85.

[21] Robinson (1995), 68.

[22] Fairclough (1995, 284). Elite business support for racial integration of the public schools coalesced at a meeting before the start of classes in the fall of 1961. The profile of the eight participants at this meeting is suggestive: a real estate magnate, chairman of a major investment brokerage, a lawyer, a prominent real estate broker, two executives of the local Coca-Cola plant, an insurance mogul, a newspaper publisher, and an unspecified entrepreneur (Baker 1996, 458). The predominance of those interests dependent upon local consumption, investment, and development is striking, as is the absence of representatives from the oil industry or transportation.

Following the public school crisis, deference to the conformers diminished as the boosters formed, in June 1962, the Committee for a Better Louisiana to bypass the lethargic Chamber of Commerce.[23] After a lack of leadership from insulated interests, and much hesitation, the mobilization of vulnerable accommodators in New Orleans marked a turning point in the city for the civil rights movement. In both domains of movement mobilization, the catastrophic disruption costs associated with expanded protests and white supremacist countermobilization prompted vulnerable sectoral interests to support concessions. Yet, movement outcomes diverged in these domains. Slowly, Jim Crow institutions in the downtown stores were swept aside as economic actors succumbed to persistent disruption costs; at the same time, absent movement wherewithal to punish elected officials for half-measures, local politicians continued to promise white voters to keep the degree of school integration to the barest tokenism. Variation in the movement's disruptive capabilities coincided with differences in the relative scope of those changes.

Atlanta, Georgia

Stretching back decades before the eruption of protests, Atlanta had a long tradition of New South politics in which business and politics fused together in active support of economic growth and the cultivation of an image for moderation. The political leadership of Mayor William Hartsfield (1942–62) and his successor, Ivan Allen, Jr. (1962–70), had close ties to the business community, with the latter having been the president of the Atlanta Chamber of Commerce.[24] Looming in the background of local politics were the utilities, key banking institutions, insurance, a few department store interests, and various Atlanta-based companies including Coca Cola. The local economic elite, described as owners of local businesses, not engaged in manufacturing, and having "their locus of consumption in the immediate metropolitan area," were vulnerable to reputational damage and disruptions in local commerce.[25] Too, over the preceding years, the large African-American middle class had united with upper-income whites and business interests to form an "invincible coalition" in city politics. This arrangement assured the political marginalization of extreme segregationists and greater political responsiveness to the

---

[23] Inger (1968, 89).
[24] Alton Hornsby, Jr. (1982, 121).
[25] Jennings (1964, 197).

African-American leadership in the form of law enforcement committed to protecting public order and the suppression of violent white counter-mobilization. Civil rights demonstrations and racial unrest in this setting endangered the city's reputation and prospects for continued robust economic development. In the early sixties, the path for the movement to achieve public schools integration, the desegregation of public accommodations, and voter registration gains thus appeared relatively unobstructed.

Yet, each of these demands came with different constellations of disruption and concession costs for their targets. Regarding voter registration, the exceptional composition of the dominant political faction meant that civil rights demands met with unusual support from local authorities. Hartsfield had long cultivated the support of the Atlanta Negro Voters League, the traditional black political organization, in return for various policy benefits such as new city parks in black neighborhoods, hiring more black police and firefighters, and more.[26] Thus, under the auspices of the Voter Education Project in 1962 alone, a voter registration drive added an estimated ten thousand African-Americans to the rolls.[27] This contrasts starkly with Selma, Alabama, where the movement managed to register fewer than four hundred black Dallas County residents by 1965 despite years of struggle.[28] Whereas elsewhere African-American voter registration represented a threat to the dominant political faction, enhanced black electoral leverage in Atlanta promised to strengthen its position.

Similarly, the political interests of Atlanta's ruling regime and the corresponding electoral weakness of segregationist countermobilization favored a calm response to school desegregation. Allowing the integration of public schools to collapse into racial disorder and negative publicity threatened to produce considerable disaffection among African-Americans and economic elites. However, school desegregation represented a greater challenge than voter registration due to widespread white opposition and higher prospective concession costs for local officials. To reduce these costs, the school board proposed a gradual plan to integrate, beginning with the last two grades of high school and adding a grade each year thereafter. This plan delayed full integration for a decade.[29]

---

[26] Bayor (1996, 26).
[27] Walker (1963, 380).
[28] Lawson (1991, 105).
[29] Hornsby (1982, 22).

Other "pupil placement" elements of the plan, including personality and scholastic aptitude tests, were used to limit black access to white schools. The school board made these proposals after the governor had already backed away from a "massive resistance" position that demanded closure of integrated schools and had instead asked the legislature to adopt a package of bills meant to keep the schools open while assuring the continuation of maximum segregation. Extensive negotiations between black and white elites within the dominant coalition produced the "Atlanta Compromise," which led to the peaceful desegregation of the public schools in 1961 while keeping the costs imposed upon whites as small as possible. In this case, the costs for school desegregation fell most heavily upon those outside of the dominant coalition.

Yet, the response of the downtown merchants complicates the city's image as a bastion of racial moderation. Students conducted their first sit-in on March 15, 1960 and continued, with uneven intensity, over a year. Despite these protests and sympathetic initial reaction from a pivotal figure among retailers, the downtown merchants refused to integrate until after the public schools had done so, which was slated for the fall of 1961. Inverting the usual responses of business and political targets, public officials evinced greater responsiveness to movement demands than did vulnerable economic interests. Although the mayor lacked exposure to electoral reprisals from vulnerable whites, targeted merchants were exposed not only to civil rights protests, but segregationist countermobilization as well. After the resumption of student protests following a temporary truce in November, fifty to one hundred Klansmen began counterpickets at the same stores in defense of segregation. "A variety of groups flocked to the city: GUTS, various KKK groups, National States Rights Party members, etc.," recounted Oppenheimer. By early December, Georgians Unwilling to Surrender (GUTS) joined the segregationist pickets and threatened a counter-boycott against any store that hired African-Americans in response to movement demands. During this period of countermobilization, the removal of Jim Crow signs from the washrooms in a major department store reportedly triggered sixteen hundred whites to close their charge accounts.[30] These instigators drew public attention to the prospect of integration and no doubt accentuated the likely concession costs for downtown retailers.

Nor were disruption costs associated with the sit-in movement severe enough to compel swift capitulation. Three factors militated against their

---

[30] Oppenheimer (1963 [1989], 137).

effective imposition. First, student protests against downtown economic interests were sporadic. Their targets included multiple venues operated under government auspices as well as establishments within bus and train stations. After a brief flurry of activity, during which scores were arrested under a new state trespass law, students were unsure what to do next, but opted in the next month to form an organization capable of sustained action.[31] By the end of April, they began picketing at an A & P grocery store to compel the management to hire more African-Americans and promote others above menial positions. Also, in May, the students organized a large protest demonstration in which more than two thousand participants marched downtown to celebrate the anniversary of the Supreme Court's *Brown* decision.[32] Toward the close of the year, however, the degree of financial duress may have abated somewhat as students discontinued pickets except for Fridays and Saturdays from early December until February in order to concentrate on final exams. These intermittent events in the first months of protests might tarnish the city's reputation, but they had minimal impact beyond their immediate targets. Second, protests against the downtown economic elites lacked the support of the city's older traditional black leadership. Such leaders preferred to negotiate with white elites in quiet discussions instead of using "pressure tactics," such as demonstrations and boycotts.[33] While some describe the boycott as "generally effective," others suggest that the boycott reduced black consumption less than 50 percent at targeted stores due to divisions in the black community. Indeed, despite attempts to form a unified front, sharp internal dissension marked the relationship between the student activists and the more conservative black leadership. And third, some evidence suggests that Atlanta retailers were less dependent upon black customers than elsewhere. After students denounced the position of a leading merchant as "a lot of Uncle Tom business" and threatened his store with a boycott if he refused to integrate immediately, he retorted, "I don't need Negro trade" and stormed out of the meeting.[34] Although this might appear to have been bluster, other observers concurred with this assessment.[35] Based on the limited effectiveness of the movement in reducing their profits, this observation appears plausible.

---

[31] Walker (1963, 69).
[32] Oppenheimer (1963 [1989], 135).
[33] Tuck (2001, 122–3).
[34] Walker (1989A, 75); Walker (1989B, 20).
[35] Oppenheimer (1963 [1989]) suggests that downtown retail merchants were less dependent on black customers than were merchants elsewhere.

Due to these weaknesses, protests in Atlanta never precipitated losses of the same magnitude that elicited more rapid concessions in other localities. The resumption of protests after a truce and the addition of a boycott in the fall of 1960 did depress profits. Christmas sales at the downtown stores fell 16 percent from the previous year.[36] Yet elsewhere, civil rights disruptions wrought far more punishing effects on local economies. For instance, in Savannah, Georgia, civil rights demonstrations in 1963 had nearly twice the impact, dropping local trade around 30 percent.[37] Similarly, civil rights demonstrations and countermovement agitation in St. Augustine, Florida, in 1964 reduced tourism by some 40 to 60 percent and a 1965 boycott in Natchez, Mississippi, cut retail sales some 25 to 50 percent.[38] These comparative figures suggest that civil rights activities in 1960 hurt the profits of the downtown stores, but may have been insufficient to cripple them.

It was not until February 1, 1961, in commemoration of the Greensboro sit-ins the prior year, that sit-ins and other protests resumed with fresh vigor. At this time, students expanded their activities beyond their main target to picket all downtown department stores and again called for a general boycott of the entire downtown shopping area. Both civil rights agitation and white countermobilization reduced trade in the downtown stores. After only four days, the *New York Times* reported that the boycott was "100 percent effective" with the weekly profits from the previous year trimmed 12 percent, and some variety stores feeling "a far greater drop" in sales.[39] Yet again, the damage was insufficient to compel targets either to accede to movement demands or shutter their operations, except for the smaller merchants that depended heavily upon their black clientele.[40]

Accordingly, when student leaders met again with key downtown merchants, they again found them unwilling to accept immediate integration. This time, however, the older traditional black leadership persuaded the students to accept a desegregation agreement that called for an end to protests in return for the integration of lunchrooms and other facilities on "the same pattern" as school desegregation, which was set to commence in September. Ivan Allen, the Chamber of Commerce president, announced the agreement on March 8. The national press widely hailed

[36] Lincoln (1989).
[37] Tuck (2001, 136).
[38] On St. Augustine, see Colburn (1982, 231), and on Natchez, *Wall Street Journal*, October 20, 1965.
[39] *New York Times*, February 18, 1961.
[40] Walker (1963, 79).

it as evidence that Atlanta was, as Mayor Hartsfield asserted, "a city too busy to hate." Ultimately, except for a firm date to integrate the lunch counters, the final settlement was the same as what the merchants had offered the year before. Many student activists denounced the agreement, which allowed the department and variety stories to reopen their dining facilities on a segregated basis for nearly eight months. Only the personal intervention of Rev. Martin Luther King, Jr., in an emotional oration for unity prevented the repudiation of this agreement. Students urged an informal continuation of the boycott until the fall to assure compliance. Finally, on September 27, 1961, with no advance notice or fanfare, 177 public eating places in Atlanta desegregated. Despite previous segregationist resistance during the active phase of student protests, no white countermobilization resumed. With so many lunchrooms desegregated simultaneously, these businesses found a means to reduce the likelihood that one of them could be easily singled out for white backlash.

In all three domains of civil rights mobilization, the movement achieved differing degrees of success. The movement won the token integration of public schools, but achieved swifter and more substantial voter registration gains. In both cases, public officials were supportive, but the lower concession costs associated with the latter allowed for greater impact. Overall, relative to other Deep South cities, the unusual exposure of local authorities to disruption costs made them far more amenable to movement demands. For downtown merchants, by contrast, a combination of weak disruption costs and pain of prospective concession costs due to countermovement agitation led them to resist capitulation. As predicted, those most dependent upon African-American customers were most eager to settle. Ultimately, the stalemate ended once movement negotiators accepted an agreement that permitted the targets to reduce their exposure to concession costs by delaying implementation until after the schools had been integrated and through the expansion of a number of affected establishments. This account suggests that while economic disruption no doubt encouraged downtown consumption interests to negotiate over a compromise, these costs were less punishing in Atlanta than other cases and that a satisfactory explanation of the outcome in this domain must highlight the target's own strategic reduction in their exposure to concession costs.

Albany, Georgia

Situated within the heart of Georgia's rural black belt, amid the vestiges of the Old South, Albany served as a processing and transportation center for local agricultural products such as cotton, pecans, corn, and peanuts. Light industry, wholesale, and retail enterprises too made up the core of the local economy. Since few economic actors continued to depend on subordination of black labor, most interests are predicted to conform to local Jim Crow traditions. The political irrelevance of the black vote due to widespread disenfranchisement and the commitment of the white population to Jim Crow foreshadows resistance from local officials. By contrast, downtown consumption and growth-dependent interests would be expected to be vulnerable to sustained disruptions. Also, the lack of strong segregationist organization in Albany meant that local interests had less fear of white reprisals. In some ways, then, Albany resembled Greensboro, but the outcomes of civil rights activity were markedly different.

Protests began in the late fall of 1961 and stretched into August 1962. Student Nonviolent Coordinating Committee (SNCC) organizers arrived in the summer of 1961 to begin a broad campaign against "all forms of racial domination in Albany."[41] Although relations between SNCC and the local chapter of the NAACP and other organizations were tense, local activists formed the Albany Movement to bring together and coordinate the competing elements. Attempts to integrate the Albany bus terminal and train station resulted in the arrest of the participants. To protest these arrests, hundreds marched to city hall and were likewise arrested. Martin Luther King, Jr., and his organization, the Southern Christian Leadership Conference (SCLC), joined the movement in mid-December, at which time five hundred people languished in jail. His arrest generated a rush of enthusiasm, but his swift release two days later following a hollow truce confused and dispirited many.

Sporadic sit-ins were staged in the early months of 1962 and a general boycott of white merchants was intensified in March. Further protest marches followed, frequently targeting city hall, and always resulting in mass arrests. During these protests, police chief Laurie Pritchett made certain that the jails had ample capacity and that the police applied local laws without resort to brutality or violence. After many months of agitation and mass jailing, the movement floundered without achieving the integration of the city's facilities.

Unlike the early explanations of this defeat, which pointed to squabbles within the movement and poor planning, more recent commentary emphasizes Pritchett's use of nonviolent, legal strategies of repression.[42] McAdam argues that Pritchett's strategy of repression denied civil rights

---

[41] Morris (1984, 241).
[42] See in particular Barkan (1984); McAdam (1982).

activists the violent clashes with supremacists that were necessary to compel federal action. Unable to provoke the white violence, "insurgents
lacked the leverage to achieve anything more than a standoff with the
local supremacist forces in Albany."[43] Absent violent countermovement
reprisals to trigger federal intervention – McAdam's "critical dynamic" –
the movement failed. Steven Barkan too points to Pritchett's effective use
of legalistic forms of repression, but Barkan's analysis suggests a resource
depletion hypothesis. The costs of fines, bail, legal representation, and
lower movement morale resulting from harassment arrests and incarcer-
ation, Barkan argues, drained resources and thus administered the "decisive blow" against the Albany Movement. While valid, both accounts
overlook a key component in the explanation of the defeat: the inability
of the movement to impose substantial costs upon vulnerable local actors.

The cost assessment hypothesis refines McAdam's and Barkan's investigation of the Albany defeat, and clarifies how the federal government
contributes to "movement leverage." Although McAdam does not elaborate upon the concept of movement leverage below the national level,
federal support transforms the cost calculations of local movement opponents. Such intervention not only involves the obvious use of coercive
capacity; the central state can also impose fines, penalties, and necessitate costly litigation or withhold valued expenditures. Movement targets
must consider whether or not these added costs outweigh the economic or
political incentives for continued resistance. Absent federal involvement,
the task of imposing the necessary costs upon local actors falls solely
upon the movement and the tactical ingenuity of the activists. In contrast
to McAdam, who appears to assume that the movement was incapable of
victory in Albany without federal intervention, this analysis suggests that
a different outcome might have resulted from the selection of vulnerable
targets and the sustained disruptions of their interests. In this, the Albany
Movement leaders made a series of crucial strategic mistakes. In contrast to the concentrated emphasis in Greensboro and Atlanta, the erratic
choice of targets and the general lack of focus made the effective imposition of sustained disruption costs in Albany virtually impossible. This
interpretation echoes King's own assessment and that of others who have
suggested that the disparate goals "spread the Movement too thinly."[44]

---

[43] McAdam (1982, 177).
[44] Barkan (1984, 557). Chong (1991) observes that the Albany Movement's lack of clear,
winnable goals meant that the campaign would fail to produce early triumphs necessary
to stimulate and sustain broader community-wide participation.

In particular, to the extent that movement leaders fixed upon any target, they chose the wrong one: elected officials.[45] Members of the city government had few reasons for entering into good faith negotiations or making substantive concessions. Lacking a strident clamor from vulnerable economic actors, federal coercion, or a plausible threat of political reprisals, these officials had many reasons to resist capitulation. Thus the movement's irregular targeting of city officials wasted precious resources bailing out and defending those who marched to, and demonstrated in front of, city hall. Relatively few direct action events disrupted business operations and, to the extent that they were tried, they were uncoordinated with other efforts and used only after the movement was already reeling from prior setbacks. As Lewis notes, the boycott "pained … but did not seriously cripple the merchants."[46] Had the many hundreds who were arrested in large demonstrations before the city government targeted those vulnerable to disruption costs, the outcome of the Albany Movement might have been substantially different even without federal intervention.

The outcome of the bus boycott is instructive. In January 1962, SNCC launched a bus boycott in Albany that, three weeks later, resulted in the closure of the bus line.[47] Before the failure of this business, the president of the bus line explained in a telephone conversation with the Albany mayor that "the company would rather grant the movement's request than go out of business" – reinforcing the general point that vulnerable economic actors preferred to desegregate rather than sacrifice their businesses. Yet, instead of accepting the proffered bargain with the company, the movement leadership insisted that the city commissioners endorse this agreement, which it flatly refused to do.[48] The movement's decision to involve the city government, a body minimally exposed to electoral threats from civil rights supporters, was unwise.

Indeed, King ultimately arrived at strikingly similar conclusions about the failure of the Albany Movement. Summing up King's analysis,

---

[45] The movement defeat in Danville, Virginia, which Barkan also addresses, shares many similarities with Albany. Although not explored here, it is worth mentioning that this movement failure stemmed from a similarly misplaced use of protests conducted at city hall. As suggested for Albany, against these insulated targets, these protests resulted in costly arrests but imposed minimal disruption costs upon their targets. Conventional accounts neglect to address the differences in target vulnerabilities.

[46] Lewis (1970, 155).

[47] Williams (1988, 171).

[48] Garrow (1986, 192).

Garrow states that the Albany Movement would have been more successful . . .

> . . . if the movement had targeted Albany's business leaders, rather than the city's elected officials. The boycott of downtown stores had been an effective but limited tactic, King decided, because the movement's direct action efforts had not been combined with the boycott so as to inflict a maximum penalty upon those business leaders.[49]

King likewise argued the marches to city hall were misplaced. Instead, he suggested that, due to the political weakness of blacks in Albany, the marches should have been directed at "the businesses in the city" because "the political power structure listens to the economic power structure."[50] While Pritchett's strategies reduced the likelihood of federal intervention and depleted movement resources, as McAdam and Barkan assert, the strategic mistakes of the movement's leaders made a difficult situation far more likely to end in defeat. King drew important lessons from the defeat in Albany and carried these lessons with him to Birmingham, Alabama. Next time, he reasoned, the movement should seek out an adversary less likely to respond with nonviolence and target downtown business interests at the outset. After much contemplation following the defeat in Albany, the movement went to Birmingham in 1963, and then to Selma in 1965.

Birmingham, Alabama

As the "the Pittsburgh of the South," Birmingham's iron and steel interests dominated this industrial city. The local managers and owners of these enterprises supported Jim Crow as a means of keeping wages low and they opposed efforts to attract new industry to Birmingham as this was thought to increase the competition for workers and raise labor costs. These industrialists had supported the election of the notorious T. Eugene "Bull" Connor in the 1930s to the city commission "to crush the Communist–integrationist menace" represented by the Congress of Industrial Organizations.[51] Absentee ownership of the United States Steel Corporation and its subsidiaries, which overshadowed the urban political economy, further reduced the potential for indigenous reform leadership. Such interests, unconcerned about attracting external investment

[49] Ibid., 226.
[50] Quoted in Garrow (1986, 226).
[51] Thornton (1991, 47).

and shielded from the disruptions of movement agitation, lacked incentives to bargain or compromise. The unusual sway of vulnerable lower-status whites in city politics further strengthened local resistance to civil rights gains.[52] For these whites, a vote for Connor meant that blacks would be kept "in their place."[53] Uncoincidentally, a Klan chapter operated in Birmingham and the vicinity such that the city had earned the nickname of "Bombingham."

While iron and steel interests benefited from insulation from disruption, other actors were far less sheltered, and movement activists appreciated this weakness. As elsewhere, a worsening racial situation caused growing concern among consumer and service interests, and it was from these sectors that opposition to the likes of Bull Connor eventually coalesced.[54] These actors, concentrated in real estate, services, and downtown consumption, sought to expand and diversify the city's economic base. Sidney Smyer, a real estate executive and former head of the local Chamber of Commerce, organized the successful political drive to change the structure of city government in an indirect move to unseat reactionary elements like Connor. After Connor lost the 1963 election, he, along with the other city commissioners, refused to step down; consequently, for several months, the city had two separate governments representing differing economic factions. As Bartley explains, "The basic rift was between the iron aristocracy, which identified segregation with low wages and a docile work force, and service-sector businessmen, whose goals were economic growth and maximizing of real estate values."[55]

The rise of mass protest in 1963 widened this split. As demonstrations, boycotts, and general disorder continued in April and May, graphic incidents of police repression drew enormous negative publicity and cost downtown retailers an estimated weekly loss of $750,000.[56] Continued disorder, the trade association of the merchants concluded, "would have a drastic and far-reaching economic effect on the metropolitan area."[57] Having learned from the defeat in Albany, King explained that these

---

[52] Eskew (1997). See also Nunnelly (1991).

[53] Sitkoff (1981, 130).

[54] Eskew (1997); McWhorter (2001).

[55] 1995, 332–3.

[56] *Time*, June 7, 1963, quoted in Patterson, "The Price We Pay" (1964). This report identifies similar stories in *Business Week*, the *Wall Street Journal*, and the *Washington Post*. Asked about the boycott, a merchant candidly observed, "It's on and it's hurting." See McWhorter (2001, 266).

[57] McWhorter (2001, 268).

economic consequences were deliberate: "You don't win against a political power structure where you don't have the votes. But you can win against an economic power structure when you have the economic power to make the difference between a merchant's profit and loss."[58] Even as regular operations for iron and steel interests continued, the racial crisis engulfed the city and devastated downtown commercial activity.

Beleaguered merchants hesitated due to fear of white reprisals, but deteriorating economic conditions eventually compelled them to agree in early May to a settlement on the condition that the city's economic leadership publicly support the agreement.[59] Although steel interests resisted concessions, a committee of economic elites eventually endorsed the agreement that accepted the movement's principal demands: the desegregation of various downtown facilities, the hiring of more blacks in non-menial positions and job promotions, the release of jailed demonstrators, and the creation of a biracial committee to continue discussions. With the endorsement of a major faction of the city's economic leadership and additional disruptive protests to compel compliance, vacillating interests reduced their exposure to concession costs and charted a jagged course to a position of accommodation.

The Birmingham case corroborates key elements of this argument. Iron and steel manufacturers, being insulated from disruption costs but presuming concessions to be at least somewhat costly, behaved principally as conformers but with a general preference against concessions. Vulnerable working-class whites, who often occupied a critical position in the dominant political coalition, offered more vigorous resistance. Thus, although Connor's outbursts are often treated as a matter of individual temperament, this approach suggests a political explanation for the use of reactionary violence. Specifically, a combination of insulated economic elites and marginal working-class whites in the governing coalition provided strong political incentives for unleashing brutal violence, even if

---

[58] Quoted in Bloom (1987, 174).

[59] Eskew (1997); Morris (1993). The sectoral logic is evidenced as well in the merchants' attempt to enlist the support of the broader business community. White negotiators knew that segregationists might attempt to single out those entities that agreed to desegregate for punishment and that downtown retailers "had merchandise that was vulnerable to the bomb, the torch, and the razor." As soon as a desegregation decision was announced, one participant surmised that "the hounds will start chasing the foxes," and therefore, "'We need to give them some good foxes to chase that are fairly invulnerable foxes' – the mortgage bankers, the real estate folks, the power company." See McWhorter (2001, 401). Although these interests might be exposed to the costs of diminished local growth, these were not directly susceptible to protest activities or reprisals by blue-collar whites.

this conduct might be counterproductive for the segregationist cause more generally. Further corroboration is found in the composition of the political faction supporting conciliation. After initial vacillation due to fear of reprisal by disaffected whites, downtown merchants, service, and real estate interests, among others, rebelled against the resisters and shifted toward accommodation to negotiate an agreement under as much collective cover as possible. The accommodators were, as predicted, clustered in those sectors that were most sensitive to disruption costs, most eager to promote local growth, and lacking an economic interest in defending segregation. The fate of the Birmingham struggle demonstrated the value of targeting vulnerable interests with severe disruption.

Greenwood, Mississippi

While the dramatic clashes in Birmingham are widely remembered, a band of dedicated activists and their supporters also encountered strong opposition in Greenwood, Mississippi. Situated in Leflore County at the edge of the vast plantations of the Delta, Greenwood served as a major center for the cultivation and trading of cotton. With Delta planters dependent upon cheap black agricultural labor, the civil rights movement potentially posed a fundamental challenge to these economic interests. At the same time, however, the mechanization of cotton agriculture was rapidly reducing the demand for farm labor. Thus concession costs were declining swiftly in this period as planters became far less dependent upon African-American agricultural workers. On the other side, declining dependence on black labor and the corresponding economic vulnerability of tenant farmers and sharecroppers meant that the local movement was unable to impose disruption costs upon planters to coerce capitulation.[60] This convergence of factors predicts for resistance from plantation interests but declining in fervor as agricultural mechanization shifted their position from staunch resisters to conformers. As elsewhere, downtown merchants, especially in a city with a large black population, were vulnerable to disruption costs. To the extent that organized white resistance elevated the costs of conceding to movement demands, vacillation could

---

[60] Before committing to voter registration, SNCC organizers had discussed the possibility of organizing a strike among black agricultural workers, but decided against this because of the many anticipated difficulties including the likelihood planters might mechanize their operations more rapidly in reprisal (McMillen 1977). A strike among a limited number of plantation workers was attempted in 1965, but local planters united and, with the assistance of local law enforcement, easily crushed the strike (Cobb 1994).

be expected. With this mixture of resisters, conformers, and vacillators, movement success depended upon external intervention or a weakening of resistance among the opponents based upon declining concession costs.

Consistent with predictions, Greenwood economic and political elites resisted change at the outset, indeed long before protests even began. In the wake of the 1954 *Brown* decision, local planters and their allies enthusiastically organized a chapter of the segregationist White Citizens' Council, which later served as state headquarters in the 1960s.[61] Nor was this pattern exceptional among plantation counties. As discussed in Chapter 2, across the South, it was in those localities most dependent on labor-intensive agriculture that the Citizens' Council found the greatest support and where the defense of white supremacy was most entrenched.[62] Often depicted as the upper-class variant of the Ku Klux Klan, the Council relied upon more sophisticated modes of coercion. Whereas Klansmen resorted to private violence, Councilors used their influence over local livelihoods, and law enforcement, as weapons against agitators and to keep whites in line.[63] In the years after *Brown*, such threats of economic reprisal against those involved in civil rights activities were especially common in plantation counties.[64] Further bolstering planter political leverage in Greenwood was the election as mayor in 1957 of Charles Sampson, a Citizens' Council member and representative of plantation interests.[65] Thus, SNCC's foray into the Mississippi Delta "appeared foolhardy, if not suicidal."[66]

Despite this resistance and enticed by the possibility of breaching this fortress of white supremacy, SNCC chose Greenwood to be the site of a major voter registration campaign in 1962 and the state organizational headquarters in 1964. Yet rather than protesting for the integration of public accommodations, SNCC activists were instead committed

---

[61] The city also served as the temporary headquarters of the national association – the Citizens' Council of America (McMillen 1971). The Greenwood unit of the Citizens' Council paid for the legal expenses of Byron de la Beckwith, a Greenwood fertilizer salesman and the recently convicted assassin of Mississippi NAACP chief Medgar Evers (*New York Times*, July 9, 1963).

[62] James (1988); McMillen (1971).

[63] In the middle 1960s, violence against civil rights activists and supporters was perhaps more common in southwest Mississippi, where the resurgent Klan operated unchecked. There, in a pattern similar to that of Birmingham, working-class white mobilization against integration encouraged vacillation among business interests.

[64] *New York Times*, April 9, 1955.

[65] Payne (1995, 135).

[66] Dittmer (1994, 124).

to grassroots organizing and the cultivation of local leadership for durable political engagement. Eschewing sit-in demonstrations and the like, key organizers believed that white dominance in black majority counties was "most vulnerable...at the ballot box."[67] Greenwood organizers canvassed local residents to encourage them to register to vote, held regular meetings, and marched to the courthouse with potential registrants. All of these activities helped to build up an organizational base, fostered a greater sense of solidarity, and reduced fears of challenging the status quo. However, as in Albany, the targeting of political actors was ineffective at achieving movement goals. After a year of struggle, some fifteen hundred local blacks had attempted to register, but only fifty had been added to the voting rolls.[68] Perhaps not surprisingly, Dittmer (1995, 213) reports that by the end of 1963 the local movement was thoroughly demoralized.

The registration drives in 1963 and 1964 produced some disruptions in public order, and generated media coverage of anti-rights intimidation and violence, but they were insufficient to harm enterprises that were potentially vulnerable. As a newspaper correspondent reported in 1963, "Greenwood has felt no repercussions from the unfavorable headlines it has been winning in the northern press because it is not making any real effort to attract new industry." Rather, the manufacturing industries that had already been lured to Leflore County "seemed happy enough."[69] Commenting the following year on the difficulties of bringing about change in places such as Greenwood, a staff member of the U.S. Civil Rights Commission noted, "The process of change usually begins when community leadership decides the price of keeping the status quo is too high. Unfortunately, the price can be quite low in a small town where the loss of new industry or convention business may not be important factors."[70] Despite the continued willingness of hundreds of locals to brave the threats associated with attempting to register to vote, the absence of significant costs imposed on vulnerable business interests, the reticence of the federal government, and the corresponding intransigence of local public officials made even modest gains elusive.

The enactment of the Civil Rights Act of 1964 furnished activists with new weapons to impose greater costs upon noncompliant enterprises, but resistance continued. As Jim Crow barriers fell across the South,

[67] Ibid.
[68] Branch (1988, 725).
[69] *New York Times*, July 9, 1963.
[70] *Wall Street Journal*, August 27, 1964.

including Jackson, Mississippi, the new civil rights law failed to sweep away segregation in Greenwood. To "test" for compliance with the newly enacted law, a few local activists unaffiliated with SNCC – the McGhee brothers and their followers – attempted to desegregate public accommodations through direct action. In response, restaurant owners converted their establishments to private clubs, and lunch counters and soda fountains were removed for fear of a loss of white business.[71] A single movie theater, belonging to a larger chain, integrated only to have organized segregationists form a picket to accost both black and white patrons. During several visits to the theater, maverick activists had repeated encounters with a hostile crowd of three hundred whites. On one occasion, Jake McGhee was dragged from his seat and beaten; a few weeks later he was again injured by flying glass when a bottle crashed through the window of the car taking their group from the theater. Days later, three whites abducted and beat Silas McGhee and, in a separate incident, an unidentified white shot him in the head as he sat in his car. Not only blacks were terrorized. "Would-be white patrons of the Leflore [Theater] were challenged at the theater entrance. Many turned back. Those who went in often faced more harassment when they emerged from the theater after dark." Threats of violent reprisal forced the newspaper editor of the *Greenwood Commonwealth* to leave town after he mildly criticized extremism in print and crossed the picket line at the theater.[72] Caught between the movement and recalcitrant whites, the theater eventually closed. Further gains in Greenwood awaited the development of a sustained boycott against downtown economic interests in 1968. At that time, the movement's capabilities to impose severe economic pain upon downtown businesses precipitated a break between them and their erstwhile plantation allies. Too, the full mechanization of cotton agriculture had dampened the opposition of rural economic elites, which allowed desegregation finally to proceed.

Selma, Alabama

"They picked Selma just like a movie producer would pick a set," declared the city mayor in retrospect.[73] Aware of the value of provocative confrontations, particularly after the events in Birmingham, King and his

---

[71] *New York Times*, August 27, 1964.
[72] *New York Times*, August 11, 1964.
[73] Mayor Joseph Smitherman quoted in Williams (1988, 272).

associates chose Selma for a major voter registration drive because of the high likelihood of anti-rights violence in defense of egregious inequalities. The prospects in Selma, situated in the heart of the Alabama black belt, for a hostile response to civil rights mobilization seemed promising indeed. The economic base of Dallas County, where Selma is located, was historically closely tied to labor-intensive agricultural production (including cotton), and rural white reliance on black tenant farmers persisted. Though nearly all were denied voting rights, African-Americans made up about half of the city's thirty thousand residents. Under these conditions, white mobilization to protect Jim Crow against black voter registration was hardly surprising. In contrast to the weak segregationist movement found in Georgia, both the Citizens' Council and the Klan had strongholds in Alabama.

Dallas County provided the Citizens' Council with especially robust support. In 1954, "1,200 Dallas Countians gathered" to hear the call for organization and six hundred "became charter members of the Dallas County Citizens' Council" – the first such entity in the state after the *Brown* decision. After a single year, the local organization claimed a membership of fifteen hundred – one quarter of all adult white males in the county – and the mayor "immediately led his municipal machine into a firm alliance with the new segregationist organization."[74] In 1958, state senator Walter Givhan, the head of the Dallas County Council and member of the segregationist Alabama State Sovereignty Commission, assumed leadership of the state association and relocated the headquarters to Selma.[75] Although the organization had been in decline since 1958 and exerted leverage in only a few counties, it seems reasonable to assume that the organization was strongest in the city in which its headquarters was located. Due to this segregationist mobilization and the ties to local officials, key conditions for harsh reprisals were met. As Thornton confirms:

The close association that was thus established from the outset between the Citizens' Council on the one hand and the Selma city government, the county Democratic party, and various local officials and state legislators on the other appears to have been the principal source of the unusually aggressive and unanimous commitment of the white community of Dallas County to an extremist racial position.[76]

---

[74] Thornton (1991, 55). Unlike the many studies that overlook the subtleties of local politics, Thornton's essay is a rare gem. His research is fleshed out further in Thornton 2002.

[75] McMillen, (1971, 57).

[76] Thornton (1991, 55).

None of the various Klan factions had a local unit in Dallas County; nevertheless the Klan had sufficient statewide membership to be a factor in electoral calculations. George Wallace actively cultivated the support of white supremacist organizations during his 1962 gubernatorial bid.[77] This degree of segregationist mobilization had made taking even slightly moderate positions politically untenable. Although in Georgia weakly organized segregationists allowed Governor Vandiver to assist Pritchett in keeping order, Wallace's political support in Alabama from white supremacist organizations likely inclined him against using the state police to keep violent whites in check.

Local economic interests in the mid-sixties split over the best response to civil rights demands. Closely tied to the conservative political machine that had dominated city politics, the Dallas County Chamber of Commerce lacked any interest in providing leadership. However, other business interests were less satisfied with the machine's lackluster efforts to attract new business investments to the city. Joseph T. Smitherman, a local merchant and political insurgent, helped to organize "a committee of businessmen to seek new industry for the county."[78] Smitherman subsequently challenged and defeated the machine candidate in the mayoral election of 1964. Even before Smitherman's inauguration in October 1964, key business leaders with a "passion for industrial development" and who were afraid of negative publicity arranged to meet with representatives of the movement and agreed to continue to do so regularly.[79] To implement his plan to burnish the city's image, Smitherman created the position of director of public safety (with jurisdiction within the city limits though not around the county courthouse) and appointed Wilson Baker, a racial moderate, to the post. With the mobilization of supportive urban business interests, the defeat of the machine candidate, and the installation of a new head of law enforcement, an ostensibly hostile situation appeared at least somewhat more ambiguous.

In this setting, ongoing civil rights activities escalated with King's arrival in early January 1965, to inaugurate a massive voter registration drive.[80] In the weeks to follow, thousands marched to the county

[77] Carter (1995).
[78] Thornton (1991, 57).
[79] Ibid., 59.
[80] Descriptions of these events can be found in various reports in the *New York Times*. See, for instance, January 3, 20, 23, and 27, 1965; February 2, 3, 4, 6, 1965. Multiple studies address the events in Selma. See, in particular, Thornton (2002).

courthouse to register to vote, often to be arrested by the hundreds. For local officials, the political weakness of the African-American population combined with the likelihood of electoral reprisals for capitulation predicts for resistance.[81] Elite divisions introduced uncertainty regarding the precise manner of white response: the soft suppression witnessed in Albany, Georgia, or the dramatic clashes of Birmingham. Either way, without federal assistance to transform the cost calculations of local officeholders, the movement's prospects for obtaining substantive concessions were dismal. King and his lieutenants no doubt anticipated this outcome. Thus, although the goal of voter registration meant that the county courthouse registrar was nominally the movement's target, they made clear that their principal target was actually the federal government and that their larger goal was the enactment of voting rights legislation. In contrast to previous struggles, then, in which activists concentrated on achieving local victories, it is more accurate to regard the Selma campaign, as the mayor himself indicated, as a set upon which a morality play was to be staged. In the place of Birmingham's Bull Connor, it was hoped that Dallas County Sheriff Jim Clark might provide the national media with the violent incidents necessary to rivet national attention to the problem of black disenfranchisement.

For a time, Clark resisted the impulse to respond with violence; yet the Selma campaign will always be remembered for "Bloody Sunday." On March 7, 1965, as over five hundred civil rights marchers departed the city across the Edmund Pettus Bridge toward the state capital to demonstrate for voting rights, state troopers and Clark's volunteer posse set upon them using teargas and wielding batons. At the end of the melee, dozens were injured and the nation had once again witnessed the raw brutality of Jim Crow. This event, more than any other, pushed forward the Voting Rights Act of 1965.[82] Only eight days later, in a joint session of Congress, President Johnson condemned the violence in Selma and declared his resolute support for voting rights legislation. Yet, since the city government had shifted toward a more accommodating posture, the ferocity of this anti-rights violence is perhaps puzzling.

---

[81] According to his obituary in the *New York Times* (September 13, 2005), Smitherman declared in retrospect that "political imperatives forced him to hide what he said had always been tolerant racial feelings." This assertion, however questionable, is consistent with the argument presented here that political incentives, particularly segregationist political mobilization, compelled officials to pursue policies with which they themselves disagreed.

[82] For the detailed argument for this case, see Garrow (1978).

Several factors explain the severity of Bloody Sunday. First, as suggested above, economic elites were divided. The Dallas County Chamber of Commerce was uncommitted to attracting outside investment, and other economic interests in favor of growth and moderation had not yet gained a sufficient measure of political control to keep Clark in check. At the state level, business organizations were just beginning to argue against anti-rights violence, and only belatedly, after numerous disruptions had already taken place and the escalation of federal involvement was imminent. Thus, few political gains went to those speaking on behalf of greater moderation.

Second, organized segregationists provided political rewards to those who resisted the civil rights movement with greater fervor, and Sheriff Clark depended on these rewards. A central aspect in the analysis of Selma, then, is the distinction between the relatively moderate city police under Baker and the county authorities under Clark. Whereas Smitherman appointed Baker, Clark relied heavily upon the political support of the rural hinterlands. In the 1958 primary election for sheriff, "The balloting revealed a deep distrust between county and city residents; Clark carried fourteen of the sixteen rural boxes while eight of the ten boxes carried by Baker were in the city."[83] Although Clark eventually won a majority in the city, the lopsided two-to-one majority for Clark in the county suggests that business moderates were politically irrelevant beyond the city limits. In addition, organized segregationists in the rural hinterlands furnished Clark with strong incentives for persistent intransigence. With the business community divided, extremist opposition to moderation "provided a potent counterweight to the demands of the blacks."[84]

Third, whereas state authorities in other states checked the excessive violence of local police, Wallace and his Alabama state troopers supported and participated in the brutal suppression of civil rights marchers. In statewide politics, segregationist organizations wielded sufficient political clout to affect electoral outcomes, and business interests had not organized to urge Wallace to adopt a less aggressive stance toward the civil rights movement. Only after the horrific violence at the Edmund Pettus Bridge did the Alabama State Chamber of Commerce and local Chambers advocate compliance with the Civil Rights Act and support

[83] Thornton (1991, 56).
[84] Garrow (1978, 122).

for voting rights.[85] Despite sporadic general statements against violence, reticent economic actors offered Wallace no encouragement to retreat from his posture of defiance. Although Wallace resented the negative attention following the assault upon the marchers, he did not discipline or dismiss those responsible, as this might have been seen as an acknowledgement of a mistake, "nor would he have wanted to rupture his ties with constituents who viewed the attack on the marchers as appropriate."[86] After federal intervention compelled Wallace to accept the inevitability of the Selma to Montgomery march, he urged Alabama citizens to eschew violence even as he refused to provide the marchers with protection.

Because Clark has attracted most of the historical attention, some important distinctions are seldom made. In many ways, Baker behaved like Pritchett in that he followed procedures to arrest civil rights demonstrators in a nonviolent manner. Typically overlooked is Baker's connection to urban business interests and Clark's electoral reliance on rural black belt whites who were organized and committed to the preservation of white dominance. Despite Smitherman's victory, ardent segregationists continued to have electoral leverage at the county level and the Dallas County sheriff therefore had no intention of making concessions. Thus, the convergence of insufficient capacity of local business interests to contain violent whites and the strength of organized segregationists – against a backdrop of statewide support for intransigence – produced the political conditions that made possible the shocking events on Bloody Sunday. Against targets insulated from disruption and poised to suffer severe concession costs, fierce opposition was all but inevitable. Indeed, in the case of Selma, movement strategists sought not a local triumph but instead to produce an evocative tableau of racial injustice.[87] In this, despite the local defeat, they won a striking victory.

Summary

Clearly, costs motivated targets to respond. References to cost considerations abound across the various case studies as targets routinely contemplated the degree to which activities of social movements, their allies, and opponents threatened their interests. Downtown merchants, for instance, smarted under economic boycotts while they fretted over

[85] Ibid.
[86] Permaloff and Grafton (1995, 214).
[87] Garrow (1978, 267).

the prospective loss of white customers. The combination of high disruption and relatively low costs for capitulation enabled the movement to extract concessions from their targets, as was often the case with vulnerable economic actors. Conversely, except in the unusual cases in which African-Americans amounted to more than a negligible share of the target's electoral coalition, elected officials often lacked an interest in negotiation. The behavior of third parties affected target perceptions regarding the magnitude of both costs. Each of the cases surveyed above confirms aspects of the principal theoretical propositions of this analysis. For instance, favorable federal intervention on behalf of public school desegregation bolstered the disruption costs for targeted political actors as the unruliness of movement antagonists hurt local commerce. On the other side, targets weigh the magnitude of concession costs based on the specific movement demand as well as the behavior of third parties. Lunch-counter operators lacked an intrinsic economic interest in segregation but feared third party reprisals and the loss of white customers.

The success against downtown merchants in Greensboro may be regarded as a case in which movement activists hit vulnerable interests with severe disruption costs and third parties offered minimal organized countermobilization to resist change. However, even without effective countermobilization, success depended upon putting the vulnerable targets nearly out of business. This highlights the effectiveness of sit-ins and boycotts as movement tactics as well as the high threshold necessary for these economic targets to be induced to concede.

By contrast, the initial sit-in movement against local merchants in New Orleans faltered because of the movement's inability to impose potent disruption costs, extensive third party mobilization against capitulation, and the insulation of dominant elites from disruption. A second agitation phase to integrate downtown facilities benefited from movement litigation to compel public-school desegregation, which generated massive tumult, negative publicity, and a more severe local economic disruption. This combination of heightened civil rights protests and disorders stemming from school desegregation placed not only merchants but also many other vulnerable interests in tourism, real estate, services, development, and banking in the position of reluctant accommodators. In this case, federal coercion and economic destabilization impelled local elites to offer concessions over the strenuous objections of organized opponents as well as those working-class whites from the impacted schools. To keep concession costs low, downtown merchants gave ground slowly and, with the collusion of the local media, sought to reduce white attentiveness to the changes taking place.

The indifference of key business interests in New Orleans that allowed for the drift toward extremism contrasts sharply with the case of Atlanta, where powerful economic actors were matched against weak segregationist organizations. Unlike the New Orleans elite, which displayed a marked disinterest in the attraction of external investment, vulnerable pro-growth interests dominated Atlanta's business leadership. With African-American voters incorporated into the dominant political coalition and an economic commitment to be regarded as a "city too busy to hate," the movement found the political targets and third parties more amenable to change than was the case in most Deep South cities. Unlike those cities that obstructed black voter registration, Atlanta officials permitted significant gains, as the concession costs were low.[88] Also, despite considerable delay, token school desegregation proceeded in an orderly fashion. Yet, in the domain of public accommodations, movement strategists struggled to impose punishing disruption costs on their economic targets. Irrespective of the city's reputation for racial moderation, the movement won an agreement to integrate certain downtown facilities only after the escalation of downtown protests and, even then, the process was postponed until the public schools had been desegregated.

The stunning civil rights defeat in Albany demonstrates the simple point that strategic decisions matter. Serious tactical mistakes, in particular, concentrating on public officials insulated from movement disruption costs, encouraged economic interests to conform to local customs during months of protest. Whereas the economic stress associated with interactions between movement and countermovement brought victory in New Orleans, the movement's sporadic and diffuse protests against downtown businesses in Albany were insufficient to produce serious economic strain and ultimately led to defeat. Also striking, the weakness of organized political demands for fierce repression provided local officials with the tactical maneuverability to devise an effective response to neutralize civil rights disturbances. Contrary to prior accounts, which concentrate almost entirely on Pritchett's disposition and tactical cleverness, I suggest that it

---

[88] In this case, movement targets acceded less due to costs than prospective political benefits. The account presented here does not preclude this possibility, though it is assumed to be uncommon and that essentially consensual movement goals are less likely to generate collective action for the purpose of extracting concessions in the first place.

was the peculiar absence of local segregationist and business mobilization that gave him the strategic flexibility to maintain segregation. While Pritchett's response was not an automatic outcome of this situation, his use of nonviolent legal repression depended upon the feebleness of state and local segregationist organizations. Specifically, local law enforcement met protests with soft legal repression in the form of nonviolent mass arrests. Coupled with ineffectual tactics, the lack of spectacular clashes between civil rights supporters and their antagonists deprived local agitators of media attention and broader external support.

Taking stock of the setback in Albany, movement activists tried something different in Birmingham. Instead of focusing on public officials, the movement targeted specific downtown businesses and deliberately enlisted the unwitting assistance of the intemperate chief of local law enforcement to produce massive disorders and correspondingly severe disruption costs. Although segregationist countermobilization and the unwillingness of industrial interests to support a compromise caused the targets to vacillate, the rapid escalation of disruption costs compelled a coalition of vulnerable businesses in consumption, services, banking, and real estate to successfully challenge steel interests and make possible a shift toward accommodation. As is well known, the visible segregationist violence unleashed on nonviolent demonstrators propelled forward the movement's national legislative agenda, a point explored in greater detail in subsequent chapters.

The struggle in Greenwood for enfranchisement produced patterns resembling those seen in Albany and Birmingham, respectively. As in Albany, civil rights organizers largely neglected downtown businesses, while organized opposition made certain that the movement won no substantive gains. Although the enactment of federal civil rights legislation allowed maverick activists to integrate the local movie theater, segregationist countermobilization eventually forced the venue to close. Tactics shifted in the latter 1960s with the implementation of an effective boycott against downtown businesses. This time, rising economic distress compelled merchants and other interests concerned about economic development to make concessions.

Even in this Deep South community, the responses of various interests in Selma confirm the predicted sectoral variation among economic interests. Vulnerable interests, as in New Orleans, came to appreciate the dire economic implications of racial turmoil and sought to reform local practices enough to forestall the eruption of violence. Nevertheless, their incomplete control of local affairs allowed intransigent elements to shape the responses of law enforcement to civil rights protests – a weakness that the civil rights movement deftly exploited. Savvy to the benefits of attracting broader national attention, the movement in Selma, Alabama, concentrated upon the daunting task of voter registration. Although the registration campaign largely failed, it succeeded brilliantly at eliciting brutal repression from the reactionary elements of local and state police. Here, the strategic choices of movement activists evinced an appreciation for the two-level game of the struggle such that a highly visible defeat at the local level contributed to gains for the movement's national legislative agenda. Put another way, only nominally were local officials the targets in Selma; instead, they were props in a performance for a national audience meant to augment the salience of voting rights violations, thereby imposing high disruption costs upon national politicians.

Finally, this analysis hints at a political explanation to resolve to a historical puzzle. Although violent outbursts against the movement have often been identified as the fundamental impetus behind the enactment of civil and voting rights legislation, most accounts do not explain them. These violent eruptions are either assumed to be ubiquitous across the South or treated as due to the temperament of specific personalities, such as the hotheaded "Bull" Connor. Even though a personalistic explanation has some merit, it elides the question of why voters select such individuals for public office. Further, southern officials generally understood that violent repression was damaging to the segregationist cause and, in any case, such visible clashes between demonstrators and authorities were uncommon. By contrast, this analysis suggests that these incidents stemmed from a distinctly political convergence in which organized segregationists possessed significant political sway in local contests, often incorporated into prevailing coalitions, and moderate business elements were unwilling or unable to operate as a counterbalance. These conditions encouraged the selection of a harsh brand of segregationist for office, and provided political rewards for officials to respond severely to movement challenges. From this perspective, public officials responded less to the general interest in defending Jim Crow against federal incursion and more to their specific local political incentives.[89]

In brief, these cases are rich in insight and empirical confirmation of the principal theoretical propositions of this analysis. They depict how target selection and vulnerabilities, movement tactics, and the mobilization of third parties defined the disruption and concession costs that

---

[89] See Luders (2005) for a more detailed version of this argument.

shaped the responses of diverse economic and political interests. The cases indicate that the sustained movement agitation to desegregate public accommodations often met with success, but voter registration drives in hostile Deep South settings had a negligible impact. Outcomes for public school desegregation fell somewhere in between with success severely circumscribed within the confines of tokenism. While the posture of local economic interests and the vigor of countermobilization appears to have affected the turbulence of the school desegregation process, the outcomes (before elevated federal intervention in the latter 1960s) were limited by the willingness of officials to countenance only the most minimal change. The configuration of local politics, too, affected the likelihood of violent repression by authorities. Suggestive as the patterns in these case studies may be, for this analysis to be persuasive, they must be supplemented with further investigation of the pattern of movement outcomes across the broader region.

5

Patterns of Regional Change

Civil rights agitation produced diverse outcomes across southern localities and against different targets. Sit-in protests in Greensboro ended segregated seating at the downtown lunch counters after several months of struggle. Activists won public school desegregation in Atlanta with relative ease compared to the protracted struggle in New Orleans against significant white countermobilization, although in both localities, despite the different paths taken, only token changes in the public schools were achieved. Voter registration drives in Atlanta successfully expanded black voter registration, whereas similar activities in Greenwood met with stunning defeat. In sum, the case studies in the preceding chapter elucidate how the exposure of targets to specific combinations of disruption and concession costs shaped their responses to movement mobilization. They document the pattern of sectoral variation in the exposure of economic actors to movement disruption costs and explicate the constellations of third parties that intervened to shape movement-target interactions.

While case studies depict specific targets weighing their cost exposure and responding accordingly, they are less useful for assessing the robustness of this relationship. Further, although social movements are often discussed as if they were unitary entities, they encompass disparate bundles of demands and tactics.[1] I suggest that each bundle necessarily imposes distinctive *combinations* of disruption and concession costs on targets and third parties that, in turn, shape their behavior. In the case of civil rights, the movement sought in particular to desegregate southern society and win political rights denied under Jim Crow. Although

[1] Banaszak (2006).

disparate movement demands might seem to be inextricably intermingled with a generalized challenge to Jim Crow, the interest in defending the discrete elements of white dominance differed. Certain demands involved costs that were larger, more visible, and immediate, and therefore more likely to attract the attention of targets and bystanders as well as provoke countermobilization. Likewise, different movement activities disrupted the interests of certain targets and bystanders and not others. The case studies offered evidence for the differing responses based upon targets' uneven cost exposure. In this chapter I evaluate the broader pattern of movement outcomes across the region through an investigation of three major domains of civil rights mobilization: public school integration, voter registration, and the desegregation of public accommodations. While each demand challenged Jim Crow, the exposure of targets and third parties varied across these three domains. This chapter thus assesses the strength of the causal relationships discussed in the previous chapter and further explores the variation in outcomes across these three movement demands.

I survey these differences both before and after the escalation of federal intervention in the 1960s. For each demand, the principal theoretical task is the delineation of the relevant costs, beginning with the specification of the main targets, their interests, movement tactics, and the likelihood and manner of third party intervention. A key distinction between school desegregation and voter registration, on the one hand, and the integration of public accommodations, on the other, is that the former involved extracting concessions from public officials while the latter mainly concerned economic actors. In previous chapters I deployed a sectoral analysis to explore the differences in relative cost exposure among economic actors, and the relative movement success in disrupting certain interests to elicit concessions. Except for the general point that targeted downtown consumption interests were particularly vulnerable to disruption and therefore often under enormous pressure to offer concessions, the sectoral argument will not be repeated here. Rather, this chapter investigates the general effectiveness of sit-ins, boycotts, and other disruptions targeted at economic actors to desegregate public accommodations. Next, I explicate the responses of elected officials to the civil rights mobilization to bring about public school desegregation and voter registration. To do this, I turn to studies that address the behavior of elected officials in response to benefit-seeking organizations. From the premise that political targets respond to electoral calculations, I explain the divergent responses of southern elected officials to civil rights demands. As shown below, in the domain of public school desegregation, the movement obtained token integration, accomplished with greater or lesser degrees of opposition. In contrast, voter registration drives achieved highly variable outcomes ranging from significant gains in African-American registration to negligible additions to the voting rolls, despite tenacious agitation. Divergence in outcomes, and the responses of political targets more generally, can be explained based on the convergence of public preferences, attentiveness, and the magnitude of countermobilization.

Interpreting Political Costs

While movement demands challenged Jim Crow in both public education and voting rights, the differences in outcome stem from variation in the exposure of the targets and third parties to the unique combinations of disruption and concession costs generated by each. This analysis relies on the conventional assumption that elected officials are concerned mainly about their reelection, and therefore they interpret costs based on their net electoral impact.[2] Accordingly, as political targets tabulate disruption costs, social movements and other organized interests matter to them insofar as they control votes, campaign contributions, volunteers, or other electorally useful resources.[3] The greater the share of votes or other valuable resources controlled by the movement, which they can withhold or shift to an opponent, the more capable the movement will be of threatening targets with significant disruption costs. Too, public opinion and attentiveness shape these cost perceptions.

Along with these disruption cost calculations, elected officials estimate the damage of acceding to movement demands. Specifically, politicians must assess the likelihood that there will be an electoral reprisal for granting concessions. The electoral ramifications of allocating new benefits to social movements or any other organized interest depend upon three key factors: mass voter preferences, their attentiveness, and the extent of organized opposition. If the majority supports a movement's demands, the main task for movement activists is attracting mass attention to boost the salience of the issue and thereby encourage elected officials to respond to majoritarian preferences. If the public is opposed to benefit-seekers' demands and attentive, then organized interests are unlikely to

---

[2] Kingdon (1973) [1989]; Mayhew (1974).
[3] Harvey (1998).

be successful as elected officials conform to majoritarian preferences.[4] However, if these publics are inattentive, indifferent, and likely to remain so, legislators are likely to weigh the relative electoral leverage of competing benefit-seekers to their reelection coalition.[5] For elected officials, then, it is useful to know what their constituents want, which issues are likely to become salient, and the extent of countermobilization.

Prior research suggests that salience of an issue in the public's awareness and organized opposition may depend upon certain attributes of a public policy.[6] Specifically, mass publics are prone to overlook costs that are small, abstract, or felt only well after the policy has been enacted and, conversely, are likely to perceive and respond negatively to the imposition of costs that are large, visible, and immediate. Countermobilization is more likely to ensue in response to the threatened imposition of the latter. Elected officials, aware of these sensibilities, may embrace the former for electoral advantage but shun the latter for precisely the same reason. In other words, an explanation of the response of an elected official to movement demands may depend upon characteristics inherent in the public policy under consideration. The activities of organized opponents or extensive media coverage may draw attention to certain issues as well. In sum, elected officials consider the electoral threats associated with movement mobilization against the prospect of electoral reprisals for conceding from attentive constituents or opposition interests.

This brief overview suggests that differing cost calculations determined the divergent target responses in the domains of voter registration and school desegregation. Targeted officials considered the impact of mobilization on their own reelection prospects, including the cost of protracted civil rights agitation and litigation. The same officials weighed the electoral implications associated with the likely responses of white voters for capitulating. This calculation necessarily entailed an assessment of mass preferences, and those of attentive citizens in particular. In historical studies of southern racial politics, the conventional assumption is that mass preferences correspond to the relative size of the local African-American population with white opposition to racial equality rising as the black population share increases.[7] Yet, insofar as civil rights proponents achieved greater success on voter registration than school

---

[4] Burstein (1999); Downs (1957).
[5] Hansen (1991).
[6] Arnold (1990).
[7] Key (1949); Matthews and Prothro (1966).

desegregation prior to the period of heightened federal support, this conventional approach is not wholly satisfactory. The divergence suggests that the concession costs for public officials were greater for school desegregation than for voter registration. Although civil rights mobilization threatened southern racial institutions, I argue that whites distinguished among these challenges and that some prospective changes were regarded as more costly, visible, and immediate than others. I speculate that, except in those localities in which African-Americans would gain a decisive electoral advantage, the costs of voter registration for white publics were generally small, abstract, and delayed. By contrast, white publics are assumed to regard the enrollment of African-American children in all-white schools as costly, clear, and immediate. In both cases, certain attributes of movement demands made them more or less perceptible as costly. Below, I flesh out this reasoning to argue that the differences in movement outcomes in these two domains can be traced back to the convergence of constituent preferences (public opinion), attentiveness, and the scope of organized countermobilization relative to movement disruptions.

Following a similar logic, elected officials had few incentives to intercede unbidden into local conflicts over public accommodations. As bystanders, they were less exposed to prospective electoral punishment if desegregation ensued, and instead often had a political interest in deferring to the preferences of local business. If targeted firms called upon public authorities to clamp down on protests, they willingly obliged. Conversely, in the absence of white countermobilization, officials lacked a political imperative to thwart an integration agreement. Should accommodations be desegregated, local economic interests absorbed the blame for the change and could be counted upon to provide political cover as needed to officials who lent their tacit support. However, as described in Chapter 4, a combination of active segregationist mobilization and weak or absent business mobilization for compromise encouraged officials to move against specific economic actors who buckled under economic distress. Generally speaking, then, public officials provided local businesses with wide latitude in responding to civil rights demonstrations.

Movement Outcomes in Public School Desegregation

An inspection of the constellation of costs associated with school desegregation suggests that only limited steps might be achieved in the absence of committed federal intervention. The movement's capabilities to impose large disruption costs upon southern officials were profoundly limited. In those localities in which African-Americans comprised a small percentage of the population, their weak electoral clout meant that their interests could be discounted in favor of white majority preferences. Conversely, it was precisely in those localities in which African-Americans were heavily concentrated that local officials most assiduously kept them off the voting rolls. Lacking the franchise, local blacks were unable to deliver electoral reprisals against those officeholders blocking integration. In addition, civil rights organizations seldom resorted to direct-action tactics to compel public school desegregation. Rather, most efforts involved NAACP lawsuits in federal courts to produce court orders to be implemented by a reluctant executive branch. As I argue elsewhere at greater length, the electoral logic in national politics was structured against bold action to compel southern whites to accept integrated schools.[8] Under these circumstances, the movement's ability to obtain favorable federal court rulings was the principal device for imposing disruption costs on unreceptive local authorities.

White constituent preferences, particularly those of attentive voters, defined the concession costs for local elected officials. Overall, white southerners overwhelmingly opposed federal compulsion to desegregate the schools. A 1964 survey found that almost three-quarters of southern whites were in opposition to federal action to compel integration.[9] White preferences and attentiveness to public school integration roughly corresponded to the relative size of the local African-American population.[10] Likewise, organized countermobilization was greater in localities with larger African-American populations. Where the black population was minuscule, whites were less concerned about desegregation; therefore, the political costs for integration were negligible. In those places, the threat of litigation or a federal court order to integrate might impose sufficient disruption costs upon targeted authorities to produce token desegregation under the guise of pupil-placement or "freedom of choice" plans. These arrangements, in nominal compliance with the 1954 *Brown v. Board of Education* ruling, served to preempt costly litigation. By contrast, in those places in which African-Americans made up a large proportion of the population, and where they lacked political leverage, white opposition and attentiveness gave elected officials strong political reasons

[8] Luders (2000).
[9] Black and Black (1987, 158).
[10] Giles (1975); Harris (1968); Pettigrew (1957); Vanfossen (1968).

to resist public school desegregation. For whites in such localities, the imposition of what most regarded as substantial, visible, and immediate costs might incite them to punish those officials appearing to countenance desegregation. In the Deep South or in communities in which African-Americans were basically disenfranchised, the advance of public school desegregation could therefore be expected to be glacial.

Under these circumstances, only the intervention of third parties could provide the necessary political rewards or reduce the political costs for movement gains to be made. The federal government possessed the authority to overcome local opposition. If federal coercion were used to compel compliance with civil or voting rights, then the disruption costs for local opponents would be insurmountable; at the same time, the political costs of racial change to accept integration would be diminished as blame fell upon federal authorities. Also, state and local business leaders might provide overt support for token integration to avert costly public disorder or a general closure of the public schools. For example, after witnessing the deleterious economic impact of racial strife in Little Rock in 1957, such business elites in Atlanta threw their support behind peaceful token integration. Similarly, in Norfolk, Virginia, the spectacle of public school closures and growing awareness about the catastrophic economic implications of this course inspired business elites to mobilize.[11] It is predicted then that the integration of the public schools would take place only in those places in which there were minimal political risks for implementing the *Brown* decision and that, in those places in which the political costs of implementation were high, only token gains would be achieved, and this due to federal coercion or business mobilization.

In describing the process of public school desegregation from 1954 into the 1970s, Black and Black (1987) identify three phases that delineate the shifting responses of southern officials over time. In the first phase, during the ten years after the *Brown* decision (1954–1965), hostile southern white opinion and countermobilization exposed public officials who dared to comply with the ruling to steep concession costs. Indeed, office-seekers might have benefited from offering the most outspoken defense of segregated schools. Perhaps unsurprisingly, most southern governors and legislators obligingly responded with "massive resistance" in the form of hundreds of new laws to block or delay all efforts to integrate the public schools as well as measures to harass civil rights organizations, particularly the NAACP. Without federal legislative support or executive

[11] Cramer (1963); Muse (1964).

leadership, the implementation of *Brown* fell to civil rights groups, as well as federal circuit and district court judges who generally disagreed with the ruling and lacked the capacity to enforce a broad mandate for change. Thus, despite relentless litigation and the heroic willingness of African-American children to risk intimidation and violence, barely over 2 percent were enrolled in integrated schools in 1965. "If integrationists achieved scattered symbolic victories in the first phase of desegregation, successful opposition was the characteristic southern response."[12]

During this phase, limited gains were made only in specific circumstances consistent with the pattern of disruption and concession costs. First, most of the integration that did occur happened in states and localities with negligible black populations, and in which concession costs for public officials were consequently low.[13] Second, token integration was achieved in cases in which organized segregationists were weak and business interests rallied behind *limited* desegregation to preserve public order and maintain a favorable business climate. For example, after word spread about the decline in new investment in Little Rock in 1957, vulnerable economic actors across the South were more eager to maintain public order and the image of amicable race relations. Likewise, as indicated above, after the public schools were closed to resist integration in Norfolk, Virginia, major economic interests rallied to the defense of public education.[14] This economic rationale facilitated the orderly integration of Clemson College in South Carolina. This pattern of support for open schools and limited integration from elements of the business community also appeared in such metropolitan centers as Atlanta, Dallas, and Tampa. Other business elites supported public schools and the maintenance of order only after severe disruptions caused significant economic harm, as witnessed in New Orleans.

Finally, in the absence of local political support for open schools and where there was extensive white opposition to desegregation, the political logic encouraged officials to offer the most intransigent opposition. Under these circumstances, the barest token desegregation depended upon decisive federal coercion to sweep aside this resistance. During the dramatic confrontations between federal and state authorities in Little Rock in 1957, the University of Mississippi (Ole Miss) in 1962, and the University of Alabama in 1963, Presidents Eisenhower and Kennedy were

[12] Black and Black (1987, 154).
[13] Vanfossen (1968).
[14] Abbott (1982); Muse (1964).

compelled to use federal troops in order to vindicate the supremacy of federal court orders. For their part, southern officials sometimes sought to choreograph their interactions with the federal government to be able to claim credit for defending segregation to the bitter end and shift the blame for integration fully to the federal government. For instance, in the case of the integration of Ole Miss in 1962, Governor Ross Barnett asked the Kennedy administration to stage a performance in which all of the arriving federal marshals would draw their guns to force the state authorities to step aside. Barnett pleaded over the phone with Attorney General Robert F. Kennedy: "We got a big crowd here and if one [marshal] pulls his gun and we all turn it would be very embarrassing . . . They must all draw their guns. Then they should point their guns at us and then we could step aside. This could be very embarrassing down here for us. It is necessary."[15] Beyond these extraordinary cases of federal compulsion, southern obstructionism persisted in the most resistant localities and, as important as these victories were, only the slightest desegregation was accomplished. Thus, despite a decade of litigation and the support of the federal judiciary, the high concession costs for public officials and the absence of significant disruption costs meant that the struggle to desegregate southern public schools had achieved virtually no local gains beyond tokenism.

The second phase began with the enactment of the Civil Rights Act of 1964 and the Primary and Secondary School Act of 1965, which placed the Department of Health, Education, and Welfare (HEW) in charge of federal enforcement efforts. This second phase, from 1965 to 1968, coincided with relatively rapid advances in desegregation far beyond what had been achieved in the preceding decade (see Figure 5.1). In just two years, from 1964 to 1966, the percentage of all southern black students in public schools with whites jumped from 2.3 in 1964 to 16.8. Unlike the period of judicial enforcement, the new legislation obliged HEW administrators to withhold federal school funding from noncompliant districts and gave the attorney general the authority to pursue desegregation suits on behalf of individuals. With the threat of far larger disruption costs to local districts than merely NAACP litigation, many began to desegregate. "In many communities in which rigid local leadership had said 'NEVER,' the pressure of Federal money had changed the slogan to a less certain 'maybe a little.'"[16] With federal coercion to

---

[15] Belknap (1991, 413).
[16] Orfield (1969, 113).

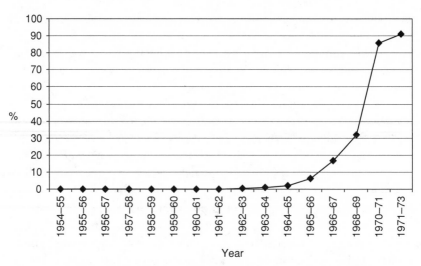

FIGURE 5.1. Percentage of black school children attending school with whites, 1954–72, selected years. *Source:* Rosenberg (1991, 51).

blame for the change, the political costs for local officials might be shifted as well. Until that time, even with the support of the federal courts, local struggles were incapable of bringing about substantive desegregation; rather, it was the movement's national legislative achievements that made possible substantive gains in desegregation in recalcitrant school districts.

The final phase, beginning in 1968–69 and extending to the present, involved judicial intervention to coerce compliance coupled with stepped-up administrative assertiveness. Federal acceptance of "freedom of choice" plans, which permitted white evasion of desegregation orders, initially hampered implementation in the most resistant localities. Then, in 1968, the Supreme Court decision *Green v. New Kent County, Virginia,* ruled that freedom of choice was impermissible unless substantial desegregation followed. The prior standard of "all deliberate speed" articulated in the Supreme Court's implementation decision (known as *Brown II*) gave way to demands for immediate desegregation from the courts and executive branch officials. Disruption costs were consequently augmented as well. In a 1969 case against 81 Georgia school districts and the Georgia Department of Education, the Justice Department argued successfully for withholding not only federal funds, but also state education funds from recalcitrant districts. This success emboldened the Justice Department to pursue similar lawsuits in other states. Again, desegregation surged. "By 1976–77, nearly four out of every five black students in the South were attending public schools in which whites constituted at least 10 percent – and usually a much higher proportion – of the student body."[17] Stepped-up enforcement, however, did not wholly eliminate school segregation in pockets of resistance in certain multiple school-district cities and in the rural black belt. Local administrators often pursued various subterfuges to maintain segregation within nominally integrated schools. Also, in the wake of the *Green* decision, whites-only private schools proliferated to maintain a largely segregated education system. Too, white flight diminished the movement's ostensible success. Regardless, in this domain, the changes in political costs for public officials shaped variation in movement outcomes over time.

In the third phase, in which the federal judiciary bolstered administrative action, these changes achieved another plateau in desegregation. At this point, the new advantages stemmed from a political logic of implementation based upon public support (including growing acceptance among whites) and the political leverage of civil rights organizations and their allies to urge federal officials to strictly enforce the law.

Movement Outcomes in Voter Registration

As with school desegregation, civil rights mobilization to obtain the franchise suffered critical weaknesses due to the insulation of local officials from disruption costs. Movement agitation concentrated upon a number of basic tactics: litigation, rallies, marches, sit-ins, pickets, boycotts, and voter mobilization. Except for electoral activities, none of these forms directly threatened a public official's reelection and, in those localities in which African-Americans had been excluded from any meaningful political participation, the effective imposition of disruption costs could be exceedingly difficult. Since local authorities in resistant localities permitted few African-Americans to register, the electoral threat associated with resistance to voter registration must be regarded as low. Nor did ostensible federal support prior to the mid-sixties appear to make a significant difference in these calculations. Despite the enactment of the Civil Rights Act of 1957, the Justice Department filed only a handful of cases of voter discrimination, and litigation of those cases might be protracted for years. Fear of federal compulsion therefore hardly mattered

---

[17] Black and Black (1987, 154–5). This figure is lower than the percentage depicted in Figure 5.1 because the threshold for considering a school integrated is higher, at 10 percent.

to southern officials in determining their response to voter registration efforts. The Civil Rights Act of 1960 likewise produced minimal results. By the close of 1962, only seventeen thousand blacks had been added to the registration rolls. So long as reelection constituencies supported ongoing opposition to the movement and federal authorities lacked additional weapons to make legalistic evasions and foot-dragging more costly, local officials could safely ignore marches and pickets to thwart voter registration drives. On the contrary, fierce resistance to the civil rights movement could be electorally advantageous. Furthermore, in rural counties in which African-Americans outnumbered whites, these prospective registrants were vulnerable to white economic reprisals for challenging Jim Crow.[18] Unable to impose disruption costs upon local registrars or other officials, movement activists had few prospects for compelling their targets to surrender benefits.

However, relative to the considerable resistance to public school desegregation, southern whites were less opposed to black enfranchisement. Amid the tumultuous Selma demonstrations, a 1965 Gallup poll found 49 percent of southern whites supported the enactment of a voting rights bill with only 37 percent opposed.[19] Clearly, the political costs of acquiescence were lower in localities in which white preferences evinced disinterest in the defense of black political exclusion. As with school desegregation, these preferences are often thought to vary according to the relative size of the local black population. Key (1949) and countless other analysts of southern politics have thoroughly documented the point that opposition to civil rights gains was greatest in states and localities with relatively large black populations, such as Alabama, Louisiana, and Mississippi.[20] In places in which blacks had no prospect of affecting local electoral outcomes, the diffuse and delayed costs for white constituents resulting from African-American voting likely discouraged opposition, attentiveness, and countermobilization. By contrast, concession costs rise as the relative size of the African-American population achieves political significance in localities with large black pluralities or majorities. (Some research [Matthews and Prothro 1963] suggests that 25 to 30 percent African-American is the critical threshold at which whites began to resist black voter registration.) The fear of "Negro domination" at the polls prompted whites in these localities to offer greater support for official

[18] Salamon and Van Evera (1973).
[19] Lawson (1991, 111).
[20] Black (1978); Matthews and Prothro (1963).

resistance to black enfranchisement and punish those who behaved otherwise. Claude Sitton of the *New York Times* reported that, for example, a registrar in Canton, Mississippi, who had permitted some 475 African-Americans to register to vote, was ousted in the next election. Elected officials thus clearly had their own self-interested motivations for defending the color line beyond the representation of white constituent preferences, as their own political fortunes depended upon exclusionary politics.

In general, then, public officials are therefore predicted to accept movement demands for black voter registration if the entrance of these voters is unlikely to either affect their reelection or damage the interests of organized supporters. Such indifferent targets were more concentrated in the Peripheral South and some Deep South cities. On the other side, in the rural black belt as well as in those Deep South cities with large black populations and active segregationist mobilization, fierce opposition can be anticipated from those officials whose political fortunes might be devastated if African-Americans were to vote. Under these daunting circumstances, local movement successes were unlikely. For substantive gains to be won against recalcitrant officials, the movement depended upon eliciting supportive federal intervention to augment the movement's disruption costs. Thus, greater registration gains are to be expected in those places in which the concession cost of black enfranchisement was low, with only negligible success in localities in which black voting represented a political threat.

In early 1962 only about 29 percent of African-Americans were registered across the South with considerable variation from state to state from a low of barely over 5 percent in Mississippi to a high of approximately 50 percent in Tennessee (see Figure 5.2, p. 130). Many civil rights activists believed that emancipation from oppression and the political self-assertion of southern blacks depended upon the vote. The exclusion of African-Americans from southern politics seemed to be responsible for political rhetoric based on crude racism and the willingness of local officials to deprive African-Americans of other basic citizenship rights. Open the ballot box to black votes, so the argument went, and a politics of racial discrimination would be swept away.

National political considerations supported African-American voter registration. Averse to offending the southern Democrats, the Kennedy administration sought to channel movement insurgency into conventional political activities, which was thought to get demonstrators off the streets and therefore be less likely to result in the sort of white supremacist violence that obliged federal intervention. Supporting indigenous political reform allowed the administration to appear to promote a civil rights agenda without getting drawn into dramatic clashes with authorities that might alienate southern white voters. Thus, in the aftermath of the violent attacks upon the Freedom Riders in 1961–62, the Kennedy administration sought funding from various philanthropic foundations for a coordinated voter registration drive involving the "big four" civil rights organizations – NAACP, Southern Christian Leadership Conference (SCLC), SNCC, and CORE as well as the Urban League. The voter registration drive, known as the Voter Education Project (VEP), had funding for two and a half years, from March 1962 into late 1964. To win the vote, civil rights organizations established VEP initiatives across the South from the metropolitan centers to the black belt hinterlands. There, they went door-to-door to canvass prospective registrants, asked local leaders to speak in favor of registration, conducted workshops on taking the registration examination, and at times marched to the courthouse to register.

To the challenge of the VEP, target responses differed. In the Peripheral South, where the African-American population was generally small, local officials permitted large numbers to register without throwing up extraordinary obstacles. The movement therefore achieved the greatest gains in registration in these localities. For instance, in Tennessee, the registration rate rose from 50 to 69.5 percent *before* the enactment of the 1965 Voting Right Act. In 1964, "majorities of blacks were registered in Tennessee, Florida, and Texas; and almost half of eligible blacks were registered in Arkansas; and around 45 percent were registered in North Carolina, Virginia, and Georgia."[21] Conversely, targets in the Deep South largely thwarted movement demands. The difficulties encountered in Canton, Mississippi, exemplified the pattern of official resistance. In a county in which African-Americans made up 72 percent of the population, only "121 Negroes, or 1.1 per cent of those in Madison County of voting age, were registered in 1962. By contrast, some 97 percent of whites were registered."[22] Here, instead of overt violence, registrars often used massive delays and legalistic evasion to deter registration. Long lines formed as applicants waited for hours to take an examination that included interpreting the finer legal points of the Mississippi state constitution. A reporter for the *New York Times* described the scene: "Only one Negro applicant at a time is permitted in the registrar's office. Of the more than 260 who waited outside Friday and the more than 50 there on Saturday,

---

[21] Black and Black (1987, 123).
[22] *New York Times*, March 2, 1964.

only seven finally got inside to take the test."[23] Inside, a White Citizens' Council sticker on the window of the registrar's office foreshadowed the futility of the exercise. Of the one thousand attempts to register, a VEP organizer observed, only thirty were added to the rolls. Similarly, local authorities pushed back against the registration drive in Dallas County, Alabama, where, after years of voter mobilization and legal action, fewer than four hundred local blacks were added to the rolls.[24]

Along with foot-dragging, political targets and other whites responded in some places with intimidation and violence against civil rights activists and supporters. As described in previous chapters, civil rights activists in hardcore areas risked beatings, bombings, sniper fire, arson, and outright murder. Although unaffiliated with the VEP, the 1964 Mississippi Summer Project – known in retrospect as "Freedom Summer" – concentrated on voter registration. This struggle provoked vicious reprisals. During that summer, activists and supporters suffered "1000 arrests, 35 shooting incidents, 30 buildings bombed, 35 churches burned, 80 people beaten, and at least six murdered."[25] In Greenwood, nearly two years of mobilization against fierce opposition added few new voters to the rolls despite hundreds of attempts. Regarding the fledgling VEP project in Mississippi in 1962, Robert Moses reported that "we are powerless to register people in significant numbers anywhere in the state and will remain so until the power of the Citizens Councils over state politics is broken, the Department of Justice secures for Negroes across the board the right to register, or Negroes rise up en masse with an unsophisticated blatant demand for immediate registration to vote. Very likely all three will be necessary before a breakthrough can be obtained."[26]

At the conclusion of the VEP in the fall of 1964, black voter registration across the South had risen by 668,000 from 29.4 to 43.1 percent.[27] Of this increase, Lawson estimates that a sizable 43 percent of the change stemmed from VEP activities. Yet, most striking were the differences in white responses to movement demands and the geographic pattern of movement gains (see Figure 5.2). Although the bulk of VEP expenditures went to the more resistant counties of the Deep South, the greatest gains from 1962 to 1964 were achieved in Florida, where registration rates went up from 27 to 50.2 percent, and in Tennessee, where black

[23] Ibid.
[24] Lawson (1991, 105).
[25] Woodward (1955 [1979], 186).
[26] Quoted in Watters and Cleghorn (1967, 65).
[27] Lawson (1991, 80).

voter registration surged from about 50 percent to nearly 70 percent. At the same time, black voter registration in Alabama went from around 13 percent to only 23 percent and registration rates in Mississippi barely budged – rising from 5.3 percent to 6.7 percent. On closer inspection, the movement met the strongest opposition and made the fewest gains against targets exposed to high concession costs. Registration gains were concentrated in the urban centers of the Peripheral South, "where extensive black mobilization could not conceivably result in black control of the primary decisionmaking institutions."[28] In addition to their own political calculus, the demands of white supremacist organizations and economic elites tied to plantation agriculture provided further political incentives to elected officials to take an intransigent position. Accordingly, James, in summing up his political economic analysis of the differences between black and white voter registration rates based on county-level data, writes:

When the racial state was under massive attack by the civil rights movement of the 1960s, it remained strongest in those areas where white farm owners and planters dominated local class structures. No other variables were as strongly or consistently related to the differences between black and white voter registration rates as were the combined effects of the concentration of white farm owners and the black farmer tenants and laborers who typically worked for white farm owners.[29]

In Mississippi, a hotbed of opposition to African-American enfranchisement, the VEP director suspended funding in early 1964 because the situation was deemed hopeless.[30] Thus, despite extensive mobilization and the willingness of many to take great risks, few tangible gains in registration were won.

The outcome of the movement for voter registration prior to expansive federal legislation was a significant enlargement in prospective African-American voters in some places, but far less in hostile communities. As Watters and Cleghorn (1967, 50) observe:

A most important research finding was its demonstration, day by day for two and a half years, of the need for federal legislation if Negro enfranchisement were ever to be fully achieved for the present generations in the South. For there was rarely success, no Negro registration to amount to anything in any place where whites seriously resisted it.

The lack of credible electoral threat, general federal unwillingness to augment the movement's leverage, and organized opposition from the

---

[28] Black and Black (1987, 122).
[29] 1988, 205.
[30] Watters and Cleghorn (1967, 48).

Citizens' Councils combined to block movement gains. The perspective here suggests that local movement successes might be won indirectly by enlisting the unwilling support from vulnerable economic interests in dealing with city hall. Otherwise, under these unfavorable circumstances, federal coercion would be critical to overcome the obstructionism of local registrars.

With heightened national attention in the aftermath of the brutal assault upon civil rights marchers in Selma, Alabama, in 1965, Congress finally passed comprehensive voting rights legislation. The Voting Rights Act (VRA) of 1965 contained several provisions that made continued discrimination more costly for local officials, in particular the displacement of local registrars by federal examiners. The law forbade the use of tests for literacy, educational attainment, or good character, as well as other devices that had been used to thwart black registration. The enactment of the VRA marked the beginning of a tectonic shift in African-American voter registration in resistant communities. In eight months, some three hundred thousand new black voters were added to the rolls.

Three of the Deep South cities with the worst reputations for equitable treatment of potential black voters – Birmingham, Jackson, and Montgomery – received federal registrars, and the most spectacular improvements occurred in Jackson, where the proportion of registered black voters jumped from 16 percent in 1964 to 67 percent three years later.[31]

The displacement of local registrars was particularly effective across the diehard states of Alabama, Louisiana, and Mississippi.

The office in Demopolis, Alabama, Marengo County, had opened in the morning of August 10. When the four Civil Service Commission employees serving as the examiners had arrived at seven-thirty, at least 150 Negroes were already there waiting for them at the post office headquarters. When the doors opened an hour later, there were 250; by 10:00 A.M., 300; and when the doors closed at 4:30 P.M., there were at least 150 who had to be told to come back the next morning. The scene repeated itself day by day there for at least a month, and in most of the other examiner offices.[32]

Shortly after the new law went into effect, black voter registration surged from one thousand to eighty-five hundred in Dallas County, the site of the brutal assault upon civil rights marchers as they left from Selma, Alabama, heading to Montgomery.[33] Although federal examiners were sent to around 60 of the 533 counties covered under the Act, some have

---

[31] Ibid., 138.
[32] Watters and Cleghorn (1967, 244–5).
[33] Lawson (1991, 112).

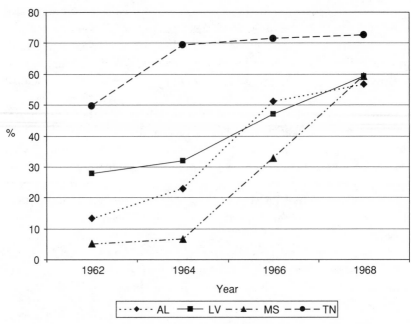

FIGURE 5.2. Black voter registration in Alabama, Louisiana, Mississippi, and Tennessee, 1962–68. *Sources:* Watters and Cleghorn (1967, App. II); Garrow (1978, 189).

suggested that just the fear of federal displacement prompted many to adopt standards consistent with the provisions of the Act. In the four years after the Voting Rights Act, southern black voter registration rates went from 43 to 65 percent.[34]

Although there appears to be a steady secular increase in black voter registration from 1962 to 1970, actually two distinct surges can be discerned. In the period before the VRA from 1962 to 1964, the Voter Education Project accomplished a significant increase in black registration in the least resistant localities without achieving change in more truculent states and localities. Following the passage of the VRA, a stunning boost in black voter registration was witnessed in the die-hard states of Alabama, Louisiana, and Mississippi, with only modest changes in the more tolerant states. Figure 5.2 depicts the spike in new registration in Tennessee pre-VRA followed by a stable plateau in the period after 1965, as well as the minimal gains in enrollment in resistant states during the

[34] Rodgers and Bullock (1972, 30).

TABLE 5.1. *Percentage of Blacks Registered to Vote in Select Southern Counties, 1968*

	Registration (% of voting age blacks)		
	Alabama	Mississippi	South Carolina
Federal Examiners and Voter Education Project	69.5	51.7	67.0
Federal Examiners only	63.7	41.2	71.4
Voter Education Project only	57.6	34.9	51.6
Neither agency	45.4	24.2	48.8

Source: Rodgers and Bullock (1972, 34).

heyday of the VEP mobilization and then the upsurge in these same states after 1965.

After enactment, the Southern Regional Council launched a second Voter Education Project to conduct over two hundred registration drives across the South from 1966 to 1968. Other civil rights organizations initiated many similar drives as well. Again, the pattern of advances in voter registration is suggestive. While the displacement of local registrars coincided with significant registration gains, the combination of federal examiners and VEP mobilization produced even larger increases.[35] Voter registration drives without federal registrars were somewhat less effective and the gains were lowest in the absence of both external examiners and registration drives (see Table 5.1).

In other words, with the formal obstacles to voter registration largely eliminated, the main challenge in the pursuit of black political participation was effective mobilization to overcome apathy and fear of white reprisals. Salamon and Van Evera (1973, 1301) declare: "Not the intensity of local white hostility, but the strength of the local black community is thus the key to dissipating fear and hence encouraging participation." In Mississippi, Andrews (2004) likewise found that the combination of federal displacement of local officials and prior movement mobilization fostered more political participation than a visit from federal registrars alone. This suggests that federal activities augmented the disruption costs to compel compliance, but that the achievement of movement goals is hardly automatic and necessarily depends upon robust mobilization to deliver African-Americans to the courthouse to register.

[35] Lawson (1991, 112); also Timpone (1995).

Movement Outcomes in Public Accommodations

Although there had been previous scattered skirmishes, the direct-action assault upon Jim Crow in public accommodations escalated sharply with the wave of sit-in protests that began in February 1960 in Greensboro, North Carolina. Eventually coalescing into the Student Nonviolent Coordinating Committee (SNCC), students from black colleges formed the nucleus of the protest movement, though they often benefited from assistance from other organizations. Activists sometimes combined sit-in protests with boycotts of downtown merchants to further augment the economic impact of recalcitrance. With the start of the Greensboro sit-ins, the student movement and the tactic diffused rapidly. In less than three months, every southern state and more than one hundred cities had been targeted for sit-ins. After a single year, some seventy thousand blacks and whites actively participated, and after two years, the figure climbed to an estimated 100,000 to 125,000.[36] These protests targeted public accommodations mainly in the larger cities of the Peripheral South, primarily segregated lunch counters.[37] With the movement challenging segregated public accommodations, public officials were largely insulated from electoral reprisals, providing them with few incentives to take the initiative in advocating or blocking local changes. In some cases, segregationist mobilization pressured public officials to pass local ordinances or state laws to strengthen the punishments for parading without a permit, refusing to leave an establishment upon request, picketing, promoting a boycott, and other such devices meant to weaken movement operations. Despite such measures, movement activities nonetheless threatened to disrupt the routine economic transactions of vulnerable downtown merchants, as detailed in Chapter 3. Commenting on the relative efficacy of the sit-in tactics, Rodgers and Bullock (1972, 60) suggest that whereas "marches had at most caused whites only the temporary inconvenience of traffic congestion, sit-ins touched the business community in its most vulnerable spot, the pocket book." If capable of mounting persistent sit-ins, pickets, and boycotts, local African-Americans possessed the means to interfere with local commerce and thereby impose severe disruption costs on targets in consumer markets. Further, civil rights contention threatened the interests of pro-growth third parties eager to attract new investment and

---

[36] Laue (1965 [1989], 8); Southern Regional Council (1961, 3).

[37] Oppenheimer (1963 [1989], 94) reports that demonstrations occurred in 69 localities, a majority (36) in cities with populations over 100,000.

fearful that racial disturbances would undermine their promotional activities. Mounting disruption costs often impelled these vulnerable interests to respond to movement demands directly or push others to do so.

As there were no intrinsic economic benefits derived from the color line in the provision of public accommodations, the magnitude of concession costs for these economic targets depended upon general public preferences, attentiveness, and organized segregationist opposition. The immediacy and visibility of the integration of public places presented targets with a significant challenge as these characteristics are associated with greater attentiveness. In cases in which whites were strongly opposed, more attentiveness threatened higher concession costs as whites might refuse to patronize integrated facilities. Following the conventional understanding for other aspects of the color line, white preferences for segregation are assumed to correspond roughly to the proportion of the population that is African-American. Thus, opposition and attentiveness should be lower in communities in which whites amounted to overwhelming majorities.[38] Conversely, as the proportion of African-Americans rises, so too should white preferences for "strict segregation," as well as the magnitude of organized opposition from third parties. In these localities, which were concentrated in the black belt of the Deep South, the prospect of integration would be associated with higher concession costs for targets.[39] With the convergence of both high disruption and concession costs, targets may be expected to vacillate. These vacillators have but four options: exit by moving away if possible, hunker down in the hope that the movement will dwindle before they are put out of business, ally with the resisters to crush the movement, or push for integration despite white opposition.[40] This last approach might involve pursuing strategies meant to reduce white attentiveness to the change, including the quiet desegregation of facilities while protesting college students are away during the summer, or limiting media coverage. Overall then, the movement's prospects for obtaining new benefits in the realm of public accommodations prior to the enactment of federal legislation

---

[38] With the threatened integration of downtown amenities, the cost of defending segregation fell to individual whites. They could abandon their patronage of these facilities, participate in countermobilization to discourage the merchants from capitulating, or punish them for doing so.

[39] On southern white opinion, see Matthews and Prothro (1962).

[40] Vacillators in fact possess an option in which they take bold action to shift to a new cost structure, either through support for movement repression or the marginalization of intransigent whites.

varied roughly with the relative share of the black population, the vigor of white opposition, and the tenacity of sit-in protesters. Analogous to the predictions for voter registration, gains in desegregation should be greatest in urban communities in which African-Americans constitute a small proportion of the population; however, unlike voter registration, sustained protests threatened targets with damaging disruption costs and therefore often compelled greater responsiveness.

The preponderance of historical evidence documents the considerable effectiveness of demonstrations and boycotts in the integration of targeted southern public accommodations. Chafe (1980, 71) reports that "within a year, more than one hundred cities had engaged in at least some desegregation of public facilities in response to student-led demonstrations." From February 1960 to February 1961, sit-ins caused racial segregation to be abandoned at "thousands of lunch counters and other facilities" in approximately 150 cities.[41] Using conservative estimates for desegregation, Laue found that by September 1, 1961, 175 cities had desegregated "lunch counters and other facilities." In his tabulation of outcomes of sit-in campaigns in 69 communities during the first year of protests, Oppenheimer (1963 [1989], 178) calculated a success rate slightly over 56 percent. Anecdotal evaluations similarly find that the sit-ins were widely effective. Black and Black (1987, 103) observe that the sit-in movement won "notable gains" and Lytle (1966) declared the sit-in movement to be "a great success." McAdam (1983) likewise attributes the popularity of the sit-in tactic to the simple fact that "it worked." He notes, "By late 1961, facilities in 93 cities in ten southern states had been desegregated as a *direct* result of sit-in demonstrations. In at least 45 other locales the desire to avoid disruptive sit-ins was enough to occasion the integration of some facilities."[42] Reporting on the student protest movement, the authoritative Southern Regional Council declared, "The year-and-a-half sit-in activity has penetrated racial barriers in public accommodations with unprecedented speed" (1961, 3). During the next surge in agitation in 1963, civil rights demonstrations prompted a "measurable desegregation of facilities... in 186 localities."[43] Other contemporaneous accounts suggest that concerted action often produced victories – albeit a checkerboard pattern of desegregation – against their specific targets.

---

[41] Laue (1965 [1989], 2).
[42] McAdam (1983, 743) (notes omitted).
[43] Laue (1965, 357–8).

The broader geographic pattern in outcomes coincides with predictions. After one year, sit-ins in more populous cities in the Peripheral South achieved significant gains. After all, this is where the movement had been concentrated. In sharp contrast, the sit-ins met with stronger opposition and often defeat in the Deep South and in those communities with larger black populations. Oppenheimer found that the success rates for sit-in protests declined as the proportion of the African-American population rose. In such cases, public opposition, more widespread countermobilization, and greater attentiveness (often due to the actions of organized opponents) reduced the prospects for movement gains. Summing up the general pattern, Black and Black (1987, 103) declare, "Desegregation was more likely in larger cities than smaller towns, in the Peripheral South than the Deep South, and in businesses owned outside the region."

Unfortunately, systematic data on the efficacy of sit-ins beyond February 1961 is limited; however, case studies suggest that sustained movement mobilization often delivered victories against targeted firms even in the Deep South communities, as seen in Atlanta and Birmingham. Likewise, the Southern Regional Council reported that, in Georgia, desegregation gains had been won in 1961–62 in Macon, Savannah, and Columbia.[44] In South Carolina, merchants had defied movement demands in the first wave of sit-ins, but strengthened protests and boycotts in 1963 brought about the integration of many facilities, and concessions to other demands as well, in Rock Hill, Spartanburg, Charleston, and Columbia. In localities with extensive white countermobilization, these victories were often won only due to the intense economic costs imposed upon movement targets.[45] In Savannah, for instance, the protests and boycott of the downtown merchants, which reduced profits by 30 percent, lasted for 18 months before the business owners capitulated.[46] Elsewhere, word of economic catastrophe encouraged rapid accommodation by some economic elites to preempt the disruptive effects of racial turmoil. For instance, movement demands in 1963 achieved swift desegregation in the Georgia cities of Rome and Brunswick.[47] Even the patchwork desegregation of public accommodations surpassed the lackluster gains achieved in public school integration. Likewise, in communities in which minimal

---

[44] Southern Regional Council Papers, Series III, Reel 123, Document 508, 1054. For Savannah, see also *New York Times*, July 9, 1961.
[45] Cox (1996).
[46] Tuck (2001, 134).
[47] Ibid., 138.

voter registration gains were won, local activists cracked the color line in segregated public facilities.

The enactment of the Civil Rights Act of 1964 recast the constellation of disruption and concession costs to shift the advantage in favor of civil rights protesters. The legislation furnished these activists with new legal weapons to impose significant disruption costs upon recalcitrant firms and further accelerate the abandonment of segregated public accommodation. The amplification of disruption costs due to increased federal support was compelling. Perhaps equally important, concession costs also fell sharply. For those members of the business community worried about the economic implications of civil rights protests, boycotts, and racial turmoil but fearing white reprisals, there was at last a plausible justification for making a change that shifted the blame to the federal government. Indeed, overt elite support for defiance of federal law was more muted than the reaction to *Brown*. Unlike the constitutional arguments that had been used to argue against *Brown*, southern elites were unable to attribute this latest federal command to an unelected, imperial judiciary. If whites were unable to defect en masse through a concerted boycott, these enterprises had little economic incentive to alienate their prospective black clientele. Thus, the new configuration of disruption and concession costs favored acquiescence to the law. Summing up this shift, Rodgers and Bullock (1972) attribute the high rates of compliance to two main factors: the eagerness of southern business operators to attract black patronage, and the relatively weaker white commitment to defending this aspect of Jim Crow. Similarly, as stated by a Mississippi restaurateur, "Desegregation of public accommodations does not basically alter the pattern of social life anywhere. That is why it has been accomplished as easily as it has."[48]

In a sense, the new legislation resolved a collective action problem deterring individual business operators from capitulating. Individual operators might reason that, if they yielded unilaterally to movement demands, they could be singled out for white reprisals. Thus, in the negotiation process with demonstrators, downtown merchants often sought ways to unite the business community behind broader desegregation plans and thereby diffuse the blame for bringing about unwanted changes as well as make the task of punishing these firms more daunting for civil rights opponents. Disgruntled customers might choose to abandon a valued public space or engage in collective action to compel the operator to reverse policies. Both options are personally costly to patrons. The

---

[48] *New York Times*, December 20, 1964.

new legislation provided these operators with the impetus to unite in the simultaneous desegregation of downtown facilities. President Kennedy, in his speech announcing his intention to submit civil rights legislation to Congress, described precisely this logic.

> I have recently met with scores of business leaders urging them to take voluntary action to end this discrimination, and I have been encouraged by their response. In the last two weeks over seventy-five cities have seen progress made in desegregating these kinds of facilities. But many are unwilling to act alone, and for this reason, nationwide legislation is needed if we are to move this problem from the streets to the courts.[49]

With the collective abandonment of segregation at lunch counters, restaurants, hotels, movie theaters, and the rest, these operators limited the prospect of being singled out for punishment for abandoning Jim Crow. For these reasons, compliance with the Act was swift and widespread.

Movement Demands and Cost Configurations

This analysis highlights the basic argument that although each specific movement demand might appear to be a general challenge to Jim Crow, the logic behind target responses to the various aspects of white dominance differed based on their *distinctive* cost assessments. In the domains of school desegregation and voter registration, the movement struggled to overcome daunting challenges, producing mixed outcomes. In both cases, the general lack of African-American electoral leverage substantially limited the movement's capacity to impose disruption costs directly upon their political targets. To motivate recalcitrant officials, the movement thus needed to obtain assistance from third parties, principally an unwilling federal government or those indigenous economic actors fearful of the implications of racial tumult. Even with the support of these reluctant allies, prior to the enactment of landmark civil and voting rights legislation in the mid-sixties, the additional disruption costs brought to bear upon local officials were limited, as there were no incentives to support more than token gains. The degree of overall movement success in these domains depended less upon disruption costs than on how these political targets weighed the relative costs of conceding to civil rights demands. In sharp contrast, the movement's general effectiveness in interfering with

---

[49] Available at: http://www.pbs.org/wgbh/amex/presidents/35_kennedy/psources/ps_civilrights.html (accessed July 26, 2008).

the operations of public accommodations allowed activists to more effectively extract concessions.

For elected officials, the concession costs associated with school desegregation and voter registration depended heavily on their perceptions about constituent preferences. With school desegregation, the cost of integration rose roughly in tandem with the proportion of the African-American population as well as the presence of instigators to organize cohesive opposition. Thus, white publics in localities with very few African-Americans were less likely to regard the costs of school integration as significant and were therefore less prone to organize against desegregation. Nevertheless, public officials, ever apprehensive about provoking an electoral reprisal, were motivated to respond often only after a federal court order, and even then kept integration to a minimum. Greater integration beyond the minimum necessary to achieve nominal compliance might attract negative attention from mass publics and expose the official to unnecessary risk. In communities with relatively large black populations and open opposition among white publics, local officials anticipated an electoral punishment for any response less than a full-throated defense of segregation. These cost constellations produced official responses to demands for school desegregation that ranged from the barest tokenism to obdurate opposition. Ultimately, without assistance from federal officials to trump local intransigence, most school desegregation struggles generally concluded in failure with minimal integration.

A different cost configuration produced greater variation in movement outcomes in the domain of voter registration before 1965. Movement disruption costs were limited mainly to those incurred by the need to respond to movement- or government-initiated litigation for unimpeded voter registration under the various civil rights laws. Local elites might deplore negative press attention that risked producing unwanted reputational damage. While not trivial, these were hardly sufficient to overcome the opposition of determined public officials fearing electoral retribution. Nevertheless, more variation in movement outcomes can be seen in the domain of voter registration due to wide differences in concern among local politicians. Up to the point that African-Americans achieved a visible electoral advantage, mass white publics were unlikely to deem black voter registration as particularly costly and were therefore inattentive. Unthreatened by either white electoral reprisals or the prospect of black political leverage, elected officials accommodated to movement demands and allowed unimpeded voter registration. Indeed, so long as it was doubtful that whites would punish an officeholder for permitting black voter registration and registered black voters might plausibly reward the official with their newly obtained votes, officeholders might seek to cultivate a new voting bloc.[50] Only in places in which African-Americans might obtain significant electoral leverage were attentive white publics or public officials inclined to thwart black voter registration. Without enhanced federal coercion, black registration gains under these circumstances were minimal and won after great struggle.

These cost configurations produced fairly consistent patterns. In heavily African-American localities, local officials fiercely resisted *both* school desegregation and voter registration. Movement gains against public officials in these resistant localities, which were concentrated in the black belt of the Deep South, were negligible in the absence of more aggressive assistance from third parties. Thus, before the enactment of federal civil and voting rights legislation, the wall of segregation in such communities had barely been breached in these two domains despite years of courageous and tenacious civil rights mobilization. The outcomes of the extraordinary struggles in Alabama and Mississippi attest to this pattern. Among communities with a large percentage of African-Americans, token school desegregation might be achieved without tumult only insofar as economic elites were more committed to economic development than the protection of lily-white schools, as in Atlanta. In localities with fewer African-Americans, the pattern of movement outcomes in the two domains diverged with mere tokenism in school desegregation, on the one hand, but significant gains in voter registration, on the other. This striking contrast could be seen most starkly in Tennessee, where by 1963–64 only 2.7 percent of black students were in classes with whites but black voter registration rates from 1962 to 1964 soared from 50 percent to nearly 70 percent.

In public accommodations across the South, movement agitation effectively wedged open previously closed institutions. As with public school desegregation and voting rights, racial segregation collapsed most rapidly in Peripheral South communities in which there were fewer African-Americans and a weaker white commitment to defend Jim Crow. Yet, even in the urban Deep South, sustained agitation cracked racial barriers

---

[50] As mentioned previously, although costs are mainly assumed to shape the behavior of targets and third parties, benefit-seeking behavior should not be ruled out. This behavior is most likely to occur in cases in which targets and third parties can choose among minimally costly options. Other things being equal, conformers can engage in benefit-seeking because concession costs are not determinative. Too, vacillators may engage in benefit-seeking behavior insofar as they choose the "least bad" option.

in the most obdurate communities. (While rural black belt localities often defied this trend, the pattern appears partly due to an emphasis upon voter registration in these inhospitable settings.) As the movement increasingly concentrated upon public accommodations in these holdout communities, economic pressures again achieved significant victories.

Summary

The analysis presented here bolsters the general point that movement outcomes are explicable. In schematic form: targets perform a cost calculation in which they weigh movement disruption costs against those of conceding to movement demands. The critical task, then, is discerning how targets interpret these costs. In particular, it is necessary to consider not only movement activities, but also how the responses of third parties affect target cost calculations. These bystanders too weigh the costs of both movement disruptions and the concessions sought from the movement's targets. In the explanation of the responsiveness of political targets, constituent preferences, attentiveness, and third party mobilization are key. In many cases, movement demands upon their political targets are sufficiently small, abstract, and delayed that bystanders – potential third party participants – do not register a meaningful political preference. Under these circumstances, movement targets will be more inclined to acquiesce to organized demands. On the other hand, if the costs imposed upon bystander constituents are significant, direct, and immediate, then their disapproval and anticipated electoral reprisal will encourage adherence to mass preferences. Thus, although an explanation of the outcomes of political movements begins with the electoral calculations of public officials, elements of this decision can be traced back to constituent cost perceptions and further still to the attributes of movement demands. As shown in this chapter, the divergent outcomes of the civil rights movement in school desegregation and voting rights stem in part from this variation in constituent cost perceptions, these differences deriving from specific features of the movement's three principal policy demands. Although social movement impact is often treated as something distinct from conventional politics, the perspective here assumes that the factors determining the outcomes of movements and interest organizations are identical.

The broader pattern of civil rights outcomes after the peak in movement activism conforms to this logic as well. With the expansion of the franchise, the logic of movement outcomes began to more closely resemble

conventional political struggles with larger electoral factions capable of
obtaining new political gains.[51] Along these lines, the decline in the scope
of civil rights victories in the latter 1960s is telling. As McAdam argues,
as civil rights agitation shifted during this period from racial integration
and routine access to the ordinary aspects of social life toward a more
fundamental restructuring of the allocation of economic advantages, the
movement ceased to win additional expansive victories.[52] The general
challenge to economic class stratification threatened to impose significant,
visible costs upon a broader share of the population (including nonsoutherners) and therefore provoked widespread opposition. Research on the
roll-call votes of House representatives on civil rights legislation from
1957 to 1991 confirms the argument that legislators respond to the real
or assumed cost perceptions of white constituents with the likelihood of
passage declining for measures deemed to be costly.[53] Thus, an explanation for the outcomes of the civil rights movement necessitates discerning
the changing relative magnitude of the disruption and concession costs
associated with specific demands over time.

[51] Stein and Condrey (1987); also Santoro (2002).
[52] McAdam (1982, 164).
[53] Sanders (1997).

6

Federal Responses to Civil Rights Mobilization

In spectacular fashion, Lyndon Johnson signed the landmark Civil Rights Act of 1964, a decade after the Supreme Court in *Brown v. Board of Education* had declared segregation unconstitutional and after hundreds of civil rights protests had awakened the nation to the profound injustices in the Jim Crow South. The civil rights movement had won a sweeping victory and, the following year, achieved another success in the Voting Rights Act. Other major acts followed. Studies of the outcomes of political movements in general and the civil rights movement in particular offer different explanations for these events, though most concentrate on disruption costs in the form of movement events, public opinion, and mass attentiveness as well as contextual political opportunities (such as the partisan composition in Congress).[1] Research specifically on the civil rights movement has documented a "critical dynamic" in which segregationist violence elevated national attentiveness that, in turn, prompted supportive federal intervention. This research explains movement outcomes based on the convergence of supportive public opinion and issue salience stemming from the movement's effective provocation of dramatic events.[2] These studies are informative, their arguments compelling,

[1] See, for instance, Agnone (2007); Amenta (2006); Burstein (1979); Costain and Majstorovic (1994); Giugni (2004); McAdam (1982); Soule and Olzak (2004).
[2] Burstein (1985); McAdam (1982). McAdam coined the term "critical dynamic." See also Agnone (2007) and Santoro (2002). This analysis supports Morris (1993) in his contention that the local triumph in Birmingham depended upon the unity and effectiveness of the movement in inflicting economic pain upon Birmingham economic elites, and was not simply a result of federal intervention in response to white violence. In some measure, however, the debate over the "violence thesis" is misplaced in that there are two distinct

and therefore my intent is not to displace them. Yet, despite their many virtues, certain aspects of the civil rights struggle merit closer scrutiny.

Perhaps due to an emphasis on protests and dramatic episodes of violence, the full range of disruption costs is seldom sufficiently addressed, particularly the place of conventional political leverage in winning policy gains.[3] Separate from the incidents that capture media attention, voting blocs are mobilized and lobbies urge elected officials to act upon their demands. Put another way, benefit-seekers can wield disruption costs in the form of routine political inducements in the absence of dramatic events.[4] Here the line between social movements and interest organizations blurs as the policy impact of both is presumed to depend upon the same political logic. As Louis Martin, an advisor in the Kennedy administration on racial matters, explained to Charles Evers of the NAACP before a meeting with Lyndon Johnson, "Now, there ain't no point in ya'll spending your time to tell the Vice President what your demands are or what you're going to have.... What the Vice President wants to know, like the President, is how many votes you can produce at election time."[5] Accordingly, the growth or actuation of benefit-seeking organizations that command significant voting blocs, along with increased competition

victories that emerge from the Birmingham struggle: one local and the other national. Indigenous elites proffered concessions due to the disastrous economic implications of movement disruptions, including the boycott. Connor's repressive violence amplified the shockwaves of these disruptions in downtown business activity, but federal intervention does not appear to have been crucial to the local outcome. At the same time, the media spectacle of local authorities using police dogs and fire hoses against nonviolent demonstrators elevated national attentiveness to the civil rights movement and accelerated the push for federal legislation, as proponents of the violence thesis suggest; see Burstein (1985); McAdam (1982). In this two-level game, sustained movement contention and reactive violence augmented disruption costs for both vulnerable local economic interests and national elected officials, and contributed to a successful movement impact on both levels.

[3] For exceptions to this general description, see Burstein (1985); Costain and Majstorovic (1994); Santoro (2002).

[4] Hansen (1991); Harvey (1997). This point is hardly controversial as this is precisely what interest organizations seek to do. Interestingly, Harvey suggests that a political party's interest in attracting the support of a voting bloc is insufficient to produce policy concessions, if this support can be obtained using symbolic gestures and social inducements (such as an endorsement from a trusted information source or cue-giver within the targeted group). She maintains that only the mobilization of voters by independent benefit-seeking organizations, not political parties, can induce rational office-seekers to concede substantive policy benefits.

[5] Evers (1974). Martin, a journalist and newspaper editor, served as Deputy Chairman of the Democratic National Committee during the Kennedy and Johnson administrations (1961 to 1969).

for African-American votes, can foster growing responsiveness to civil rights issues. I argue, then, for the fuller inclusion of conventional political factors in explanations of movement outcomes.

Also, since greater attention is paid to dramatic disruptions, there has been a corresponding underemphasis of the concession costs associated with specific movement demands and why targets might be more or less resistant to capitulation. As argued throughout, both costs must be considered together to explain target responses. In the domain of national politics, greater attention to these costs produces three additional insights about the responsiveness of the movement's political targets. Specifically, variation in presidential support for equal rights follows from broad changes in the overall disruption and concession costs over time. I evaluate this proposition by surveying the changing presidential responses to demands for greater racial equality from the close of Reconstruction to the 1960s, focusing in particular on the administrations from Truman to Johnson. I trace how variations in disruption and concession costs over time caused the presidential position on equal rights to shift from resistance to a vacillating attempt to appease both southern whites and civil rights benefit-seekers, and, eventually, to accommodation to civil rights demands.

Next, taking a closer look at concession costs draws attention to a movement's opponents.[6] This consideration too is often overlooked. In this case, the virtual absence of organized nonsouthern opposition meant that these legislators could vote for major civil and voting rights bills without much fear of electoral retribution. Such a perspective points to the strikingly low concession costs for most lawmakers due to the lack of business opposition to civil rights gains, and thus clarifies the legislative processes that led to specific movement outcomes during the period of greater presidential support in the 1960s. Finally, greater attention to concession costs reveals aspects of the legislative bargaining process as well as the *content* of the measures that were ultimately enacted. This point is documented below in an analysis of the role of "pivotal" Republican

---

[6] Although public opinion and attentiveness may be regarded as determining the magnitude of aggregate concession costs (mirroring disruption costs), the political leverage of the organized opposition must be included as well. It is likely that public opinion has emerged as a particularly significant factor in the explanation of social movement impact for the precise reason that it taps into both disruption and concession costs. Nevertheless, I contend that organized benefit-seekers often operate within circumstances of low attentiveness (or indifference) and that conventional political factors (such as controlling large voting blocs) can be crucial.

legislators whose support was critical for the enactment of civil and voting rights measures but who lacked a strong electoral impetus to concede.[7] Obtaining their support during the legislative bargaining process produced a set of compromises that weakened the legislation and, in particular, often concentrated the chief impact of the measures on southern constituencies. Variation in movement impact, it is argued, will be decisively affected by the political calculations of these pivotal legislators. Movement studies that address political outcomes seldom delve into the legislative bargaining processes that generate specific pieces of legislation and, as such, insufficient attention is devoted to the role of these pivotal legislators. In brief, in this chapter I present an argument for the consideration of the full range of disruption and concession costs to bring into clearer focus the factors affecting changes in presidential behavior, shaping legislative bargaining processes, and delineating the substance of these accomplishments.

The Development of Civil Rights

In the domain of citizenship rights, it has long been axiomatic that federalism limits the actions of the national government. The 1833 Supreme Court decision *Barron v. Baltimore* narrowed the application of the Bill of Rights to the federal government and only slowly did the Court reverse this position.[8] This decision gave citizens two sets of rights – national and state rights – with the latter to vary widely across the nation. Even after the ratification of the Reconstruction amendments and passage of civil rights laws, the nineteenth-century Supreme Court limited the nationalization of citizenship by narrowly construing the scope of federal civil rights.[9] In addition, federalism vested the states with "police powers" to protect the health, safety, and welfare of the citizenry. Indeed, the Court affirmed in *Plessy v. Ferguson* (1896) that segregation was a legitimate expression of state police powers.[10] Insofar as states and localities refused

---

[7] Krehbiel (1998); Rodriguez and Weingast (2003).

[8] 7 *Peters* 243 (1833).

[9] In a series of decisions from 1873 to 1883, the Supreme Court adjudicated Reconstruction amendments and statutes. For example, the 1873 *Slaughterhouse Cases* 83 U.S. 36 limited the scope of national citizenship and the civil rights under the Fourteenth Amendment. The *Civil Rights Cases* (1883) voided key sections of the Civil Rights Act of 1875. In this decision, the Court stated that the equal protection and due process clauses of the Fourteenth Amendment applied to discriminatory state action, but not to that of private individuals. See also *United States v. Cruikshank* 92 U.S. 542 (1876).

[10] 163 U.S. 537 (1896).

to grant full citizenship rights, the rigidity of the federal-state split was crucial. As Daniel Elazar points out:

In the United States, the immediate problems of overcoming racial discrimination are inevitably linked to the enduring questions of federalism. No consideration of these problems as political issues can escape questions of federal jurisdiction, states' rights, the role of the United States Supreme Court as an arbiter of federal-state relations, constitutional guarantees of internal autonomy of the states, and the constitutionally guaranteed power of the states and localities in national politics.[11]

With the escalation of civil rights agitation and the commensurate rise in anti–civil rights activity in the fifties and sixties, liberals clamored for federal action to halt southern opposition to school desegregation and to protect protesters from the brutality of public authorities and private citizens. In response to any attempts by the national government to expand the citizenship rights of African-Americans, southern whites harshly denounced such actions as infringements upon states' rights. The controversy thus involved not only African-American citizenship rights but also, as E. E. Schattschneider (1960, 8) remarked, "the rights of 'outsiders' to intervene."

These rights of outside intervention were significantly circumscribed. For instance, federal jurisdiction in cases of anti–civil rights violence rested primarily upon two Reconstruction statutes against official brutality and private violence – Title 18 USC Sections 241 and 242. Section 241 proscribed conspiracies against the rights of citizens and Section 242 addressed "willful" deprivations of rights "under color of law." In a series of cases, the Supreme Court limited the potential reach of both these statutes.[12] These precedents made obtaining convictions of the perpetrators of anti–civil rights violence extremely difficult. Federal laws permitting civil suits were likewise limited in coverage and the costs were to be borne by the plaintiff.[13] Therefore to the extent that federal authorities sought to punish anti–civil rights activists, and thus to enforce national citizenship rights, they were seriously constrained.

[11] 1966, 5.
[12] In *United States v. Williams* 341 U.S. 70 (1951), the Court ruled that Fourteenth Amendment rights were not covered under Section 19 (the predecessor of Section 241). In *Screws* 325 U.S. 91 (1945), the Court weakened Section 242 by offering a restricted interpretation of "willful" such that the plaintiff was required to prove the prior intent of the defendant to abridge another of their constitutional rights. Congressional Quarterly (hereafter CQ) (1968, 9); Belknap (1987); Burns (1965, 228–54).
[13] CQ (1968, 9).

Yet, if federal authority were indeed lacking, why had not the necessary civil rights legislation been passed to broaden federal jurisdiction? In some measure, structural difficulties inhibited federal action. Decentralization of national political institutions and decision-making multiplies the numbers of "veto points" at which organized interests can block major policy initiatives, thus making bold action far more difficult.[14] In addition, as a set of policies with redistributive implications, the success of civil rights legislation depended upon presidential leadership to sweep aside congressional parochialism.[15] The question "why no jurisdiction?" thus shifts to another level. If sufficient federal authority did not exist and executive leadership was necessary to enlarge federal jurisdiction over these matters, why did president after president *refrain* from pushing for the passage of civil rights legislation?

An account of the structure of political institutions alone cannot explain the low level of federal support – and especially presidential backing – or the eventual expansion of African-American citizenship rights. It will perhaps be no surprise that, for reasons of electoral and legislative expedience, post-Reconstruction presidents reacted to heinous violations of constitutional rights with the argument that federalism strictly limited national jurisdiction over matters of local law enforcement.[16] The advance of racially charged policies depended less upon formal structures than on the configuration of political interests. Unwillingness, more than inability, kept the central state from acting to protect the constitutional rights of African-Americans.

The Politics of Resistance

Reconstruction marked a decisive break in American race policy.[17] After the abolition of slavery, the federal government under Republican rule sought to reshape the southern political economy and to expand the citizenship rights of African-Americans. During Reconstruction, Republicans enforced a variety of measures designed to enfranchise the newly freed slaves, to suppress Klan violence, and to provide a national basis for citizenship. The Reconstruction amendments to the Constitution and

---

[14] Krehbiel (1998).
[15] Ripley and Franklin (1976, 121–2).
[16] Logan (1965).
[17] On this period generally, Bensel (1990, 303–65); Stampp (1965); Valelly (2004); and thereafter, Woodward (1951) and Woodward (1955) [1979].

enforcement acts described above gave the government new authority to nationalize African-American citizenship rights. For a time, the coercive capacities of the federal government were deployed to prosecute those responsible for abridging the rights of African-Americans. However, this commitment proved to be short-lived. An ensemble of political and economic factors – including Democratic party resurgence, the high cost of maintaining the Union army in the South, economic stagnation after the financial panic of 1873, and declining northern interest in the plight of ex-slaves – conspired to bring Reconstruction to a close in 1877. Republican interests in southern party-building had abated, as it was increasingly clear that black votes were unnecessary to maintain national political dominance. The withdrawal of Union troops not only signaled the Republican abandonment of the region, but doomed the citizenship rights of southern blacks for many decades to come. In addition, as indicated above, a series of Supreme Court decisions reduced the impact of the Reconstruction amendments and supporting legislation. In the *Civil Rights Cases* (1883), for instance, the Court affirmed that although the Fourteenth Amendment prohibited state actions that deprived citizens of their fundamental rights, it did not apply to the discriminatory actions of private individuals.[18] In addition, toward the close of the century, southern legislatures began adopting a set of laws designed to disenfranchise blacks and erect the segregated racial order known as Jim Crow.[19] As if to mark the complete abdication of federal intervention in southern race relations, the Supreme Court's affirmation of segregation in *Plessy* was based on finding that "separate but equal" accommodations did not violate the equal protection clause of the Fourteenth Amendment.[20]

As southern Democrats recaptured control over Dixie politics, another logic emerged to discourage national support for racial equality. Once returned to Congress, southern Democrats sought to preserve *local* control over civil rights and black labor. Without much complaint from Republicans legislators, for instance, federal anti-lynching bills died in congressional committees at the hands of southern representatives, or they were filibustered to death in the Senate. Accordingly, of the 248 anti-lynching bills introduced between 1882 and 1951, none passed.[21]

---

[18] 109 U.S. 3 (1883).

[19] See generally, Kousser (1974). These laws included poll taxes, literacy tests, and property requirements.

[20] 163 U.S. 537 (1896). In 1898, the Court likewise upheld the constitutionality of literacy tests used in the South to hinder black voter registration.

[21] Belknap (1987, 18).

Even though the southern congressional delegation might split over certain issues, on civil rights the "solid South" truly lived up to its reputation. The northern wing of the Democratic party was seldom eager to upset their southern brethren. Differ as they might over civil rights policy, for obvious reasons northern Democrats knew the success of their legislative agenda rested on the cooperation of southerners. Likewise, the reliance upon the southern votes in presidential elections discouraged executive action on behalf of African-Americans. This ensemble of political factors severely weakened federal support for the nationalization of black citizenship rights.

These inhibitions were nowhere more evident than during the New Deal period, even though African-Americans were increasingly leaving the party of Lincoln to support the redistributive thrust of the Democratic party. The South supplied Franklin D. Roosevelt with a vital base of congressional support. Largely dominated by the plantation elite, the southern wing of the Democratic Party had the power to obstruct various components of the New Deal. This potential for a "southern veto," which encouraged intense negotiation between the party's northern and southern wings, contributed to the New Deal's peculiar blend of regulatory, labor, and social welfare initiatives.[22] Through a set of concessions designed to mollify southern agrarian interests, the northern labor wing of the party won support for their legislative agenda. Simply put, southern support for the New Deal was purchased at the price of excluding southern blacks from coverage under its major legislative enactments.[23]

In order to accommodate the regional divisions within the Democratic party, agricultural and domestic laborers were excluded from the nationalizing impact of the Social Security Act, the Fair Labor Standards Act, and the National Labor Relations Act. In addition to the exclusion of particular occupational categories, "each Act stipulated regional forms of public administration geared to preserve local customs and fortify the white-dominated south."[24] For example, the determination of eligibility and benefits levels for Aid to Dependent Children (later AFDC) was left to local governments. At the time of the cotton harvest, planter-dominated county governments cut recipients off to silently coerce blacks into the

---

[22] See Katznelson, Geiger, and Kryder (1993); Watters and Cleghorn (1967, 210–44).
[23] Lieberman (2001).
[24] Katznelson et al. (1993, 4–5). See also Lieberman (1995); Mettler (1998); for a dissenting opinion, see Davies and Derthick (1997).

fields.[25] Thus, if progressive policies were enacted, either blacks were excluded outright or the administrative authority was devolved to southern whites. With respect to federal intervention to punish racial violence, Roosevelt did nothing. Two lynchings in Florida and Mississippi, clearly actionable under the Lindbergh Kidnapping Act, went unprosecuted.[26] Finally, neither did Roosevelt submit nor did Congress pass any civil rights legislation.[27] While the New Deal provided other citizens with the full benefit of new national policies, the improvement of the lot of southern blacks was often limited and, on occasion, federal action made matters even worse. Only under the threat of an immense march on Washington during a period of intense war mobilization did Roosevelt issue an executive order to prohibit discrimination in employment of African-Americans in government or defense industries.[28] To enforce the order, Roosevelt created the Fair Employment Practices Commission (FEPC) to receive and act upon complaints of discrimination. Yet even the administration of the FEPC was sufficiently decentralized to limit federal intervention into southern race relations.[29] Thus, after Reconstruction, a lack of public support for federal action to promote racial equality, the intense opposition of southern elites, and the political weakness of African-Americans meant that concession costs remained high, disruption costs low, and inaction was the national policy on civil rights.

The Politics of Vacillation

After World War II, a new configuration of factors foreshadowed greater instability in civil rights policy.[30] In particular, the emergence of a significant black voting bloc in the North, favorable Supreme Court reaction to NAACP attacks upon Jim Crow institutions, and Cold War foreign policy concerns pushed civil rights slowly toward center stage.[31] Persistent African-American migration to northern urban centers, without

---

[25] Bensel and Sanders (1986); Raper (1968, 254–69).
[26] Belknap (1987, 19).
[27] Wolk (1971, 31).
[28] Klinkner and Smith (1999).
[29] Kryder (2001).
[30] McAdam (1982, 73–86); also Piven and Cloward (1977, 181–263).
[31] Notable cases include *Smith v. Allwright* 321 U.S. 649 (1944), which banned "white primaries"; *Shelley v. Kraemer* 334 U.S. 1 (1948), in which the Court ruled against state enforcement of restrictive covenants; and *Sweatt v. Painter* 339 U.S. 629 (1950), in which the Court questioned the equality of segregated facilities. See Greenberg (1994); Kluger (1977); on the limits of judicial action, see Rosenberg (1991).

suffrage restrictions, made the black vote a more critical factor in presidential elections. Further, the concentration of the black population in states of decisive importance in the electoral college, such as California, Illinois, Michigan, Ohio, and Pennsylvania, accentuated this prospective leverage.[32] Clark Clifford, a Truman advisor and architect of his 1948 presidential campaign, similarly pointed to precisely this geographic concentration as the main justification for courting African-American support.[33] In 1948, under the aegis of the Progressive party, Henry Wallace's challenge from the left threatened to capture enough black votes to cost Truman the election. To preempt Wallace, Truman's aides had devised a tactical response: the introduction of a major legislative initiative. Thus, even before Wallace announced his candidacy, Truman proposed anti-lynching, anti–poll tax, anti–transportation segregation, and FEPC legislation.[34] Although this riled southern Democrats, it was a necessary risk.[35] On election day, despite the defection of the Dixiecrats, Truman narrowly won with the support of the party liberals along with a large percentage of the non-southern African-American voters.

The explosive growth of the NAACP no doubt contributed to rising interest in civil rights initiatives. Surging from roughly fifty thousand members in 1940 to over four hundred thousand by the end of the decade, the NAACP and its allies might credibly threaten the electoral fortunes of indifferent lawmakers in an increasing number of northern districts and states.[36] The organization specifically sought to pursue a "balance of power" strategy to extract civil rights commitments from both parties.[37]

[32] Berman (1970, 6–9, 133); McAdam (1982); Moon (1948); Stone (1968).

[33] McCullough (1992, 590).

[34] Berman (1970); CQ (1968). The strategic logic behind Truman's early positions on these issues is revealed in a comment that Truman made as a senator to a southern colleague regarding the 1938 anti-lynching bill. "You know I am against this bill, but if it comes to a vote, I'll have to vote for it. All my sympathies are with you but the Negro vote in Kansas City and St. Louis is too important." Quoted in Berman (1970, 10). On other occasions, Truman spoke strongly in favor of the principle of equality for African-Americans.

[35] During the national convention, the "Dixiecrats" bolted. In the 1948 presidential election, Strom Thurmond (D-SC), the candidate of the States' Rights Democrats, took the electoral college votes of Alabama, Louisiana, Mississippi, South Carolina, and a single elector from eastern Tennessee.

[36] McAdam (1982, 102). During the critical years from 1960 to 1970, NAACP membership averaged around 450,000 but peaked to over 500,000 in 1963 as the pace of civil rights protests quickened in the early 1960s (Marger 1984). Weak membership gains may have been due in part to the ferocious assault upon the organization by southern state governments.

[37] Moon (1948).

"Even though we didn't advocate voting for or against a candidate," explained the organization's executive secretary, the NAACP could "create the kind of climate in which certain candidates would find it difficult to maneuver."[38] While Republican party leaders were divided over whether to court the large black populations in northern urban centers or pursue southern whites disillusioned with the Democratic party, they opted (for a time) for the former strategy. Republicans decided to court African-American voters and, if possible, divide the Democrats with renewed support for civil rights legislation. Although the Senate Majority Leader, Lyndon B. Johnson (D-TX), scuttled the administration's 1956 civil rights bill to defuse the situation, the results of the 1956 presidential election appeared to vindicate the Republican strategy.[39] In that election, northern African-Americans, while more supportive of the Democratic party, had shifted in greater numbers in favor of the Republican candidate.

For the Democrats, their historical dilemma persisted: appease the South and risk the defection of northern African-American voters to the beckoning Republicans or satisfy African-Americans only to splinter the Democratic coalition.[40] At the same time, the strategy of attempting to contain civil rights controversies was becoming more difficult to sustain as the black vote destabilized. As Piven and Cloward assert, it was not "the rise of a substantial African-American electoral bloc in the southern states that finally set the stage for civil rights concessions; it was the rise of black defections."[41]

In addition to electoral instability, domestic racial oppression weakened the strategic position of the United States in the emerging Cold War struggle to influence the numerous post-colonial nations.[42] The escalation of civil rights agitation put pressure on the federal government to redress these grievances. In the competition with the Soviet Union for international political leverage – particularly in Africa and Asia – the brutality of Jim Crow repeatedly embarrassed presidents and foreign

---

[38] Roy Wilkins Oral History Interview (1969, 3).

[39] Burk (1984, 209). Democrats suspected the Republicans of introducing a civil rights bill during a presidential election year to cause intra-party squabbling and to weaken the standing of the Democrats among African-American voters. At a cabinet meeting in December 1955, Vice President Nixon supported Brownell's call for submitting civil rights legislation for precisely this reason.

[40] On the regional bipolarity in the Democratic party, see Bensel (1984).

[41] Piven and Cloward (1977, 217).

[42] Dudziak (2000); Klinkner and Smith (1999). Cold War imperatives appear in legal briefs and arguments from the Justice Department to the Supreme Court concerning the need to dismantle white supremacist institutions in the South.

policymakers abroad. After each atrocity in the South, the Soviet Union took the opportunity to broadcast the hypocrisies of American democracy around the globe. To combat this international threat, Truman declared at an NAACP rally:

The support of desperate populations of battle ravaged countries must be won for the free way of life.... They may surrender to the false security offered so temptingly by totalitarian regimes unless we can prove the superiority of democracy. Our case for democracy should be as strong as we can make it. It should rest on practical evidence that we have been able to put our own house in order.[43]

To fulfill this promise (and to maintain the support of liberal Democrats), Truman issued executive orders to desegregate the armed forces and to forbid discrimination in federal employment or under government contract. The constant pressure to keep southern race relations out of the international press encouraged successive presidents to engage in intense behind-the-scenes bargaining with southern authorities and civil rights activists and, on rare occasions, to take action in favor of black civil rights. Thus, the developing commitment of the national state to African-American civil rights came about more because of political calculation and national security interests than from a shift in moral conviction.

After the Supreme Court's 1954 decision in *Brown*, the contestation over race policy entered a period of greater federal involvement, with the courts leading the way. With this decision, the Supreme Court drove a wedge into the southern racial order and left an unwilling executive branch to hammer away at the privileged position of the white South. President Eisenhower had no particular enthusiasm for enlarging the coercive capacities of the federal government and even less for doing so to expand African-American citizenship rights. Indeed, Eisenhower refused to show public support for the ruling, usually expressing the opinion that morality cannot be legislated. This ambivalence pleased southerners and aggravated liberals who believed that the president ought to provide greater moral leadership to combat mounting southern opposition to the ruling. In private, Eisenhower condemned the decision as a serious blow to the development of southern Republicanism.[44] Still, despite the rising clamor from southern resistance forces, during his 1956 reelection campaign, Eisenhower endorsed components of a civil rights bill

---

[43] O'Reilly (1995, 154).
[44] Ibid., 170. On the plus side, Eisenhower supported other civil rights measures such as further desegregating the military, and also nominated jurists to the Supreme Court who were not supportive of segregation, in particular Chief Justice Earl Warren.

that would enhance federal authority to combat black disenfranchisement. Although the president seldom made much of this endorsement, Vice President Nixon sought to do so. On the campaign trail in Harlem, Nixon affirmed Republican support for the passage of civil rights measures and castigated the Democrats for their opposition. The Republican platform affirmed support for the *Brown* decision and called for the passage of Eisenhower's 1956 civil rights program. While the Democratic party platform accepted *Brown*, it rejected "all proposals for the use of force" to implement the decision and made no mention of civil rights legislation.

The implementation of *Brown* ruptured southern race relations and heightened the pressure on the Eisenhower administration to do something decisive to protect the constitutional rights of African-Americans. Yet, the costs associated with political action for Eisenhower resembled those for Roosevelt and Truman. Assertive enforcement of the decision could only imperil nascent Republican gains in the region. At the same time, instability in the black vote in the North promised another route to electoral advantage and an outright rebuff of African-American demands threatening the wholesale defection of an attractive voting bloc. These circumstances again dictated a cautious approach meant to placate both sides. For example, Eisenhower continued the desegregation of the armed forces initiated under Truman and issued additional executive orders to further desegregation in areas under federal jurisdiction, such as within the District of Columbia. In contrast, perhaps to shore up his southern support, Eisenhower assured Governor Byrnes of South Carolina that he planned to go slowly on public school desegregation.[45] Such timidity encouraged southern segregationists to believe that the president was not committed to enforcing the *Brown* decision. "Just as Andrew Johnson had given cues to former confederates that they could reassert control over the South without interference from the White House," suggests William Chafe, "so President Eisenhower, through his reticence and ambiguity, encouraged segregationists to believe that they had free rein to resist the Supreme Court."[46] After a brief period of apparent resignation, white reaction against the prospect of public school desegregation hardened. In 1956, southern elected officials – including 19 senators and 82 representatives – signed the "Southern Manifesto," a pledge to "use all lawful means to bring a reversal of this decision which is contrary to the

---

[45] Burk(1984).
[46] Chafe (1986, 150–1).

Constitution and to prevent the use of force in its implementation."[47] Southern authorities passed dozens of new laws and proposed numerous state constitutional amendments designed to block or delay *Brown*'s implementation. Private citizens reacted as well by organizing into segregationist organizations, as detailed in Chapter 2.

The outcome of the 1956 presidential election again demonstrated the disruptive potential of the electoral instability among African-American voters, and likely contributed to the advance of civil rights legislation. Not only were African-Americans heavily concentrated in key states of the electoral college, they held a balance of power in 61 congressional districts.[48] In that election, the estimated African-American vote for Eisenhower rose to nearly 39 percent, a margin that alarmed Democratic candidates and encouraged Republicans to continue to speak in support of civil rights initiatives.

The 1956 election results in large Northern industrial cities convinced many observers in both the Democratic and Republican parties that the Negro vote had reached substantial proportions and that the traditional Northern Negro vote for the Democratic party was swinging toward the Republicans. Neither party felt that this trend could be ignored. (Wilhoit 1973, 53)

After years in the political wilderness, some Republican party strategists reasoned, if they could win back the northern black vote, they might return as "America's majority party."[49] Assessing the situation, Senator Hubert Humphrey (D-MN) lamented, "Democrats are digging their own grave by inaction in the field of civil rights."[50]

After the election, Eisenhower expressed his support for a more expansive civil rights bill in his State of the Union address, but thereafter he abandoned the school desegregation provisions.[51] The lack of executive leadership is witnessed in the administration's changing posture toward the implementation of *Brown*. Before the election, in the fall of 1956, Texas Governor Allan Shivers developed the prototypical response to a federal court order: allow white crowds to assemble, let them create a hostile and dangerous situation, then call off the desegregation process as a public safety measure. In public statements, Eisenhower accepted the

---

[47] Wilhoit (1973, 52–3). This sum amounted to 101 of the 128 member southern delegation in Congress.
[48] Lawson (1991, 151).
[49] Caro (2002, 777).
[50] Sundquist (1968, 230).
[51] Lawson (1991, 54).

actions of the Texas authorities. On another occasion, he declared, "I can't imagine any set of circumstances that would ever induce me to send Federal troops . . . into any area to enforce the order of a federal court."[52] Shivers's approach to blocking integration set a precedent that other governors sought to emulate. Thus it was in Little Rock. There, in September 1957, Governor Orval Faubus deployed the Arkansas National Guard to block the entry of black students into Central High School on the grounds that he was protecting public order against possible mob violence.[53] Unimpressed with Faubus's assertions about impending riots, a federal court ordered Faubus to allow the students to enter. In response, Faubus removed the Guardsmen and departed for a conference of southern governors, thereby abdicating state responsibility for the maintenance of law and order. The burden of law enforcement fell to the city police force. Hours after the students entered the school, a belligerent crowd formed and the police secreted the students out of the building. Outside, reporters, black and white alike, were harassed and beaten. The mayor of Little Rock repeatedly called upon the federal government for assistance. Attorney General Herbert Brownell assured the president that he possessed the constitutional authority to take charge of the situation and, at length, Eisenhower relented.

Although Eisenhower wanted no involvement in the desegregation process or the turmoil caused by local compliance with *Brown*, a fundamental challenge to national supremacy was unacceptable. Administration officials urged the president to take action. In addition, Eisenhower had met personally with Faubus to secure what he took to be a desegregation agreement, and the apparent breach of that agreement angered the president. Also, the 1956 election had passed and the electoral significance of Arkansas was relatively slight (unlike Texas the previous year). Thus, central state intervention in Little Rock came about not because of a policy concern for desegregation but because of a combination of factors including a frontal assault on national supremacy, the lack of foreseeable electoral reprisals, and a personal dislike for Faubus and his deception. For the first time since Reconstruction, this combination of factors pushed a president to send in federal troops.

---

[52] Burk (1984, 173).

[53] Faubus employed an anti-integration strategy that had been successfully applied in Mansfield, Texas. In that situation, in 1956, Governor Allan Shivers likewise deployed the Texas Rangers to block integration based upon threats to order. Yet during the Mansfield crisis, Eisenhower chose not to intervene, citing the local responsibility for law enforcement.

This action was highly exceptional for the administration. Instead of extending federal authority into southern states to preserve order, administration officials typically sought to enhance African-American voting rights. "Armed with the ballot," it was argued, "blacks would not need the administration to undertake intervention actions it deemed politically risky and philosophically objectionable."[54] Yet this measured enthusiasm for voting rights legislation came not from the president, but from Attorney General Brownell, who believed the party's fortunes lay in cultivation of the black vote.[55] In 1956, the administration submitted legislation that contained provisions to create the Civil Rights Commission (to investigate civil rights issues and make recommendations), to elevate the civil rights section of the Justice Department to division status, and two proposals designed to protect black voting rights. However, the voting rights provisions were not included in the original legislation that Eisenhower had approved but were added – somewhat surreptitiously – by Brownell "in direct violation of the explicit instructions of the White House."[56]

Unlike the organizational components of the bill, the voting rights measures involved using federal authority to challenge southern electoral practices that served to keep African-Americans from voting. The most controversial aspect of the 1957 civil rights bill involved enabling the attorney general to file suits to seek injunctions against those who sought to deprive a person of any civil right, a provision known as Part III.[57] The broad legislative language implied vesting the attorney general with vast authority not only to compel school desegregation but to defend against the encroachment of any constitutionally protected civil right. Southern Democrats railed against the extension of federal authority, played up the likelihood of the use of federal troops in the South, and compared the legislation to the "force acts" of Reconstruction. Another point of contention involved the question of whether or not those accused of civil rights violations (on a charge of criminal contempt) were entitled to a jury trial as opposed to a trial before a federal judge. Southern Democrats,

---

[54] Burk (1984, 204).

[55] Lawson (1991, 150–2). As the former chair of the Republican National Committee, Brownell had conducted an analysis of the 1944 presidential election and determined the decisive influence of the black vote on the outcome. See Moon (1948, 35–6).

[56] Anderson 1964. In his transmittal letter conveying the civil rights bills to Congress, the attorney general "transmitted the two approved bills but left in his transmittal letter the arguments for all four." Sundquist (1968, 227).

[57] CQ (1968, 27); Sundquist (1968, 226).

aware of the difficulties of obtaining convictions among southern juries in their region, supported jury trials.

Congressional representatives had competing imperatives. Northern Democratic and many Republican legislators supported the legislation to maintain the support of numerous organizations and reduce the defections of black voters. A collection of more than 20 pro-rights organizations, operating under the auspices of the Leadership Conference on Civil Rights (LCCR), lobbied for the measure.[58] Southern countermobilization against civil rights as well as their personal political fortunes vested Southern Democrats with a keen interest in thwarting any civil rights legislation, through a Senate filibuster if necessary. In the Senate, majority leader Lyndon Johnson (D-TX) "sought to fashion a bill that would be acceptable to both liberal and conservative wings of the party, one which northern Democrats could claim as a victory for civil rights and southerners could accept as least objectionable."[59] Rather than blocking the 1957 civil rights bill outright, Johnson sought passage of a weakened version of the bill that eliminated Part III and severely limited the penalties that federal judges might impose for criminal contempt in cases of civil rights violations.[60] Both moves restricted the impact of the legislation on the South and continued to leave southern whites with the capacity to define the citizenship rights of southern blacks. Ultimately, southerners emerged victorious in the congressional struggle over the expansion of federal authority. Senator Richard Russell (D-GA) deemed the evisceration of the bill to be "the sweetest victory in my twenty-five years as a Senator."[61]

Despite the weakening of the bill, the LCCR agreed to accept the measure as a small victory, arguing that it signaled an important shift in national civil rights policy. Not since Reconstruction had a civil rights measure passed in Congress. As the competition for the votes of northern blacks intensified and economic and political disruption costs mounted, the classic strategy of suppressing civil rights measures no longer appeared tenable. With the threat of black defections, civil rights proponents continued to press both parties, in particular the Democratic party, toward

---

[58] Sundquist (1968, 237). The LCCR, founded in 1950, emerged from the National Emergency Civil Rights Mobilization that lobbied in 1949 for fair employment legislation.

[59] Lawson (1991, 54).

[60] CQ (1968, 27–30). The compromise allowed for judges to decide criminal contempt cases so long as the penalty was not more than $300 and 45 days' imprisonment. If the penalty were greater, the defendant could have another trial by jury.

[61] Sundquist (1968, 237).

positive action. This time, the Democratic coalition had survived based on passing legislation that granted concessions to both sides. "Henceforth," Piven and Cloward observe, "the struggle would be over the substance of those concessions."[62]

This struggle resumed in 1959. As the next presidential election approached, the Republican administration submitted a more expansive legislative package including an anti-mob bill, an anti-bombing bill, and a bill to give the Justice Department the ability to inspect voting records.[63] Northern Democrats, including House Judiciary Committee Chairman Emanuel Celler (D-NY), and Republicans proposed even stronger legislation to enable the federal government to coerce school desegregation and give Part III authority to Justice. The LCCR, now a congregation of some 50 organizations, pushed for these measures as well.[64] A bloc of pivotal congressional moderates kept the bill from being entirely watered down by southerners or strengthened by northern liberals.

Of the two factions, the southerners were more successful in extracting provisions than civil rights proponents were in inserting strengthening amendments. In the House Judiciary Committee, southern members moved to eliminate two items: the creation of a permanent anti-discrimination Commission on Equal Job Opportunity Under Government Contracts, and a provision to provide technical assistance to desegregating schools. On the Senate floor, southerners filibustered against the Part III provisions of the 1960 civil rights bill, which would have given the attorney general authority to seek injunctions to protect civil rights. After the emergence of a moderate consensus, both chambers moved to pass the limited act. Ultimately, the legislation modestly reinforced black voting rights and included stronger penalties for interfering with federal court orders, making bomb threats, and detonating bombs. Southerners were again pleased that more severe measures had been resisted and Senator Harry Byrd (D-VA) declared, "In the main the result has been a victory for the South."[65] Although the new law gave the national government additional authority, "it represented a rather minimal federal intrusion

---

[62] Piven and Cloward (1977, 218–19).

[63] In addition, the bill extended the life of the Civil Rights Commission for another two years, and provisions to offer technical and financial assistance to localities faced with school desegregation. CQ (1968, 30–6). The administration's 1959 bill, however, did not contain Part III, perhaps due to Brownell's departure in late 1957 and the appointment of William Rogers as attorney general.

[64] Berman (1962, 10).

[65] Sundquist (1968, 249–50). See generally CQ (1968, 42–3).

into law enforcement in the southern states."[66] Also, in many ways, this bargaining process foreshadowed episodes to follow in which pivotal legislators with weak incentives to support tough legislation pursued a strategy of evincing concern over civil rights while supporting measures with weak enforcement provisions.

Back at the Justice Department, despite Brownell's support for civil rights legislation, the Eisenhower administration adopted a timid policy of detachment with respect to the desegregation process. Even after repeated pleas from local authorities in the Peripheral South for assistance, especially to combat racial violence, Justice asserted that law enforcement was primarily a state and local responsibility. As early as June 1955, the Justice Department had directed local U.S. attorneys "not to have integration disturbances investigated as possible violations of civil rights statutes."[67] In other areas, the Eisenhower administration was equally reserved. With regard to litigation of civil rights violations, the Justice Department pursued "a more conservative prosecution policy than the state of the law required."[68] The unwillingness of the federal government to punish those who abridged black civil rights invited the infringement of those rights and allowed southern racial violence to go virtually unchecked. In summing up the civil rights activities of the Eisenhower administration, Burk notes that "Eisenhower and his subordinates had displayed a consistent pattern of hesitancy and extreme political caution in defending black legal rights."[69] Even more bluntly, Garrow asserts:

From events large and small – particularly the administration's very grudging role in *Brown I* and its hesitant, tardy intervention in Little Rock – one could build a powerful argument that the administration's conduct gave important indirect assistance to the segregationist backlash that emerged as so powerful a political force across the South between 1955 and 1959.[70]

For Eisenhower, partisan competition for the electoral support of both southern whites and northern blacks encouraged him to support civil rights, but within limited confines. Political expedience encouraged vacillation and thus favored the enactment of symbolic legislation without great substance.

---

[66] Belknap (1987, 68).
[67] Ibid., 37.
[68] Ibid., 35.
[69] Burk (1984, 263).
[70] Garrow (1989, 363).

The next phase of civil rights contestation began on February 1, 1960, in Greensboro, North Carolina, when four black college freshmen sat down at a lunch counter reserved for whites. This action set in motion a wave of civil rights agitation that fundamentally challenged the traditions of the Old South. Sit-in demonstrations and heightened appreciation of the importance of the black vote in the North pushed civil rights into the forefront of the 1960 presidential elections. At their national conventions, both major parties adopted strong civil rights planks offering an array of legislative and executive measures to hasten school desegregation, enhance voting rights, and reduce employment discrimination. Although allied with liberal and labor organizations, Democratic party presidential nominee Senator John Kennedy (MA) did not have much prestige among civil rights groups. He appeared to be courting southern political leaders, and in the Senate he was an inconsistent supporter of civil rights legislation. Kennedy's selection of Lyndon B. Johnson as his vice-presidential running mate – a selection that stunned Kennedy's liberal supporters who believed that Hubert Humphrey had already been chosen – was meant to solidify southern electoral support. Nevertheless, during the campaign, Kennedy sought to broaden his electoral appeal among African-Americans through meetings with civil rights leaders. Martin describes a meeting with the Kennedy campaign staff: "Eisenhower had made some inroads into the Negro vote in the election before, and it was a tight contest. It was felt that every vote was precious, and the minority vote, the black vote, was terribly important to them."[71] Vice President Nixon, in contrast, already had some measure of popularity. As a senator, he had supported civil rights and, as Vice President, had chaired the commission devoted to eliminating discrimination in the federal workforce and among government contractors, and had endorsed civil rights legislation. In fact, both Nixon and Kennedy carefully calibrated their appeals to straddle the racial division between southern whites and northern blacks.

The critical shift in Kennedy's favor took place after Georgia authorities arrested Martin Luther King, Jr., for driving with an out-of-state license. Whereas Nixon dodged the matter after weighing "the potential electoral gains and losses of intervening," Kennedy placed a call to King's wife, Coretta Scott King, to console her, and Robert Kennedy placed another call to the Georgia authorities seeking King's release.[72] Both of

[71] Martin (1969, 4).
[72] Piven and Cloward (1977, 225).

these calls provided Kennedy with the leverage he needed. After being released, King made a public statement thanking Kennedy for his intervention, and the Kennedy campaign made wide use of this statement to reinforce support among African-American voters. Martin Luther King, Sr., announced, "It's time for all of us to take off our Nixon button."[73] With blacks voting overwhelmingly Democratic, Kennedy went on to win the election by a razor-thin margin.

As civil rights agitation escalated, so too rose the incidence of anti–civil rights contention. Following the same precepts as their predecessor, the Kennedy administration vacillated, insisting that the authority to punish the perpetrators of racial violence lay with state and local authorities. Federalism, administration officials asserted, did not give the central state a role in the matters of local law enforcement. Accordingly, prosecution of cases of anti–civil rights violence "increased only slightly from what it had been during Eisenhower's presidency."[74] Yet despite the weaknesses of USC Sections 241 and 242, other sources of federal jurisdiction were tenable. Additional Reconstruction-era statutes (10 USC Sections 332 and 333) gave the president substantial authority to use the armed forces in cases of local lawlessness.[75] In a telling memorandum, Nicholas Katzenbach, the deputy attorney general and attorney general under Presidents Kennedy and Johnson, respectively, observed in 1964 that, based

---

[73] Williams (1988, 143).

[74] Belknap (1987, 76).

[75] 10 USC 332. "Whenever the President considers that unlawful obstructions, combinations, or assemblages, or rebellion against the authority of the United States, make it impracticable to enforce the laws of the United States in any State or Territory by the ordinary course of judicial proceedings, he may call into Federal service such of the militia of any State, and use such of the armed forces, as he considers necessary to enforce those laws or to suppress the rebellion."

10 USC 333. "The President, by using the militia or the armed forces, or both, or by any other means, shall take such measures as he considers necessary to suppress, in a State, any insurrection, domestic violence, unlawful combination, or conspiracy, if it –

(1) so hinders the execution of the laws of the State, and of the United States within the State, that any part or class of its people is deprived of a right, privilege, immunity, or protection named in the Constitution and secured by law, and the constituted authorities of that State are unable, fail, or refuse to protect right, privilege, or immunity, or to give that protection; or
(2) opposes or obstructs the execution of the laws of the United States or impedes the course of justice under those laws.

In any situation covered by clause (1), the State shall be considered to have denied the equal protection of the laws secured by the Constitution."

on "the complete breakdown of State law enforcement as a result of Klan activity and Klan connections with local sheriffs and deputies . . . the President could, as a legal matter, invoke the authority of sections 332 and 333." He concluded that "it is a mistake to base our position on a lack of legal authority" and that the obstacles to federal intervention were "more practical than legal."[76] Of course, to civil rights activists, trusting state and local authorities was no solution at all, because southern authorities often perpetrated or supported repression of the movement.[77] To these activists, the suggestion that they must rely upon state and local law enforcement must have provided cold comfort.

At first glance, the strict adherence to federalism during the Kennedy administration is perhaps more surprising than under Eisenhower. After narrowly boosting Kennedy to victory, African-American civil rights leaders expected action. Nonetheless, political considerations compelled Kennedy to reconsider his promises. Almost one-third of Kennedy's electoral college votes came from southern states and he did not wish to risk losing this critical base of support.[78] More important, in Congress, senior southern members continued to chair the most powerful committees, and the passage of Kennedy's legislative agenda depended upon their support.[79] Even before Kennedy assumed office, Roy Wilkins, the executive secretary of the NAACP, was notified that the new president would not immediately seek civil rights legislation, but he would pursue other means, particularly executive orders, to advance racial equality.[80] However, after taking office, Kennedy delayed on the implementation of his campaign promise to do away with discrimination in federally assisted housing by "a stroke of the presidential pen" until late November 1962,

---

[76] Memorandum from Katzenbach to Lee White, special assistant to the president, and "Memorandum for the President" (July 1, 1964), Johnson Presidential Library, White House Central Files, Box 26, File Jan. 1, 64, July 16, 64. Similarly, a 1964 Southern Regional Council report concluded that "the question of federal police intervention in Mississippi . . . [is] not one of power to act, but of policy." Quoted in Watters and Cleghorn (1967, 230) (italics omitted). Burke Marshall, the head of the Civil Rights Division, added that the federal government did not have a national police force and therefore, as a practical matter, the central state lacked the capacity to protect civil rights advocates.

[77] Luders (2003).

[78] This tally (81 of 303 electoral college votes) does not include West Virginia or Maryland. Tabulated from CQ (1987). For a discussion of the political concerns shaping the Kennedy and Johnson administration's civil rights policy, see Stern (1987, 49–76).

[79] Stern (1992, 40).

[80] Ibid., 42; see also Schlesinger, Jr.(1965, Chapters 35 and 36).

after the midterm election.[81] His advisors reportedly considered "the weight of the Negro vote in the North as against the possible dissident White vote in the South if he should sign a strong order."[82] Thus, even as civil rights agitation intensified and greater public attention threatened to disrupt political alliances among nonsouthern voters, the composition of the Democratic political order meant that the electoral concession costs for responding to the movement's principal demands appeared dangerously high. This vulnerability to both high disruption and concession costs kept the Kennedy administration on a cautious course of symbolic affirmations of support and strategic equivocation on substantive policy initiatives.

Practical considerations were present as well. As Burke Marshall, the head of the Civil Rights Division, had observed, the paucity and relative inexperience of federal marshals in these matters meant that they were ill-equipped to perform the task of providing protection to civil rights workers. In addition, key Justice Department officials argued that the commitment of federal marshals or the use of the military might inflame southerners and thus make matters more volatile and dangerous. Hostility among southern whites to federal intervention, it was feared, might in fact intensify local animosity toward civil rights workers. From the perspective of the Justice Department, successful law enforcement depended upon the support of the state and local police. If federal forces were deployed, state and local law enforcement might completely abdicate their responsibilities. Irrespective of jurisdiction, these considerations further discouraged central state intervention.

The fear of undermining southern Democratic support and uncertainties about the effects of federal intervention meant that, at all costs, confrontations like Little Rock were to be avoided even if this involved sacrificing black civil rights in the process. Instead of taking strong measures to halt public or private violations of national citizenship rights, the Kennedy administration sought to broker settlements between movement activists and southern authorities. "Caught between rising black electoral strength and entrenched southern white political power, President

---

[81] *Time* (November 30, 1962) reports that Kennedy believed that "the promised executive order might hurt Democrats in the South more than it would help Democrats in the North." On the timing of issuing the order, see also *New York Times*, November 20, 1962.

[82] Roy Wilkins Oral History Interview (1969, 6).

Kennedy treaded circumspectly in the field of civil rights."[83] Character-istic of the vacillation of the early years of the Kennedy administration, officials engaged in what Belknap (1987) describes as a policy of "crisis management" in which the federal government refused to become active participants in the protection of the constitutional rights of southern African-Americans until it was absolutely necessary to maintain public order.

As movement activities escalated, this approach became increasingly untenable. The initiation of the Freedom Rides in the spring of 1961 compelled President Kennedy to make critical tactical decisions about the South. In response to the 1960 Supreme Court ruling in *Boynton v. Virginia*,[84] which banned segregation in terminals for interstate carriers, the Congress of Racial Equality (CORE) organized a set of trips to south-ern bus terminals to test the decree. At the outset, Justice argued that the protection of the riders had to be entrusted to state and local authorities. Over the course of the rides, this position was sorely tested.

Trouble started in Rock Hill, South Carolina, where whites roughed up two riders. There, local police quickly arrested the attackers and, thus far, trust in local law enforcement appeared justified. However, after passing peacefully through Georgia, riders met with brutal white violence in Anniston, Alabama. In the town, a crowd of 100 to 150 whites mobbed the bus with clubs, breaking the windows and slashing the tires, as local police refused to intervene. Outside of town, after the bus stopped to repair a flat tire, a member of the crowd threw a firebomb in the rear entrance of the bus. As the riders fled the burning bus, they were beaten with chains and baseball bats. The presence of FBI agents and their inaction in Anniston during these attacks underscored federal deference to state law enforcement.

The arrival of the riders in Birmingham, Alabama, was even more contentious. Local police conspired with the Ku Klux Klan to permit a white mob to have an uninterrupted fifteen minutes in which to assault the riders. Again, federal acquiescence to the brutality was evident. Despite advance notification of the planned violence in Birmingham from an informant, the FBI took no steps to prevent bloodshed. In fact, the Bureau did not even notify Robert Kennedy, the attorney general. And, even

---

[83] Lawson (1991, 76–7). Kennedy also appears to have waited until Congress was ad-journed to deter southern members from immediately organizing against the measure.
[84] 364 U.S. 454 (1960).

though the informant also told the FBI of the ties between the Birmingham police and the Klan, the FBI passed on the Freedom Riders' schedule to local law enforcement.[85] Throughout this episode, Alabama state officials assured the Kennedy administration that state law enforcement forces could handle the situation and that federal intervention was unnecessary unless the state should call for such assistance.

Robert Kennedy and eventually the president desperately sought assurances from Alabama Governor Patterson that the riders would be protected. In the same meeting that Patterson personally assured Justice Department aide John Seigenthaler that the state of Alabama protected all visitors, the governor declared:

I'm going to tell you something. The people of this country are so goddamned tired of the mamby-pamby [sic] that's in Washington, it's a disgrace. There's nobody in the whole country that's got the spine to stand up to the goddamned niggers except me. And I'll tell you I've got more mail in the drawers of that desk over there congratulating me on the stand I've taken against Martin Luther King and these rabble rousers. I'll tell you I believe I'm more popular in this country than John Kennedy is.[86]

After the meeting, Floyd Mann, the head of the Alabama Highway Patrol, pulled Seigenthaler aside to offer additional assurances of the riders' safety on state highways.

At the city limits of Montgomery, matters changed. Despite assurances to the FBI that no violence would be allowed, local law enforcement allowed a crowd of a thousand whites to ambush the bus at the station. A major clash ensued that continued until Mann moved in and brought the violence to a halt. During the onslaught, several were badly injured, including Seigenthaler. Finally, after a call from Mann, Governor Patterson declared martial law in Montgomery. Outraged at this apparent violation of the agreement to maintain order, the president authorized the attorney general to send in several hundred federal marshals. During that evening at a rally to support the Freedom Riders at the First Baptist Church, a white crowd formed outside. The federal marshals, who had

[85] On this incident, see Belknap (1987, 80); Stern (1992, 58). Throughout the period, the Federal Bureau of Investigation, headed by J. Edgar Hoover, had no enthusiasm for preventing racial violence or protecting civil rights activists. Quite the contrary, Hoover directed agents to infiltrate and investigate the "subversive elements" within the civil rights movement. Hoover aggressively used Bureau resources to investigate and attempt to discredit Martin Luther King, Jr. These actions are detailed in Garrow (1981) and O'Reilly (1989).

[86] Quoted in Williams (1988, 152).

surrounded the church, clashed with the mob. Following a conversation with Kennedy, the governor again declared martial law to break up the crowd of whites and escort the blacks inside the church to safety. With the conclusion of this incident, Robert Kennedy called for a cooling off period, a temporary discontinuation of the rides. The riders declined and continued to Mississippi.

After the incidents in Alabama, Robert Kennedy surrendered principle for expedience. While he had been committed to the rights of citizens to ride unhindered on interstate carriers, Kennedy accepted the offer from segregationist Senator James Eastland (D-MS) to protect the riders from mob violence on the condition that Kennedy acquiesce to their mass arrest in Jackson for violating state segregation laws. Forced to choose between protecting the constitutional rights of African-Americans and maintaining local law and order, Kennedy opted for the latter. While the civil rights movement fed upon massive disruptions covered on television and across newspaper headlines, the administration desperately sought to limit contention and federal intervention to mollify southern Democrats. As the Freedom Rides and arrests in Jackson continued, the Kennedy administration requested that the Interstate Commerce Commission issue regulations concerning interstate bus terminals in light of the 1960 Supreme Court ruling, which were subsequently produced the following September.

In the aftermath of the Freedom Rides, Kennedy officials also attempted to reduce their exposure to disruption costs by steering the movement into institutional channels deemed less likely to provoke the violence that necessitated federal action. Echoing Eisenhower's position on civil rights, they often suggested that change in the South had to emerge from state and local sources, not from coercive national action.[87] It was argued that, with ballot in hand, southern blacks would be able to obtain the remainder of their civil rights. The Justice Department stepped up the number of prosecutions of voting rights violations. The administration sought to move civil rights activities toward voter registration by helping to organize the Voter Education Project (VEP), a privately funded effort to promote black political participation (as described in Chapter 5).[88] With

---

[87] The Justice Department thus relied upon attempts to "persuade" state and local authorities to remove discrimination voluntarily prior to the use of legal action. Wolk (1970, 81–3). This theme persisted in the Johnson administration as well. See Katzenbach (1964).

[88] Stern (1992, 64). On the Voter Education Project, see Watters and Cleghorn (1967, 44–74).

the goal of voter registration, it was hoped that movement activities might shift away from confrontation and toward institutional action. "Kennedy decided to try to redirect the movement and deflect it from getting involved in violent confrontations requiring the administration's intervention."[89] Civil rights organizations divided over how to respond to these overtures. The more cautious NAACP agreed that voter registration made sense even as others argued that direct action tactics remained essential. Contrary to the administration's hopes, the VEP did not contain the movement but instead actually worsened the relationship between the activists and the Kennedy administration. After encouraging a registration campaign and stepping up the prosecutions of voting rights cases, registration workers were shocked to learn that federal authorities refused to offer them protection.[90]

Hemmed in between civil rights supporters and southern opponents, the administration attempted to reconcile the competing demands of both sides of the divide. For civil rights leaders, in addition to the VEP, Kennedy issued executive orders to strengthen provisions to eliminate discrimination in the federal government and with private employers operating under federal contracts.[91] For Dixie, Kennedy nominated southern judges to the federal bench who were outspoken in their opposition to both *Brown* and civil rights. For instance, Judge William Howard Cox – a notorious racist and close friend of Mississippi Senator Eastland – was elevated to the federal District Court. Averse to using federal marshals or the troops, the Kennedy administration sought to resolve disputes through intense negotiation and bargaining with southern authorities. With the onset of protests, Justice Department officials typically set up lines of communication with the governor and law enforcement officials to ensure the maintenance of law and order. This strategy risked playing into the hands of state authorities. Typically, the governor assured representatives of the Justice Department that federal forces were unwanted and unnecessary, which, in turn, allowed local authorities to determine the level of local intransigence toward civil rights activists. Unsurprisingly, this strategic vacillation displeased the civil rights community and southern officials alike.

The dangers of the "conflict management" approach surfaced during the next major crisis the following year at the University of Mississippi.[92]

---

[89] Williams (1988, 160).
[90] Stern (1992, 69).
[91] Piven and Cloward (1977, 228).
[92] The term comes from Belknap (1987).

In 1962, under a federal court order, the University of Mississippi in Oxford was directed to admit James Meredith, a black Air Force veteran. Kennedy administration officials sought assurances from Governor Barnett that law and order would be maintained. He gave them, but then his lieutenant governor personally blocked Meredith's entry to the university, and he excoriated the federal government in speeches for its actions. While the Kennedy administration continued to seek a quiet settlement, Barnett's harsh segregationist rhetoric worsened an already combustible situation. At length, Kennedy sent Meredith to the university with three hundred federal marshals in riot gear. After federal authorities brought Meredith onto the campus to register, a riot erupted, and although Barnett assured Robert Kennedy of the availability of the state troopers to "give every assistance," confusion at the scene caused the troopers to withdraw. Absent the buffer, the crowd assailed the marshals with bricks, bottles, and even with gunfire. Conditions deteriorated after nightfall. Following the withdrawal of the troopers and repeated calls for reinforcements, Kennedy sent in the Army. In the morning, after the tear gas had cleared, 150 marshals had been injured, including 28 who had been shot, and two civilians, a bystander and a French reporter, had been killed in the melee.[93]

As with Eisenhower in Little Rock, in cases openly challenging national authority, President Kennedy resorted to force. Faced with a combination of state opposition to *federal* court orders and a massive breakdown of law and order, the chief executive federalized the Mississippi National Guard and called in the Army. However, in the absence of a clear challenge to federal authority, national government forces were unavailable to protect the citizenship rights of African-Americans during the hundreds of demonstrations and protests elsewhere in the South. Again, the desire to demonstrate national supremacy, not an abiding concern in the cause of civil rights, precipitated federal intervention. Contradictory electoral imperatives impelled successive presidential administrations in this period to vacillate between support for the expansion of African-American civil rights and deference to southern racial hierarchies.

The Politics of Accommodation

On February 28, 1963, after two years of hesitation and delay, Kennedy gave a forceful address on civil rights in which he unveiled a fairly

---

[93] Despite social ostracism, Meredith continued at Ole Miss until graduating the following year.

unambitious set of legislative proposals to facilitate public school deseg-regation and voting rights lawsuits. While some civil rights proponents celebrated the rhetoric in favor of equality, the speech failed to touch upon either public accommodations or employment discrimination.[94] As spring approached, representatives and senators looking forward to tough reelection fights began submitting far stronger civil rights measures. It was in this setting that the next major test of the administration's willingness to intervene in southern race relations took place during April and May of 1963 in Birmingham, Alabama.

After the movement's failure in Albany, Georgia, Southern Christian Leadership Conference (SCLC) leaders selected Birmingham for massive protests in the downtown business center to provoke the violent Com-missioner of Public Safety, T. Eugene "Bull" Connor. Project C – for con-frontation – did not disappoint. Although initially Connor arrested protesters without undue violence, he soon turned police dogs and fire hoses on demonstrating youths. As described in Chapter 4, images of snarling dogs and hapless demonstrators blasted by fire hoses against a brick wall shocked whites around the country and, it was feared, stoked racial animosities nationwide. As elsewhere, the Kennedy administration sought a negotiated settlement and, despite the many calls for federal intervention, government action was limited mainly to FBI involvement in the investigation of local bombings. Eventually, amid intense protests, a committee of vulnerable business interests consented to desegregate lunch counters and agreed to hire a few black employees. This settlement, which was made public on May 10, infuriated members of the local Ku Klux Klan and, the next evening at a rally outside the city, the Grand Dragon of the KKK vowed to fight the new accord. Later that night, bombs exploded at the home of King's brother and at the motel where King was staying.[95] In reaction, blacks rioted. State troopers and Connor's police brutally quelled the riot. When order was restored, seven stores had been set on fire and 35 blacks and five whites had suffered injuries.[96] These incidents of white violence and racial contention propelled civil rights to the top of public opinion polls as the nation's "most important problem."

Although the fear of antagonizing southern Democrats had discour-aged Kennedy from taking decision action, it was becoming increasingly clear that timidity and vacillation were no longer acceptable options.

---

[94] Graham (1990, 70).
[95] Williams (1988, 193–4).
[96] Belknap (1987, 100–1).

Heightened public support and attention demanded action. Further, administration officials feared that protests were reaching dangerous, crisis proportions. In a discussion with Kennedy on May 12 about the ongoing trouble in Birmingham, Attorney General Robert Kennedy described his concerns:

You're going to have these kind of incidents: the Governor has virtually taken over the city. You're going to have his people around sticking bayonets in people, and hitting people with clubs and guns, et cetera, you're going to have rallies all over the country calling upon the President to take some forceful action, and why aren't you protecting the rights of the people in Birmingham? And we feel that based on the success that they had in Birmingham, and the feeling of Negroes generally, and reports that we get from other cities (not just in the South), but that this could trigger off a good deal of violence around the country now.[97]

Burke Marshall, the deputy attorney general, recollected: "The country was in turmoil . . . absolute turmoil because of Birmingham; it was repeating itself all over the place and everybody was on President Kennedy's neck – black people, white people, everybody was on his neck."[98] During this time, administration officials came to appreciate that inaction promised to unleash further violence and that more decisive action was imperative.[99]

Demands for a response quickened when, on June 11, Governor Wallace fulfilled his campaign promise to "stand in a schoolhouse door" by blocking the integration of the University of Alabama. This time, Kennedy quickly federalized the National Guard and integration proceeded without incident. Against a backdrop of escalating civil rights demonstrations, this latest episode of intransigence provided Kennedy with an occasion to address the nation that evening and affirm his commitment to civil rights legislation. After pointing to the moral rightness of the demands for equal rights and equal opportunities, he acknowledged that,

The events in Birmingham and elsewhere have so increased the cries for equality that no city or state or legislative body can prudently choose to ignore them. The fires of frustration and discord are burning in every city, North and South, where legal remedies are not at hand. Redress is sought in the streets, in demonstrations, parades, and protests which create tensions and threaten violence and threaten lives. (Kennedy, 1963)

[97] May 12, 1963, in Rosenberg and Karabell (2003, 98).
[98] Graham (1990, 70).
[99] Ibid., 74; Brauer (1977, 261) states that, "A principal reason for taking immediate steps to secure Negroes their rights was the threat of violence which accompanied street demonstrations."

This time, Kennedy spoke directly about the need for legislation concerning public accommodations, though again there was no mention of discrimination in employment.[100] Hours after Kennedy's speech, a white extremist gunned down Medgar Evers, the field secretary of the NAACP in Mississippi, in his driveway.

After repeated attempts to suppress fractures in the Democratic coalition, public support, rising attentiveness, and a growing fear of racial conflagration finally compelled Kennedy to advocate for a more substantial legislative response. Yet even as Kennedy signaled his support for civil rights, the administration maintained a detached attitude toward the disruptive actions of the civil rights movement. In fact, in order to facilitate passage of the legislation, in June, Deputy Attorney General Nicholas Katzenbach advised Robert Kennedy that "Burke Marshall should keep in close touch with Negro groups in an effort to channel and control their activities."[101]

The administration's legislative package included provisions to assure blacks access to public accommodations, empower the Justice Department to file suit to desegregate schools, enable the federal government to cut off funding to governmental units practicing discrimination, strengthen anti-discrimination enforcement among federal contractors, and create a Community Relations Service to foster peaceful desegregation.[102] All of these provisions were a significant step forward. However, despite much administration hand wringing over the lack of federal jurisdiction in cases of anti–civil rights violence, this legislation still lacked measures that might enable the federal government to protect citizens in the free exercise of their citizenship rights. In addition to widespread protests over the ensuing months, the civil rights movement conducted a massive March on Washington on August 28, during which an estimated 250,000 civil rights supporters, including labor and church organizations, thronged the grounds before the Lincoln Memorial. The nonviolent march for "Jobs and Freedom" culminated in King's soaring "I Have a Dream" speech. Violence in the South, however, continued

---

[100] Some have argued that Cold War competition with the Soviet Union provided an important impetus to the civil rights movement. See Dudziak (2000); Klinkner and Smith (1999). While concerns of this sort no doubt elevated administration interest in civil rights, this explanation is unsatisfactory in accounting for the timing and scope of proposed civil rights measures.

[101] Memorandum (June 29, 1963), Kennedy Presidential Library, Papers of Robert F. Kennedy, File "Civil Rights."

[102] CQ (1968, 39).

unabated. On September 16, 1963, the explosion of a massive bomb at the Sixteenth Street Baptist Church killed four African-American girls as they prepared in the basement for Sunday school. Notorious incidents such as these sustained national outrage and stimulated support for the enactment of civil rights legislation. Indeed, by October 1963, a Harris poll estimated that Kennedy's positions supporting civil rights had likely produced a net gain of 6.5 million votes over his total in the 1960 election.[103]

The assassination of John F. Kennedy on November 22, 1963, which catapulted Lyndon B. Johnson into the Oval Office, raised serious questions about the direction of the new administration's civil rights policies. Johnson quickly dispelled these doubts in his first address before Congress on November 27, during which he made the passage of Kennedy's civil rights legislation a top priority. "No memorial oration or eulogy could more eloquently honor President Kennedy's memory than the earliest possible passage of the civil rights bill for which he fought so long."[104] From the outset, Johnson wanted action. He was eager to build his support among liberal Democrats, and this response was critical. Without their support, LBJ anticipated an intra-party challenge from the left in the upcoming 1964 presidential campaign and believed embracing a civil rights law was imperative. "I knew that if I didn't get out in front on this issue [the liberals] would get me . . . I had to produce a civil rights bill that was even stronger than the one they'd have gotten if Kennedy had lived."[105] To circumvent this threat and to respond to mounting public support for the movement's demands, Johnson threw his backing behind strong civil rights legislation.[106]

The Civil Rights Act of 1964

An explanation for the passage of the Civil Rights Act, as with explanations of the outcomes of political movements more generally, depends upon the identification of the interests of targets and third parties, and

---

[103] Frymer (1999, 98). This poll found that 63 percent of white respondents nationwide favored the Kennedy civil rights bill, including 31 percent of white southerners. See Brink and Harris (1963, 142).

[104] CQ (1968, 41); Stern (1992).

[105] Dallek (1998, 114). As Dallek reports, this decision appeared justified by an April poll that revealed 57 percent of respondents approved of Johnson's handling of civil rights and only 21 disapproved.

[106] For an assessment of the competing explanations for the passage of the Civil Rights Act of 1964, see Plotke Chapter 2 (in press).

the further specification of their exposure to disruption and concession costs. Although Congress is sometimes treated as a unitary entity,
members of Congress possess different degrees of electoral vulnerability
depending upon various factors, including the characteristics of their constituents. For northern Democrats and Republicans representing more
diverse, urban constituencies, the disruption costs for inaction on civil
rights were high as multiple organizations might threaten them with
reprisals. At the same time, widespread public support for the expansion
of civil rights meant that the concession costs were negligible and indeed
many of these states had already passed fair employment laws. Nearly
all southern Democrats confronted the opposite incentives: a trivial electoral threat from African-Americans and the opposition of segregationist
constituents. Since northern Democrats lacked the necessary two-thirds
majority (67 votes) to overcome the inevitable southern filibuster in the
Senate, the crucial role of undecided Republicans in the passage of civil
rights legislation was plain to all. At the center of the bargaining process
was the Republican Minority Leader, Senator Everett Dirksen of Illinois.
At his behest, a host of conservative Midwestern and Mountain State
Republicans might be counted on to vote for cloture to end the Senate
debate and support the measure. Lyndon Johnson and others fully appreciated Dirksen's pivotal position for enactment and spared no efforts to
cultivate his support. As Johnson explained to Wilkins of the NAACP,
"You're going have to persuade Dirksen why this is in the interest of the
Republican party.... And let him know that you're going to go for the
presidential candidate that offers you the best hope and best chance of
dignity and decency in this country. And you're going with a senatorial
man who does the same thing."[107] Thus, an explanation for the successful
enactment of the Civil Rights Act entails not only accounting for ardent
supporters, but also the winning of the votes of pivotal legislators.[108]

The convergence of multiple factors amplified the disruption costs for
national political actors. Clearly, rising public support for equal rights
strengthened the hand of the movement. According to public opinion
polls, large majorities backed the principle of equal rights. By December
1963, 75 percent of northern whites supported public school integration
and 88 percent approved of desegregated public transportation.[109] By

---

[107] Beschloss (1997, 148); also, Kotz (2005).
[108] I borrow the terminology of ardent supporters, opponents, and pivotal legislators from
Rodriguez and Weingast (2003).
[109] Hyman and Sheatsley (1964, 18–19).

1964, over 80 percent of whites favored equal employment opportunities for African-Americans.[110] Attitudes toward government action to ban segregation in public accommodations were strongly supportive, such that by February 1964, a Harris poll "showed 68 percent favoring the House-passed bill."[111] Indeed, this represented a significant increase from only 49 percent support in June 1963. Although the precise cause for this change in public opinion can be debated, the interactions between peaceful civil rights demonstrators and violent southern whites likely encouraged this dynamic.[112]

In addition to favorable public opinion, mass attentiveness had risen sharply. Mounting racial tumult, in particular, images of segregationist brutality splashed across newspapers and shown on the nightly news, added to issue salience. As President Kennedy reportedly told King in 1963, "Our judgment of Bull Connor should not be too harsh. After all, in his own way he has done a good deal for civil rights legislation this year."[113] Multiple studies demonstrate a relationship between segregationist violence, issue salience, and federal responsiveness.[114] Nor were protests confined to Birmingham; they had spread across the South and to northern cities as well. Gallup polls on "the most important problem facing the country" indicate that the Civil Rights Act of 1964 and the Voting Rights Act of 1965 were both enacted during moments of peak attentiveness. Following the events in Birmingham and elsewhere in 1963, nearly half of the respondents identified civil rights as the "most important problem."[115] After receding only slightly in 1964, the figure surpassed 50 percent in early 1965. To a lesser extent, greater attentiveness is evident as well in 1957 and 1968, during which other civil rights measures were enacted.

Along with greater national concern over civil rights, the submission of substantive civil rights legislation precipitated an unprecedented mobilization of a coalition combining civil rights advocates, organized labor, and churches.[116] Many of these organizations, nearly 80 in all by 1964 (as

---

[110] Burstein (1979, 162). Affirmations in favor of the vague principle of equal rights, however, often lagged far behind the willingness to advocate government intervention to change matters. On these complexities, see Schuman, Steeh, and Bobo (1985).

[111] Burstein (1985, 58); the Harris poll is cited in Whalen and Whalen (1985, 155).

[112] Lee (2002).

[113] Quoted in McAdam (1982, 174).

[114] McAdam (1982); Garrow (1978); Burstein (1979); Santoro (2002).

[115] McAdam (1982, 160).

[116] A broad range of organizations joined in support of the Civil Rights Act under the rubric of the Leadership Conference on Civil Rights (an aggregation of civic, labor,

opposed to approximately 50 in 1959), united under of the auspices of the LCCR.[117] For legislators, the support for the Civil Rights Act from civil rights organizations and, to a lesser extent, labor, was assumed; however, the actuation of the churches and their congregations held great import because it signaled the mobilization of activist moderates. As Lohmann (1993) argues, legislators need to know the majority preferences of their constituents and the behavior of activist moderates signals this valuable information. "The major new factor," averred a legislative strategist for the LCCR, "is the church participation." The National Council of Churches (NCC) had reportedly dedicated $400,000 to support enactment of the bill and, more importantly, the NCC elected to devote particular attention to Republicans from key Midwestern states.[118] Although civil rights advocates in these largely rural districts lacked political leverage, it was believed that church people and their moral arguments "might be especially effective."[119] Along with the NCC, the U.S. Catholic Conference and several Jewish organizations met regularly with their senators during the debate. Using data from the *New York Times* for the period from 1941 to 1972, Burstein (1985) documents a peak in meetings with pro-rights delegations in Washington, D.C., in 1963 and 1964. Across this period spanning more than three decades, more delegations came to speak on behalf of the equal employment legislation in those two years than at any other time. During this time as well, an interfaith mixture of seminary students conducted an around-the-clock vigil at the Lincoln Memorial that continued until the passage of the bill.

Many sources single out the mobilization of religious bodies and adherents as decisive. Whalen and Whalen observe, "The persistent flow of mail and personal visits from religious groups created pressures on central and western state senators that they had never felt before. And nothing is more difficult for a legislator to resist than a holy crusade led by clergy of all

and religious organizations). These included the NAACP, the American Civil Liberties Union (ACLU), Americans for Democratic Action (ADA), AFL-CIO unions, and the National Council of Churches; see Lytle (1966, 287).

[117] Lytle (1966, 287). As noted above, the NAACP's membership peaked in 1963 at slightly over 534,000. On the breadth and strength of NAACP ties to individuals and other organizations that might have facilitated the NAACP's lobbying efforts, see Aveni (1978).

[118] Findlay (1990, 74).

[119] Ibid. Branch (1998, 220) relates how the participation of Midwestern clergy in a Hattiesburg, Mississippi, voter registration campaign provided them with vivid experiences that they shared with their congregations and others. "There was no better catalyst for dormant church influence," Branch writes, "than the astonished personal accounts of Mississippi, delivered by respected ministers to colleagues, congregations, and members of Congress back home in Iowa or Minnesota."

faiths and made up of a large body of articulate followers."[120] Analyzing a sample of constituent mail to three legislators, Findlay (1990) estimates that church people (based on letterhead or text) sent from 37 to 44 percent of the total volume. Sundquist, in his extensive legislative history, observed:

> The churches supplied a civil rights constituency, for the first time, to senators from the Rocky Mountain and Great Plains states where Negroes are few and civil rights sentiments had in the past been weak – and whose senators had traditionally voted against cloture motions. And despite the "white backlash" that was apparent in some primaries, there was no organized opposition to the bill in the North to offset the church influence.[121]

As Roy Wilkins exulted with the president in the successful enactment of the bill, he declared: "It was absolutely magnificent and of course Russell put his finger on two things. First he said it was Lyndon Johnson. And second, he said it was the clergy. He hasn't been wrong – much."[122] In short, the cost of widespread constituent disaffection threatened not only ardent civil rights supporters in northern urban districts, it had implications for moderate and conservative Republicans.

Dirksen, as the minority leader, no doubt appreciated the risks of having the Republican party appear to be blocking the passage of civil rights legislation. With public support and attentiveness rising, outright Republican opposition to civil rights placed Republican presidential and congressional candidates at risk.[123] "Dirksen, like every other Congressman," his biographer observed, "had been closely watching the rising racial discord. Like them, he tried to fathom the political implications involved and how best to act in the growing crisis. He sensed national sympathy for the Negro demonstrators and the feeling that something must be done."[124] Should Republicans from urban states oppose the bill, they might lose not only black votes, but also those of white independents and moderates. A different and more delicate political balancing

---

[120] 1985, 233; on the importance of church mobilization, see also Loevy (1990, 202).

[121] Sundquist (1968, 268).

[122] Beschloss (1997, 421). Similarly, Senator Hubert Humphrey (D-MN) explained to the bill's chief civil rights lobbyists, "The secret of passing the bill is the prayer groups." Whalen and Whalen (1985, 164, 165).

[123] Whalen and Whalen (1985, 156). Graham similarly declared that Republicans were "sitting on a volcano" (1990, 143–4); MacNeil (1970, 270).

[124] MacNeil (1970, 218). Dirksen worried too that the "no" votes on cloture and final passage by Barry Goldwater, the likely Republican candidate for president, would make the Arizona senator appear to be a racist and doom his party's chances to win the White House (239–40).

act applied to the more conservative Republicans. In rural states, supportive churchgoers might be sufficiently attentive and threatening to encourage a vote for cloture and the bill.[125]

An interest in reducing their exposure to disruption costs is insufficient to provoke action if doing so exposes a legislator to even greater concession costs. Foremost among the calculation of concession costs for office-seekers are anticipated electoral responses of voters within their reelection coalition. Moderate and conservative Republicans might anticipate electoral retribution from citizens disgruntled with the intrusion of the federal government into their private affairs and conservative business interests opposed to expanding the national state's regulatory reach. The opponents of the civil rights bill sought to accentuate those concerns, particularly among the constituents of pivotal senators. Organized countermobilization, however, was weak. The Coordinating Committee for Fundamental American Freedoms (CCFAF), the only organization that lobbied heavily against the Civil Rights Act, lacked a grassroots base and appeared to be largely a construct of the Mississippi State Sovereign Commission (MSSC), on which it was almost entirely dependent for funds.[126] The chief function of the organization was a massive direct mail operation targeted at residents of key states (in business and various professions) and the publication of newspaper advertisements to foster hostile public sentiment toward the bill and stimulate letters from concerned citizens.[127]

Perhaps the most striking aspect of this countermobilization is how weak it was and ineffective it seemed to be.[128] In addition, despite fervent attempts by CCFAF to enlist the support of conservative business organizations in opposition, they declined to speak out against the bill. The National Association of Manufacturers (NAM) remained "formally

---

[125] Rodriquez and Weingast (2003) speculate Dirksen and others may have seen political benefits in hastening the breakup of the Democratic party in the South. Certainly, if a backlash resulted from the legislation, Republicans could expect to reap the political rewards.

[126] From July 1963 to February 1964, the CCFAF spent slightly over $257,000 of which $250,000 came from the Sovereignty Commission. It was claimed that the funds from the Sovereignty Commission were donated by private citizens and business interests, and that only $10,000 came directly from state coffers. See Lytle (1966), 290); also Robert Baker, "Rights for Sale," *Washington Post*, April 19, 1964. A cursory survey of Sovereignty Commission records indicates that a large share of the contributions came from Mississippi business interests and black belt whites.

[127] Strategic memoranda of the CCFAF can be found online within the archives of the Mississippi State Sovereignty Commission. See, for example, SCR ID # 6–70–0–2–8–1-1.

[128] Lytle (1966, 291).

neutral" to the bill and the Chamber of Commerce supplied the House Subcommittee on Labor a letter opposing the measure, but failed to lobby against it.[129] "Significantly missing from the list of active opponents," declared *Congressional Quarterly*, "were the major business groups."[130] Had business organizations opposed the bill, conservative Republicans might have "shied off of key titles or even refused" to support the measure. It is thus difficult to overstate the significance of this nonevent. Without business countermobilization against the bill, targeted legislators likely anticipated that their concession costs were insignificant.[131] The absence of these interests from the debate signaled that the concession costs for pivotal conservative Republican supporters were negligible.

Irrespective of organized opposition, members of Congress could have feared electoral punishment from voters who retrospectively deemed the legislation to be personally costly. However, from the outset, the civil right measures under consideration overwhelmingly impacted the South. Since the main thrust of the Civil Rights Act was banning official (de jure) segregation in schools and public accommodations, which existed only in the South, the problems that the bill purported to fix were sectional.[132] Certain aspects of the legislation, nevertheless, threatened to encroach upon nonsouthern constituencies, such as fair employment provisions embodied in Title VII. For Dirksen, obtaining the support of pivotal

---

[129] Hill (1977).

[130] CQ (1968, 57).

[131] It is unknown precisely why business groups failed to rally against the measure. Members of the Kennedy and Johnson administrations had met with business leaders to persuade them of the necessity of the civil rights measure and blunt their opposition. Lytle (1966, 291) speculates that the business community was preoccupied with the administration's pending tax bill. See also CQ (1968, 57). The preponderance of moral arguments about the bill's necessity and growing public approval might have disinclined businesspeople to speak out against the measure. See Burstein (1985, 107); Hill (1977, 4). Also, as shown in previous chapters, economic actors wished to avert the economic damage that stemmed from racial disruptions and might have been amenable to legislation on the presumption that a legislative change would reduce such interference. Finally, it is possible, as argued by Vogel (1996) and Overby and Ritchie (1991), that the business community was remarkably disorganized during this period before the regulatory state had been expanded in response to the demands of the civil rights, consumer, and environmental movements. This interpretation is consistent with the general argument presented here in which third parties behave as conformers if they suffer neither disruption nor concession costs. The costs associated with civil rights demands were nonexistent (public accommodations outside the South) or diffuse (the ban on employment discrimination), and therefore inhibited coherent business countermobilization.

[132] Graham (1990, 75).

members of his caucus depended upon proposing amendments to limit these prospective concession costs. Dirksen's changes not only weakened the bill overall but systematically reduced its impact beyond the South.[133] For instance, in proposing language that the attorney general needed to demonstrate a "pattern or practice" of employment discrimination in litigating such cases, Dirksen concentrated the emphasis on the official discrimination found in the South.[134] Other changes involved deference to state and local fair employment commissions before permitting the commencement of a federal suit. As these institutions were found exclusively outside of the South, such changes limited the regulatory domain of the legislation. Finally, his amendments sharply limited the powers of the Equal Employment Opportunity Commission (EEOC) in pursuing allegations of discrimination, and shifted the authority to initiate prosecutions to the attorney general. Additional amendments exempted racial segregation in public schools that resulted from de facto residential patterns and, again, thereby concentrated the impact of the bill on de jure segregation, which was confined to the South. These changes prompted an indignant Senator Russell to declare: the bill now "has been stripped of any pretense and stands as a purely sectional bill. . . . Provisions have been written into the bill which draw up a monumental wall . . . (protecting) the states that are north of the Mason-Dixon line."[135] Overall, then, Dirksen's amendments and others essentially negated the threat of electoral reprisals for Republican conservatives, as well as for northern Democrats who might have been concerned about federal attempts to remedy de facto school segregation based on residential patterns.[136] Thus, Dirksen's success in winning the support of pivotal Republican conservatives was attributable to a convergence of modest disruption costs from public opinion, attentiveness, and church mobilization as well as negligible political risks due to the nonexistent countermobilization beyond the South and the careful shifting of the bill's impact onto southern constituencies.

---

[133] Rodriguez and Weingast (2003, 1489). This section depends heavily on their insightful analysis of Dirksen's amendments. Graham (1990) and Sundquist (1968) make analogous arguments about the regional impact of Dirksen's amendments to the bill.

[134] Rodriguez and Weingast (2003, 1472).

[135] Quoted in Rodriguez and Weingast (2003, 1496).

[136] The concentration of the impact of the legislation upon the South clarifies the overall weakness of the countermobilization against the bill. "The southern opposition organized," Sundquist (1968, 264) explains, "but since the legislation would have an impact upon the legal and social order only in the South, organized opposition did not develop outside that region."

Following months of bargaining, the Senate invoked cloture to end debate and proceeded to pass the measure on a vote of 73 to 27. The infamous southern filibuster to block civil rights had finally been broken. Congress passed the civil rights bill which Johnson signed into law on July 2, 1964. In ten Titles, the Civil Rights Act attacked segregation in public education, housing, and public accommodations, enlarged federal authority in voting rights cases, and enabled the national state to combat employment discrimination. As if to vindicate Johnson's willingness to accept the political dangers of endorsing a strong measure, he won a landslide victory against his Republican challenger, Barry Goldwater (AZ), one of the few nonsouthern senators who voted against the Civil Rights Act of 1964. Goldwater won only his home state of Arizona and five Deep South states. Congressional elections were no less decisive as northern Democrats picked up a stunning 36 seats in the House as well as two in the Senate.

The Voting Rights Act of 1965

The dynamics that culminated in the enactment of the 1964 Civil Rights Act bear a striking resemblance to those behind the enactment of the Voting Rights Act of 1965. This similarity is no coincidence. In Birmingham, civil rights activists discovered the value of provoking hostile response to elicit federal action and they hoped to repeat this success in Selma, Alabama. At the commencement of the Selma campaign in January 1965, King announced, "We hope that, through this process, we can bring the necessary moral pressure to bear on the federal government to get federal registrars appointed in these areas."[137] As observed in Chapter 4, King and his associates in SCLC targeted Selma as the site of the voter registration campaign for the express purpose of stimulating national voting rights legislation. In this, they were highly effective.

The local struggle began with a series of marches to register at city hall. After responding initially with calm, Sheriff Jim Clark and his officers soon resorted to rougher tactics. Newspaper photographers captured striking images of this abuse, such as Clark bringing his nightstick down on the head of black woman as she lay pinned to the ground by two officers. In the nearby town of Marion, during a nighttime march, a state trooper shot down Jimmie Lee Jackson, a black man, as he defended his mother during a clash that involved demonstrators, police, and a crowd

---

[137] Williams (1988, 255).

of angry whites. At his funeral it was proposed that the movement should stage a protest march to Montgomery, the state capital. Days later, as planning for the march began, three white Unitarian ministers, who had participated in local demonstrations, were beaten in Selma and one, James Reeb, died from his injuries. After some confusion and false starts, it was eventually decided to begin the long walk to Montgomery on March 7, 1965. As some six hundred demonstrators crossed the bridge out of the city of Selma, Sheriff Jim Clark, his deputies, and state police met them. Using tear gas, cattle prods, and nightsticks, the police attacked the marchers with the national media capturing the melee. "Once again, through television and news pictures, the nation became an eye-witness to southern violence, and the outrage was instantaneous."[138] The events of "Bloody Sunday," as it was later called, would be denounced in Congress and singled out by President Johnson as evidence of the necessity of new voting rights legislation. In a March 15 speech, Johnson told a joint session of Congress:

At times, history and fate meet at a single time in a single place to shape a turning point in man's unending search for freedom. So it was at Lexington and Concord. So it was a century ago at Appomattox. So it was last week in Selma, Alabama. There, long suffering men and women peacefully protested the denial of their rights as Americans. Many of them were brutally assaulted. One good man – a man of God – was killed. (Johnson, 1965)

Johnson threw his support behind the legislation, declaring in the words of the civil rights anthem, "We shall overcome." But lofty speeches are insufficient to enact legislation; rather, a favorable combination of factors greatly benefited the movement.

Even more than the desegregation of public accommodations, public opinion overwhelmingly supported voting rights for African-Americans. Long before Selma, in a December 1963 poll, nearly 80 percent of whites supported action to ensure southern blacks could vote.[139] As civil rights activists had hoped, the events in Selma drew national (and international) attention to their cause. Media coverage of the assaults on non-violent demonstrators provoked national indignation and pushed civil rights back to the top of the public's list of important problems. In the aftermath of Bloody Sunday and sustained voting rights protests, public

---

[138] Sundquist (1968, 273).
[139] Garrow (1978, 157). Garrow's research on the impact of events in Selma on civil rights outcomes superbly captures this dynamic.

attentiveness remained high as the bill plodded through Congress.[140] The pro-rights lobby embodied in the LCCR, which now numbered more than 150 national organizations, reminded their representatives of the urgency of congressional action.[141]

Concession costs again figure into the logic of enactment. Beyond the southern delegation in Congress, no organized opposition was mounted to resist the legislation. As before, the legislative bargaining process relied on the same concentration of the bill's impact upon the South.[142] Unlike the public accommodations and fair employment aspects of the 1964 Act, the unambiguous sectional impact of the voter registration bill meant that northern whites were unlikely to regard the legislation as costly. Rather, with public sentiment in favor and attentive, the likelihood of retrospective punishment was low. Dirksen again admonished his Midwestern partisans, "This involves more than you. It's the party. Don't drop me in the mud."[143] Vulnerable northern Republicans likewise urged their conservative colleagues to capitulate and, with minimal electoral risk entailed in supporting the legislation, they did so. Thus, the combination of public support, attentiveness, civil rights mobilization, and the absence of organized nonsouthern opposition or any foreseeable political costs for support led to a decisive defeat for southern Democrats. By obliterating most state and local obstructions to political participation, this act at long last nationalized the right to vote.

Fair Housing and Equal Employment

The Fair Housing Act of 1968, after suffering previous defeats from southern filibusters in the Senate, was finally enacted with bipartisan support. Unlike previous victories, a ban on housing discrimination had greater national implications and therefore impacted not only the constituents of southern representatives. Opinion polls showed large majorities supported the principle of equal access to housing. Whereas only 42 percent of northern white respondents expressed acceptance of limited neighborhood integration in 1942, this figure had risen to 70 percent by

---

[140] Burstein (1979); Santoro (2002); Smith (1980).
[141] Jonas and Bond (2004, 224).
[142] Rodriguez and Weingast (2003); Thernstrom (1987). The triggering mechanism for coverage under the Act involved both the use of literacy tests and a voter turnout below 50 percent in the 1964 presidential election. These provisions effectively targeted the South, in particular the hardcore black belt.
[143] MacNeil (1970, 259) (italics omitted).

December 1963. By 1968, nearly 70 percent of whites agreed that blacks should be able to live where they want.[144] Nevertheless, the disruption costs fostering enactment of a discrimination ban depended upon the same convergence of factors: supportive public opinion, amplified attentiveness due to civil rights protests as well as riots, vigorous lobbying by an ensemble of pro-rights groups, and the relative weakness of the nonsouthern opposition. Supporters again depended upon Republican votes for passage.

In brokering a settlement, a closer inspection of the political logic is instructive. Liberal Republicans from states and districts with a larger percentage of African-Americans responded due to the combination of supportive public opinion and effective political mobilization by pro-rights interest organizations. These Republicans, whose reelection coalition included civil rights supporters, urged their leadership to support action or else risk the loss of seats in the upcoming election. A *Washington Post* editorial similarly noted that Republican action to defeat the bill would be "disastrous" and that Dirksen had shifted to support a bargain "for the sake of improving the Republican image in the election next November."[145] Others concurred with this assessment of the political situation. Senator Charles Mathias (R-MD), for instance, was also "concerned that the Republican Party would be blamed for killing the fair housing title."[146] Civil rights activities, including rioting, had elevated mass salience and the demands for "something" to be done. In explaining his own reversal from opposition to support, Dirksen stated, "I do not want to worsen . . . the restive condition of the United States."[147] While some whites likely opposed this legislation, they were not organized to

---

[144] Burstein (1979); Hyman and Sheatsley (1964). The previous attempt to pass fair housing legislation in 1966 coincided with a peak in public concern that the Johnson administration was "pushing integration too fast." According to Gallup, in September, 52 percent of northern whites took this position. At the time the 1968 act passed in April, only 34 percent expressed this concern, perhaps due to King's assassination that same month.

[145] Quoted in Farhang (2007, 62).

[146] Mathias (1999, 23).

[147] Quoted in Dubofsky (1969, 157). In brokering a compromise, two senators from Kentucky joined the coalition in favor of cloture. Their conversion may be partly attributable to the enactment of a state fair housing law during the same year. Other sources report that Johnson arranged for an $18 million housing grant for Anchorage, Alaska, to win the vote of Alaska Senator E. L. "Bob" Bartlett. See Kotz (2005, 391). In addition to the factors discussed above, side payments such as these obtained the votes of a small number of pivotal members of Congress. (Alaska too had already enacted state fair housing legislation.)

articulate this preference and the antagonism of real estate interests was insufficient to overcome the electoral imperatives for action. The assassination of Martin Luther King, Jr., on April 4, 1968, while the bill was languishing in the House Rules Committee, fostered a final surge in public attention to civil rights and added to concerns about the escalation in urban rioting.[148]

Enactment again depended upon gaining the support of pivotal Republican legislators to overcome the filibuster. Because these particular Republicans represented states and districts in which African-Americans amounted to a politically insignificant minority, their political calculations were subtle. A threat from black voters could be discounted because of their low numbers but, for precisely this reason, these legislators could also reasonably discount a backlash from their white constituents. As contemporaneous opinion polls demonstrated, most whites supported the general principle of open housing, but were more apprehensive if prospective changes threatened to significantly alter the racial composition of their neighborhood.[149] For white constituents in these critical districts, which were often lily-white, such concerns were baseless and therefore retrospective punishment by voters at the polls seemed highly unlikely.[150] Thus, although the Republican leadership needed to avoid blame for blocking the bill, they were in a position to bargain for the weakening of the measure's enforcement mechanisms to further insure against electoral retribution. Specifically, under the original proposal, the federal Department of Housing and Urban Development (HUD) would have been vested with power to investigate complaints and issue enforcement orders. The revised legislation provided HUD only with authority to investigate and seek voluntary conciliation. If unable to achieve a satisfactory outcome, aggrieved individuals retained the option of private litigation. Civil rights supporters accepted the weakening amendments and a bargain was brokered. Also rolled into the bill were provisions to punish rioters, which provided these marginal Republican legislators with additional political cover for their votes, if necessary. Thus, even weak disruption costs felt by pivotal legislators, such as arm-twisting from party leaders, were sufficient to win enough of their votes but only in the virtual absence of concession costs.

[148] Hunter, *New York Times*, April 6, 1968.
[149] Burstein (1979, 165).
[150] Black (1979, 678) points out that in 1971–72, only 8.9 percent of Republican House districts contained a population that was more than 10 percent African-American.

The bargaining processes resulting in enactment of the 1972 Equal Employment Opportunity Act (EEOA), which strengthened the Title VII ban on employment discrimination and expanded coverage to include state and local governments, seemed to repeat the events of previous episodes. Public opinion was strongly supportive of equal opportunities in employment, with 95 percent of respondents in favor.[151] Civil rights organizations lobbied for action from northern Democrats and Republicans. Southern Democrats waged a filibuster in the Senate only to be defeated by a bipartisan coalition. During the negotiation process, stronger enforcement measures, which would have vested the EEOC, created by the 1964 Act, with authority to hold hearings and issue "cease and desist orders," were removed and replaced with authority to initiate suits in federal court.[152] However, despite many similarities to previous episodes, circumstances differed somewhat in 1972. In contrast to prior breakthroughs, Congress enacted the 1972 EEOA in the absence of significant protests and public attentiveness. Only around 5 percent of the public continued to identify civil rights as the most important issue facing the nation. Perhaps due to an emphasis upon movement triumphs during moments of dramatic protests, humdrum conventional political processes are often overlooked.[153]

Although favorable public opinion no doubt encourages legislators to be generally supportive in the absence of issue salience, it is organized benefit-seekers who provide vulnerable legislators with the incentives to take action. The more important a benefit-seeker and his or her allies are in a reelection coalition, the more steadfast a legislator's support will be.

---

[151] Burstein (1979, 163).

[152] On these negotiations, see Farhang (2007). The EEOC could initiate litigation only after an investigation and attempts at conciliation had failed.

[153] Both Burstein (1985) and Santoro (2002) attribute this successful outcome to overwhelming public support for nondiscrimination in employment. Consistent with the explanation presented here, Santoro speculates that conventional politics, particularly black representatives behaving as "institutional activists," likely facilitated enactment. He also suggests that, once a precedent-setting legislative breakthrough is achieved, "second wave" legislation is less controversial; and it is true that the mere presence of Title VII made possible the emergence of a bipartisan consensus that the enforcement mechanism of this provision needed repair. In other words, conventional political agitation by civil rights supporters provided the necessary disruption costs for legislators to act, and the enactment of second-wave legislation entailed lower concession costs. Although his analysis is highly plausible, it does not incorporate quantitative measures for conventional political activity into the statistical analysis. Burstein's (1985) investigation does contain such quantitative measures based on *New York Times* reports, but these appear to be too crude to detect the lobbying activities that are reported in qualitative sources.

These ardent supporters, actuated by organized interests, attempt to persuade their party leadership and colleagues of the necessity for action. In particular, they endeavor to commit the leadership to attracting a sufficient number of pivotal legislators for enactment. The leadership, for its part, seeks to discern the overall electoral risks associated with action or inaction. In this case, the Republican leadership, looking to protect the seats of its vulnerable caucus members, sought to enlist the support of the pivotal legislators holding safe seats. In particular, they needed to find the legislative bargain that would both satisfy their vulnerable members and gain the support of the pivotal legislators. A bargain can be struck if the legislation to be enacted is acceptable to the benefit-seeker and does not entail significant concession costs for pivotal actors. As concession costs fall to insignificance, a settlement can more easily be achieved. In other words, a closer inspection of conventional politics and legislative bargaining processes not only clarifies how movements achieve outcomes in situations of low salience, it elucidates the substance of measures that are ultimately enacted as well.

The EEOA passed as a result of precisely this combination of favorable opinion, conventional political mobilization, and negotiation to produce an acceptable compromise. The Nixon administration, which supported reforming the provisions of existing law that were widely viewed as deficient, opposed giving the EEOC powers of administrative adjudication and instead supported the Republican compromise of vesting it with prosecutorial authority to sue in federal court as well as permitting private litigation. The Chamber of Commerce likewise opposed the expansive bill, but "vigorously campaigned" for the weaker version.[154] Ardent legislative supporters, taking their cues from pro-rights organizations (increasingly including feminist and traditional women's groups), had pushed for a hybrid enforcement mechanism that included both "cease-and-desist" authority for the EEOC and avenues for private litigation.[155] Following the enactment of the 1964 act, civil rights organizations (the NAACP in particular) had developed significant legal capabilities for pursuing high-profile discrimination cases through private litigation.[156] Under these circumstances, the promise of expanded coverage under the

---

[154] *New York Times*, September 17, 1971.
[155] Harvey (1997).
[156] Farhang (2007). More precisely, the NAACP Legal Defense Fund (LDF) pursued these cases. The cease-and-desist provision was enacted in the House in 1966 and in the Senate in 1970 but, in both cases, ultimately failed.

proposed act, even with the weakened EEOC, was too difficult to refuse. Thus, with public opinion "virtually unanimous" over the principle of equal opportunity, administration and business support for the milder measure, and the willingness of civil rights organizations to take "half a loaf," pivotal legislators could be enlisted to support passage of the weakened version. This condensed legislative history distills a critical point: benefit-seekers can obtain concessions through conventional politics, despite low attentiveness, so long as the concession costs for pivotal legislators are low. The critical limitation of a political movement's legislative impact will be these bargaining processes in which outcomes will be fundamentally defined by the political calculations of legislative pivots.

Summary

Under different guises, studies of movement outcomes often concentrate upon the effective application of disruption costs. These disruptions may assume various forms. In democratic states, it seems straightforward that political targets must be concerned about majoritarian preferences. Yet, however conducive favorable opinion may be, it is not sufficient to place an issue on the agenda; rather, something more is necessary to trigger a legislative response. Additional factors can operate as such an impetus. Movements can stage dramatic events that arouse public concern. In the case of the civil rights movement, protests, segregationist violence, and urban disorders stimulated mass attentiveness to racial inequalities. Also, against a backdrop of supportive public opinion, more mundane participation by movement supporters in conventional politics can produce disruption costs to which targets need to respond. The political instability of the black vote made inattention to civil rights politically risky. The growing political involvement of churches, liberal interests, organized labor, and civil rights groups compelled a bloc of legislators to respond to their legislative demands. Absent mass attentiveness, the activities of these organizations compelled vulnerable legislators to continue to push for the expansion of prior victories.[157] Research on the enactment of both fair employment and open housing laws at the state level similarly document the contribution of the civil rights organizations (particularly

---

[157] Within Congress, a handful of African-American representatives often behaved as political entrepreneurs in their efforts to place the concerns of their constituents on the agenda as well.

the NAACP) in the timing of their enactment.[158] In brief, the disruption costs necessary for movement gains can, and often do, assume the form of conventional activities for competitive political advantage.

While such electoral incentives are an essential impetus for action, they do not adequately predict movement outcomes without a consideration of concession costs. As suggested above, a satisfactory narrative of the historical shifts in presidential responses to civil rights demands from conformity, to vacillation, and eventual accommodation necessarily incorporates an appreciation of these concession costs. Since a one-sided emphasis on disruption is insufficient, a theory of movement outcomes must also address a benefit-seeker's leverage relative to that of its opponents. From this vantage point, a critical element in the successful enactment of civil and voting rights legislation was the virtual absence of nonsouthern countermobilization. The weakness of business opposition and the lack of a coherent conservative movement at the grassroots to counterbalance movement demands meant that nonsouthern legislators operated in a political setting nearly devoid of concession costs. Indeed, the absence or weakness of conservative countermobilization, which eventually coalesced in the early 1970s, appears to have been critical not only for the legislative breakthroughs of the civil rights movement, but for feminism and the environmental and consumer movements as well.[159] Finally, the consideration of concession costs clarifies the legislative process as well as the substance of the laws that are ultimately enacted. Such a focus draws attention to the crucial role of pivotal legislators in passing legislation. To obtain their support, successful bargaining repeatedly depended upon an overall weakening of the respective acts by substituting bureaucratic enforcement mechanisms with provisions for private litigation. Concerning the breakthrough civil and voting rights laws, Republican negotiators further reduced the concession costs by shifting the anticipated impact onto other constituencies, in particular southern whites. Other research confirms that the magnitude of concession costs influences the likelihood of a measure's enactment. In her analysis of House roll-call votes on civil rights bills from 1957 to 1991, Sanders (1997) finds that the actual

[158] See Chen and Phinney (2004) on housing and Collins (2003) on state fair employment legislation. Suggestive evidence for the political significance of the NAACP can be found in other studies as well. For instance, Andrews (1997), in his analysis of black political leverage in Mississippi after the Voting Rights Act, found NAACP membership (as well as the number of Freedom Summer volunteers) to be a strong predictor for black voter registration.
[159] Harvey (1997); Overby and Ritchie (1991).

or perceived costs to nonsouthern white constituents significantly affect the probability of passage.[160] Thus, in addition to the disruption costs that encourage action, the inclusion of concession costs in the analysis of movement outcomes promises a richer, more nuanced explanation for the responses of political targets and specifies more clearly the resulting outcomes.

---

[160] On differences in perceptions of the costliness of different civil rights objectives and congressional voting behavior, see also Black (1979).

7

Conclusion

Why do movements succeed or fail? Or, more precisely, under what conditions are movements capable of extracting desired concessions from their targets? The purpose of this book has been to answer this question. To do so, I began with the proposition that explaining movement outcomes necessitates greater attention to the targets themselves, and to the specific costs that movements impose upon them. Pushing this point further, I distinguished between the two main costs that movements directly or indirectly impose and argued that, depending upon their relative magnitude, target responses can be generally predicted. This much is simple and straightforward and, if this line of reasoning went no further, it might not prove particularly interesting or useful. Yet, from this rudimentary starting point, greater theoretical purchase on the topic can be achieved based on the consideration of *variation* in the magnitude of these costs for specific targets, as well as for third parties. In particular, I explore how actors weigh these costs and identify the main factors contributing to variation in their magnitude. The metric for assessing damage to their interests depends upon the target.

While studies of movement outcomes concentrate overwhelmingly on political targets, actual social movements routinely focus on economic actors, as seen in the mobilization concerning environmental degradation, genetically modified foods, corporate social responsibility, globalization, and so on.[1] To refine social movement theory, I present a

---

[1] Although commentators often cite Gamson's *The Strategy of Social Protest* (1975) as a pioneering investigation of movement impact, routinely overlooked is how many of the movement targets identified in that analysis were economic actors. Fully 19 of the 53

sectoral analysis that draws attention to variation in the exposure of economic actors to disruption as well as vulnerability to reprisals from third parties.[2] Certain firms are shown to be consistently more vulnerable to conventional protest activities. These include those engaged in local consumption, those dependent upon local economic development, and producers of name-brand consumer goods. Insofar as movements have sought modest concessions from such vulnerable targets, agitation has demonstrated a general pattern of effectiveness.[3]

This analysis enriches explanations for the responses of political targets as well, specifically policy outcomes. Synthesizing previous studies, I draw attention to the interactions among three main factors: public opinion, mass attentiveness, and the electoral significance of both movement supporters and their organized opponents. How these factors are variously combined fundamentally shapes a movement's chances for policy victory. As many accounts attest, the legislative triumphs of the civil rights movement in the mid-sixties depended in no small measure on the heightened national salience of southern racial inequalities that resulted from the dramatic interactions between the movement and its opponents. Multiple studies concerning a wide range of movements point to the relevance of these factors[4]; however, to my knowledge, no study of movement outcomes has argued for the inclusion of all of them and paid attention to their interaction effects. As such, they suffer from the problem of omitted variables and run the risk of biasing the findings or obscuring the relationship between these factors and the outcomes of political movements.

American social movements (approximately 36 percent) in Gamson's sample were labor unions with certain businesses as their principal targets. Further, 12 out of 20 (60 percent) of Gamson's cases of success (full response) represented labor mobilization. The overall success rate among labor unions is thus a stunning 63 percent, next to only about 20 percent for other movement types. It is noteworthy as well that those targeting businesses in high-demand markets and associated with immobile capital assets (such as steel mills, mines, ports, and so on) appear to have been particularly successful.

[2] For a similar analysis of economic dependencies among corporations, stakeholders, and third parties, see Frooman (1999).

[3] Elliott and Freeman (2004); Pruitt and Friedman (1986); Schurman (2004); Smith (1990); Spar and Le Mure (2003). For an application of social movement theory to corporate stakeholders, see King (2008). This analysis might be taken further through an investigation of diffusion processes and imitation among comparable targets; see Soule and Earl (2001).

[4] Agnone (2007); Harvey (1997); Lo (1982); Meyer and Staggenborg (1996); Santoro (2002); Soule (2004).

Finally, since the interventions of third parties can be determinative, their inclusion in the analysis of movement outcomes is crucial. Most accounts, however, treat third parties as exogenous agents. I suggest instead that that these interests respond in a manner comparable to a movement's targets, that is, based on the same logic that impels targets to conform, accommodate, vacillate, or resist. For example, even if they are not directly targeted, those suffering from high disruption costs and low concession costs will be impelled to act on behalf of the movement. For instance, stockholders of firms targeted by the anti-sweatshop movement might sell their shares if they anticipate that movement actions will tarnish a firm's reputation and hurt sales. Thus, the decision of these third parties to sell their stocks, and the resulting decline in the firm's share price, deliver a potent economic reprisal to compel a targeted firm to change its behavior.[5] By including an account of third party behavior, this approach promises to significantly increase the causal scope and leverage of explanations for movement outcomes.[6] At the end of the day, theoretical refinements are only as valuable as the empirical findings that result. Applied to the civil rights movement, the theoretical approach presented here recasts multiple aspects of conventional accounts. The following sections briefly survey these revisions in the context of the civil rights movement and then discuss the broader implications of this analysis for explanations of social movement outcomes.

Cost Variation: Disaggregating Civil Rights Demands

Even as it is conventional to speak about the civil rights movement in the singular, social movements are not unitary entities. They are, among other things, ensembles of organizations sharing some goals, but not others, and their diverse objectives necessarily entail different targets, tactics, and the actuation of diverse third parties. The constellation of costs associated with specific goals will vary so that movements might achieve significant gains in some domains but none in others. Looking at public school desegregation, voter registration, and the integration

[5] King and Soule (2007); Pruitt and Friedman (1986).
[6] As argued elsewhere, the concept of political opportunity has been criticized for lack of theoretical precision. From this perspective, the central conceptual problem with political opportunities has been the underspecification of the larger political context. In explicating the responses of targets and third parties, this analysis provides a theoretical foundation for specifying more precisely which variables can be expected to be significant.

of public accommodations, the movement achieved differing degrees of success in various settings, as described in Chapter 5. In the immediate aftermath of the 1954 *Brown v. Board of Education* decision, barriers to public school integration fell almost exclusively in the Peripheral South, in localities in which African-Americans amounted to a smattering of the local population.[7] Elsewhere, the movement achieved minimal gains with school integration often only after protracted legal struggle, court orders, and, in some notable cases, coercive federal intervention. And, despite these pressures, white officials kept the extent of integration to minimal tokenism, until federal legislation vastly enlarged the reach of national authorities.[8] In this domain, legal and political mobilization was far less effective at swaying insulated public officials than the intervention of local business elites to avert economic self-destruction.

Outcomes in voter registration struggles diverged, with easy gains in some settings and decisive defeat in others. For officials representing overwhelmingly white constituencies, the addition of a few black voters offered no electoral threat nor was white opinion likely to be attentive or opposed. Although these voter registration campaigns achieved significant gains, they are seldom described in movement histories and hardly remembered, perhaps precisely because they lacked contentiousness. Contrariwise, officials with large disenfranchised black constituencies offered implacable resistance to maintain their political advantages and minimize the threat of electoral punishment. Segregationist organizations in these localities bolstered such political imperatives. Despite the dogged commitment and bravery of black registrants, their attempts to be added to the voting rolls were swatted away with a multitude of legalistic contrivances and dilatory tactics. In these southern precincts, movement success in this domain proved elusive until federal legislation pushed aside defiant registrars or threatened to do so.

Finally, as previously discussed, the movement achieved significant gains in the desegregation of public accommodations due to sustained

[7] Far greater desegregation ensued in the Border States of Oklahoma, Missouri, Kentucky, West Virginia, Maryland, and Delaware. See Southern Education Reporting Service (SERS) "Statistical Summary" (1964). Even in the Border South, the percentage of the population that was African-American was a prime determinant of compliance (Pettigrew 1957).

[8] Orfield (1969). By 1964, ten years after *Brown*, less than 1 percent of southern blacks were enrolled in schools with whites in Arkansas, Alabama, Georgia, Mississippi, and South Carolina. Other southern states were only marginally more integrated. Texas achieved the greatest desegregation at just over 7 percent enrollment. See SERS, "Statistical Summary" (1964).

protests and boycotts. The enactment of federal civil rights legislation facilitated and accelerated this process. Thus, as this brief summary suggests, "the civil rights movement" achieved widely divergent degrees of success among domains and across southern subregions, and these differences are explicable in light of the cost analysis I have put forth here.

Third Party Activity: White Responses to Civil Rights Mobilization

Civil rights mobilization sometimes provoked fierce white resistance, though this opposition was far less robust and unified than is commonly assumed. Histories of the civil rights struggle sometimes presume uniform white opposition or present crude distinctions between and within southern states. Indeed, had southern whites mounted a more unified or savvier defense of Jim Crow, the movement might have been unable to win significant concessions prior to the enactment of sweeping federal legislation. In any case, accounts that treat southern whites as united against the movement seldom offer much nuance. At times, it is as if the region were viewed as "one large Mississippi," as Key averred regarding northern perceptions of the South.[9] While most southern whites opposed the movement's objectives, a presumption of unified or cohesive countermobilization is inaccurate and militates against the search for more subtle distinctions.

The overall patterns of southern white response coincide with the predictions of this analysis. First, this approach predicts the overall weakness of organized countermobilization against the civil rights movement due to the minimal tangible concession costs that movement demands represented to most southern whites. "The southern way of life" might be challenged, but seldom were individual livelihoods or political futures at stake. The weakness of southern countermobilization during the Second Reconstruction contrasts vividly with the opposition witnessed one hundred years prior. During the Reconstruction period following the Civil War, southern white elites engaged in a broad-based and sustained countermobilization against the bid to transform the political economy of the region. This time around, far fewer whites were similarly threatened by black gains, substantially reducing the organized regional opposition to racial egalitarianism. In no small measure, the overall success of the civil rights movement must be attributed to the reduction of the political and

[9] 1949, 229.

economic imperatives that had previously reinforced the southern white elite commitment to Jim Crow.[10]

Second, this approach predicts that the fiercest movement opponents of the Second Reconstruction would be those exposed to high concession costs and insulated from the disruption costs. And, indeed, organized white opponents were drawn overwhelmingly both from the black belt elite and from among those working-class whites in vulnerable occupational niches. Against such targets or within communities in which they predominated, success proved elusive. The vehemence of resistance, however, was not immutable, as cost perceptions were modified over time. For instance, along with other factors, the mechanization of southern cotton agriculture appears to have weakened elite opposition and diminished the organized political demands for unflinching resistance.

Either as targets or third parties, many whites reacted to civil rights disruptions with calls for negotiation and compromise. Conventional histories point toward a general business moderation hypothesis in which economic actors preferred compliance to avert the eruption of public disorders that might be damaging to the local economy. The sectoral analysis proposed here revises this hypothesis by offering more precise distinctions among economic actors and crisper predictions for their likely responses. As third parties, it was overwhelmingly vulnerable economic actors who spoke out in favor of desegregation as a necessary response to preserve local economic growth, emboldening elected officials to endorse the necessary concessions. Without this overt support, elected officials and other economic actors might have been wary of backing even modest concessions out of fear of retribution. While organized white opposition bolstered the cost for targets to concede to movement demands, these conciliatory interests provided the cover necessary to forge compromises and achieve local movement victories.

Case Studies: Civil Rights and Local Outcomes

The case studies retrace terrain familiar to students of the civil rights movement, but the theoretical perspective sheds new light on local and national movement outcomes. For example, the success of the sit-in movement in Greensboro depended upon not only the vulnerability of downtown merchants, but the weakness of organized opposition that

---

[10] For a different explanation for the divergence in the two periods, see Valelly (2004).

might have discouraged capitulation. A comparable weakness in organized opposition and the unusual incorporation of African-Americans in the ruling coalition in Atlanta provided the movement with the prospect of extracting concessions among political and economic elites in a Deep South city. The movement's defeat in Albany shows how strategic decisions matter, particularly against a savvy opponent. Although downtown merchants there were as vulnerable as elsewhere, the movement's concentration upon elected officials and irregular disruption of economic interests reduced the likelihood of winning concessions.

In addition to explicating the responses of economic targets, my analysis further incorporates a political explanation for the responses of southern authorities to civil rights disturbances. Since it was widely known that the movement fed upon violent clashes and that a Pritchett-style reaction was an effective countermeasure, it might seem puzzling that southern authorities deviated from the optimal reaction. The divergent law enforcement responses in Albany and Birmingham are usually depicted as stemming from the differing personalities of Laurie Pritchett and Bull Connor, respectively. By contrast, this research shows that the best response for local officials to thwart civil rights gains was not necessarily their politically optimal reaction due to a combination of segregationist mobilization and weak electoral demands for moderation.[11] For example, the Birmingham struggle suggests that violent outbursts against civil rights activists should not be regarded as automatic reactions to civil rights demonstrations; rather, they are attributable in no small measure to political processes. The violent incidents there ultimately depended more upon the political preferences of working-class segregationists, and their electoral leverage within the dominant coalition, than the brutality of a single individual. In the absence of organized segregationist demands for a harsh reaction to black insurgency, officials might adopt a more nimble response to blunt the movement's disruptive capabilities. Hence, from this perspective, Pritchett's calm response in Albany is attributable in particular to the striking weakness of organized political demands for a harsh reaction to black insurgency. Insofar as multiple studies point to violent white backlash as the critical impetus behind the enactment of civil rights legislation, this interpretation revises those studies that assume the outbursts of southern violence to be manifestations of hot-tempered personalities.

[11] Luders (2005).

Images of fire hoses and snarling dogs in Birmingham can sometimes obscure the reality that protesters ultimately demonstrated the effectiveness of relentless disruptions in extracting benefits from economic actors. These lessons make the strategic decision to target public officials in Selma all the more striking. In selecting Selma, organizers sought to reproduce the politics of Birmingham, in which the demands from organized segregationists for extremism were embodied in local law enforcement. Unlike other struggles in which organizers set out to win a local victory, the selection of Selma was primarily for the purpose of staging a dramatic clash necessary to win national legislation. The case studies thus not only convey how a compelling explanation for movement outcomes must integrate the strategic interactions among movement, targets, and third parties, they also recast standard accounts of the civil rights struggle, pinpointing the key elements within them.

National Legislative Responses: Public Opinion, Attentiveness, and Benefit-Seekers

As countless local struggles battered at Jim Crow institutions, the achievement of breakthroughs depended upon decisive federal action to overcome southern opposition. With courts lacking the enforcement capabilities to bring about fundamental social change, aggressive federal action necessitated presidential leadership and committed congressional majorities, but the political interests of most presidents obliged them to ignore the illiberal and undemocratic practices engendered in Jim Crow institutions. Without some imperative to compel action, president after president had ample motivation to behave as conformers. Entrenched in Congress, the southern wing of the Democratic party effectively wielded a veto over racially egalitarian measures. Caught between the political demands of civil rights supporters and southern segregationists, the Kennedy administration vacillated and made political overtures to both sides of the controversy. Rather than staking out a clear position, the administration engaged in "crisis management" and sought to guide movement activities into institutional channels that were deemed less threatening. Only extraordinary events such as direct challenges to federal authority and changing political imperatives circumvented this ineluctable logic.

Most accounts point correctly to the movement's effectiveness in attracting the attention of the national media and boosting the salience of civil rights issues.[12] While survey data suggest that most nonsoutherners supported the limited demands of the civil rights movement, their attentiveness was generally low, and concerted southern opposition was able to halt measures deemed threatening to segregation and white dominance. Matters changed following the eruptions of dramatic violence in Birmingham and Selma. Outbursts such as these drew extensive media coverage, elevated the salience of civil rights, and catapulted the issue to the top of the national political agenda. Heightened attentiveness recast the political costs of inaction to make possible significant legislative gains. These circumstances furnished a broad coalition of liberal, labor, religious, and civil rights organizations with the disruptive capabilities to threaten targets of both political parties with electoral reprisals for inaction on civil rights. Accordingly, despite significant political risks, President Johnson in particular appreciated the electoral importance of shoring up his position on civil rights issues.

At the same time, insufficient attention has been paid to the relevant concession costs associated with movement outcomes. In particular, the success of the legislative coalition in support of civil rights depended upon both the weakness of organized opposition outside the South and the willingness of pivotal Republicans to support civil rights measures. The changes in legislation Republicans demanded which allowed them to insulate their constituents from the impact of civil rights legislation intensified the regional concentration of concession costs, obliging northern Democrats to take responsibility for enacting legislation that was deeply unpopular among southern whites. Other research confirms that legislators sought to anticipate and reduce the concession costs for their constituents as they enacted racially egalitarian measures.[13]

Despite fervent segregationist entreaties to national economic organizations and nonsouthern economic elites to support their position against the enlargement of federal regulatory capacity, these appeals failed. The unwillingness of nonsouthern interests to join in opposition to civil rights legislation or organize on behalf of weaker legislation limited the concession costs for nonsouthern legislators and left the southern congressional

---

[12] Along with the studies that point to the role of protest in boosting issue salience, others suggest that it was the convergence of massive war mobilization coupled with a reform movement that brought forth a national thrust to elevate African-Americans to full citizenship. See Klinkner and Smith (1999).

[13] Sanders (1997).

delegation politically isolated. The Senate filibuster no doubt provided southern Democrats with a significant fortification for protecting Jim Crow against federal incursions, but the combination of supportive opinion, mass attentiveness, and broad-based political mobilization provided the movement with a battering-ram to smash through this obstruction at long last. Along with the specific propositions regarding the outcomes of the civil rights movement and the vulnerabilities of certain economic sectors, my analysis suggests a series of additional observations about these factors and their impact on policymaking.

Social Movements and Policy Change

Even as some research suggests a general congruence between public opinion and policy outcomes, the relationship is often more complicated due to variation in mass attentiveness.[14] Favorable public opinion alone may be insufficient for elected officials to incur the costs of taking action in a particular policy domain. True, entrepreneurial maverick legislators sometimes seek to champion particular causes in the absence of organized benefit-seekers. However, without such entrepreneurs, officeholders hesitate because significant change necessitates the expenditure of limited political capital for uncertain electoral rewards. Accordingly, other studies find that policy outcomes do not neatly conform to public opinion, and that divergence can be expected under certain circumstances.[15] As officeholders are occupied with multiple, competing demands for their attention, they prefer to respond to concerns that are highly salient for their constituents.[16] The threat of retrospective electoral punishment furnishes public officials with compelling motives to adhere to the preferences of attentive majorities. Movements with attentive majorities behind them have an overwhelming advantage over their opponents and have the most favorable circumstances for winning policy victories. It is no surprise, then, that movements backed by supportive opinion engage in "strategic dramaturgy" to stimulate mass attentiveness.[17] Interest organizations provide legislators with information or signals about public preferences, thereby bringing policy into alignment with public opinion.[18]

[14] Page and Shapiro (1983); Stimson, MacKuen, and Erikson (1995).

[15] Giugni (2004); Page and Shapiro (2000).

[16] Jones (1994); Kingdon (1973) [1989].

[17] McAdam (1996).

[18] Burstein (1999); Lohmann (1998). In the latter twentieth century, the gradual repeal of criminal sodomy statutes proceeded apace so long as this legal change was regarded as

Conversely, although sometimes seen as intrinsically conducive to social movement success, attentiveness cuts both ways and can be detrimental to movement victory if public sentiment is arrayed against the movement's goals.

Perhaps more importantly, although the combination of mass support and attentiveness favors movement victory, I suggest that movements and other benefit-seekers can win concessions from targeted public policymakers even without them.[19] Indeed, due to the low salience of most issues before mass publics, inattentiveness is the most common circumstance in which movements or interest organizations seek to shape policy outcomes. Conditions of low salience highlight the critical importance of the *electoral significance* of the movement participants and their allies within the target's reelection coalition.[20] If compelled to choose between diffuse constituent preferences or the determined opposition of highly attentive, organized voters, targeted officials may prefer to adhere to the demands of the latter. In such cases, there will be far less congruence between public opinion and policy outcomes.[21] The difficulties in enacting gun control legislation is a classic example of this pattern, where organizations such as the National Rifle Association are often effective at thwarting diffuse mass preferences for greater regulation of firearms.[22] Preferential treatment in the tax code for specific businesses or sectors is another commonplace form of this sort of policy output. Further, even if public preferences are nominally opposed to a benefit-seeker's goals, success is nonetheless possible if concessions are unlikely to be noticed, as attested, for instance, by the success of agriculture lobbies in obtaining public subsidies for farmers at the expense of consumers.[23] Due to

the simple modernization of state criminal codes. However, once sodomy decriminalization came to be seen as a gay issue and attracted the interest of traditionalist interest organizations, this reform process largely halted (Kane 2007).

[19] For a similar argument, see Denzau and Munger (1986); Stratmann (1991). Smith (1995) offers a useful review of the literature on interest group influence.

[20] Soule and Olzak (2004), for instance, find state-level pro-ERA mobilization and favorable opinion positively affected state ratification rates.

[21] Burstein (2006), a longtime advocate for the incorporation of public opinion in studies of policy outcome, has recently argued that the impact of public opinion has been overestimated in previous studies due to sampling biases in favor of more salient issues. See also Lohmann's (1998) discussion of shirking.

[22] It is worth noting that such deviations from majority policy preferences do not involve cases of government action, but rather inaction. In these cases, government policy does not so much contradict mass preferences, it simply does not respond to them.

[23] Olson (1965). On this point, see the extensive literature on distributive policy and "iron triangles" or issue networks in policymaking. Too, as Hacker and Pierson (2005)

the prevalence of policymaking in conditions of low salience, theories of movement impact that offer predictions only in cases in which mass publics are both supportive and attentive have limited value in elucidating most policy outcomes.

Yet benefit-seekers do not necessarily operate in a political field without competitors, and the activities of organized opponents to counterbalance the political demands of benefit-seeking movements cannot be overlooked. In situations with organized competition over an outcome, targeted officials will attempt to discern the implications for their reelection prospects and they will favor the benefit-seeker possessing greater electoral clout within their reelection coalition.[24] As suggested above and discussed in Chapter 6, the limited nature of congressional action on civil rights stemmed less from a lack of broad public support than from low salience coupled with ardent southern obstructionism. Thus, an account of the responsiveness of elected officials to movement demands must address the electoral leverage of countermovement opponents.

Attending to the interactions among these factors, it is possible to consider how different combinations define certain predictable paths toward success or defeat for political movements. The best prospects for victory for political movements can thus be found in the convergence of supportive public opinion, high attentiveness, and weak or absent countermobilization. Under these circumstances, disruption costs are high for public officials and concession costs are almost nonexistent. The sweeping legislative triumphs of the early environmental movement demonstrate this pattern. On the other side, the opposition of attentive mass publics and a more formidable countermovement doom a movement to certain defeat in majoritarian settings. The difficulties of winning federal or state legislation for the recognition of same-sex marriages attests to the challenge of overcoming fierce countermobilization coupled with broad public opposition.[25] Between these extremes, a movement's electoral clout relative to its opponent is critical. Thus, a movement might win concessions from political targets if the public is indifferent and the opposition is

---

demonstrate, it is further possible for legislators to devise policy *instruments* that obfuscate or conceal the principal beneficiaries of enacted policies.

[24] Hansen (1991). Due to the structure of American political institutions and the many veto points, in situations in which competing organizations possess equal electoral leverage, the interest organization attempting to bring about change will have greater difficulty than one defending the status quo (Krehbiel 1998).

[25] The successes that have been won in this domain have overwhelmingly resulted from judicial intercession, not majoritarian action in state legislatures.

relatively weak.[26] Voting rights gains in Peripheral South states conform
to this pattern.[27] However, even if public opinion is mildly supportive,
a movement might be defeated by an opponent with superior political
capabilities, as was the case with civil rights activity against organized
southern opposition in the years prior to the mid-sixties. This perspective
makes sense of outcomes that, based on a consideration of public opinion
alone, might otherwise appear perplexing.

Policy Characteristics

As suggested above, mass preferences and attentiveness affect movement
outcomes. Thus far, both have been treated as exogenous, but the logic
of my analysis clarifies the structure of public opinion as well. Insofar
as public opinion might be regarded as a third-party response to movement demands, disaggregating the costs associated with these demands
can be instructive. Drawing from studies of legislative politics, my analysis unpacks movement demands to predict how third parties (including
mass publics) will likely respond. Considerable research has shown that
demands with large, concentrated, tangible, and immediate costs are most
likely to attract negative public attention and stimulate countermobilization.[28] By contrast, demands that have smaller, diffuse, abstract, and
delayed costs generally mute public opposition and attentiveness, and
thereby impede coherent countermobilization. White indifference toward
black voting in localities with few African-Americans has already been

[26] Although not addressed in this investigation, institutional configurations shape movement outcomes. In their analysis of the absence of national health care in the United
States, Steinmo and Watts (1995) point to a profound institutional bias against comprehensive reform. Thus, institutions can present social movements, interest organizations,
and political parties with a daunting obstacle course or necessitate the formation of far
larger majorities for effective response than might otherwise be required. In a sense,
the decentralization of political institutions and relatively weak political parties in the
United States effectively multiply the number of relevant targets for public policy outcomes (Smith 2005). These institutional features similarly make it easier for an interest
organization to block action on new legislation than to obtain a favorable change in
existing policies. Organized opponents too acquire particular bargaining leverage in
their capabilities to block policy changes. The discussion of the "southern veto" over
civil rights policies exemplifies this pattern. An account of movement outcome must be
attentive to how institutional settings define the conditions necessary for a successful
outcome as well as shape the exposure of targets and relevant third parties to disruption
and concession costs. See generally, March and Olsen (1989).

[27] Feminist legislative victories to ban credit discrimination against women exemplify this
path toward success as well.

[28] Arnold (1990); Stone (2002).

mentioned, but other examples are easily identified. The women's move-ment successfully prompted Congress to enact credit discrimination legis-lation due to the relative invisibility of any costs associated with acceding to these demands, and the weakness of any organized opposition.[29] Like-wise, demands to enact laws to protect women from violence imposed costs only upon sexual predators or abusive partners and met with mini-mal countermobilization. The initial lack of clear economic implications associated with the Endangered Species Act again provided legislators with an opportunity to claim credit for protecting "fuzzy critters" from extinction without slapping any particular interests or localities with obvi-ous punitive costs.[30] This suggests that movements seeking benefits that are smaller, diffuse, or otherwise not self-evidently costly will have a greater impact than those seeking gains that provoke public opposition or countermobilization.[31]

Strategic Action and Reaction

Sweeping explanations of political outcomes run the risk of oversimplifi-cation and, specifically, omitting actual social actors from the narrative. Although some circumstances might be more or less favorable for move-ment triumph, outcomes are never preordained. A benefit-seeker's inept tactics or internal squabbles might leave a vulnerable target unscathed or, conversely, clumsy opponents can provide benefit-seekers with unex-pected advantages. The violent reaction of southern white supremacists to

[29] Gelb and Palley (1982). Jackson (1998) describes the historical diminution of the con-cession costs for male elites in his analysis of the rise of women's equality. Largely absent from his analysis, however, is the necessary imposition of disruption costs upon targets by organized benefit-seekers in accelerating the process of social change.

[30] See Fowler and Shaiko (1987) on the broad popular support for the 1978 reauthorization of the Endangered Species Act. The vote in favor on final passage for the original 1973 legislation was nearly unanimous.

[31] Insofar as movement demands involve conflicts over values, further research might address at greater length how cultural narratives affect these cost perceptions. For exam-ple, gay rights mobilization for the passage of hate crimes laws has met with less organized resistance than other civil rights protections or various forms of relationship recognition. On these cultural or interpretive aspects, see Schneider and Ingram (1993); Stone (2002). There is a burgeoning literature on framing effects in social movement theory and policy studies that clarifies how actors calculate certain costs. In many cases, the consideration of material costs is reasonably straightforward; however, in other situations, cultural perceptions and social cues shape how targets and third parties interpret the implica-tions upon norms and values of movement demands. See Donovan, Wenzel, and Bowler (2001); Wald, Owen, and Hill (1988).

civil rights demands, for instance, heightened the national salience of the movement's agenda and furthered the enactment of congressional legislation.[32] In contrast, the weakness and ineptitude of business countermobilization in the late 1960s and early 1970s in responding to challenges from environmental and consumer movements led to sweeping victories that might otherwise not have been won.[33]

Movement organizers can strategically modulate their demands to reduce their visibility or offensiveness to certain third parties.[34] Doing so reduces the concession costs for political targets and boosts the prospects for success. Incremental approaches in American politics have a long and successful history in bringing about social change.[35] Depending upon public sentiment, optimal movement strategies differ. A movement possessing broad public support has a keen incentive to pursue strategies that maximize attentiveness to bring target behavior into alignment with these preferences, a strategy that Schattschneider (1960) described as the "socialization of conflict." By contrast, indifference or diffuse public opposition encourages movements or interest organizations to pursue benefits that are just below the magnitude or visibility likely to attract notice, and therefore unlikely to trigger a hostile reaction.[36] Although a movement might be in a stronger or weaker bargaining position at the outset, outcomes nearly always depend upon the selection of appropriate strategies, the modulation of movement demands, and the relative efficacy of countermovement opponents. Rote adherence to structural explanations obscures the basic point that an adequate explanation for movement outcomes must be mindful of these strategic dimensions.

---

[32] Burstein (1979); Garrow (1978); McAdam (1982). On the selection of movement strategies to match their political or economic circumstances, see, respectively, Amenta (2006) and Frooman (1999).

[33] Rochon and Mazmanian (1993).

[34] For example, in their discussion of the policy gains of the women's movement, Gelb and Palley (1982) describe how the movement sought to define key goals as matters of basic equity, rather than as challenges to gender identities. While a considerable portion of the research on such interpretive aspects ("framing") concentrates on movement participation, this substantial literature also clarifies how movements seek to shape the perceptions of targets and third parties. See generally, Benford and Snow (2000); Gamson (1992); and Snow (2004).

[35] Hayes (1992); Szymanski (2003).

[36] In some measure, these strategic considerations might account for Burstein and Linton's (2002) finding that interest organizations and social movements appear not to have as much impact on policymaking as commonly assumed, once public opinion has been included. According to the analysis presented here, benefit-seekers might strategically modulate their visibility based on presumptions about public sentiment and attentiveness.

Policy Implementation: The Politics of Enforcement

Decisive legislative victories are not the end of the story of movement impact. The implementation phase stimulates new struggles to define the extent of the triumph.[37] A full discussion of how this theoretical approach can be translated into an analysis of policy implementation is beyond the scope of the present investigation; nevertheless, a few speculative remarks are in order. First, movements often desire tough legislation that furnishes enforcement agents with the positive or negative inducements sufficient to induce recalcitrant targets to change their behavior. As described above, they will be most successful in winning such legislation given a convergence of mass attentiveness, majoritarian opinion in favor of strong measures, and the political weakness of organized opponents. Benefit-seekers not only pursue policy victories; they agitate for effective implementation as well. This mobilization has three main forms: actuating beneficiary populations to take advantage of the new institutional openings; using newly forged legal weapons found in authorizing legislation to augment disruption costs for recalcitrant targets; and encouraging administrators, as well as courts, to engage in committed enforcement of the enabling statutes. I address each briefly in turn.

To enhance successful policy implementation, organized benefit-seekers often attempt to stimulate the beneficiary population. In the case of voter discrimination, benefit-seekers wished to assure not only the provision of equitable registrars, but also the active interest of new registrants. Accordingly, following the enactment of the Voting Rights Act of 1965, the Southern Regional Council launched another Voter Education Project to encourage African-American citizens to register. As Andrews (2001) demonstrates, a robust movement infrastructure stimulates demands among beneficiaries and facilitates their use of a newly available benefit. His analysis of county-level data in Mississippi reveals greater increases in African-American voter registration after 1965 in localities with histories of greater movement activity.

Movements and interest organizations use the new legal tools at their disposal to change the behavior of their targets and expedite compliance. In the case of the civil rights movement, activists turned their attention to litigation against operators of public accommodations that had refused

---

[37] On different aspects of political responsiveness, see Burstein, et al. (1995).

to integrate. Civil rights organizations promptly began "testing" the new law in staged visits of segregated public accommodations and facilities. They called upon the Justice Department to challenge the behavior of voter registrars in hostile localities. Individuals and organizations sued businesses for employment discrimination to expand job opportunities. In furnishing aggrieved individuals and civil rights organizations with these new legal weapons, the enactment of sweeping civil rights and voting rights legislation vastly enhanced the disruptive capabilities of the movement and supportive third parties (as well as reduced the concession costs for some as they might be able to blame the federal government for the change).[38]

Finally, activists urge implementing bureaucracies and courts to vigorously enforce provisions necessary to provide redress to beneficiary populations.[39] As the implementation phase begins, benefit-seekers increasingly concentrate upon institutional channels.[40] Organized interests and bureaucracies may operate in tandem in pursuit of their overlapping purposes. Indeed, movement actors may enter the enforcement bureaucracy to promote effective implementation.[41] For their part, activists often argue in legislative forums in favor of expanded jurisdiction for their administrative benefactors as well as larger budgets, and also provide political defense against retrenchment. Irrespective of this symbiotic relationship, the same factors identified above – public opinion, attentiveness, and organized opposition – shape and constrain the implementation process. Thus, implementation will be more aggressive if public opinion is supportive, attentiveness is high, and the organized opposition is relatively weaker.[42] Conversely, declining public support, diminished attentiveness, or assertive counter-mobilization can bring about the erosion or reversal of prior gains. In the case of school desegregation, the political backlash among whites, including nonsoutherners, against "forced busing" reduced public support for assertive measures to implement desegregation plans and indeed has allowed for the slow resegregation of the public

---

[38] The literature on the implementation of civil rights policies is vast. For a sampling, see Farhang (2007); Hochschild (1999); Minchin (1999); and Rodgers and Bullock (1972).

[39] Walton (1988).

[40] Burstein et al. (1995); Piven and Cloward (1977); Santoro (2002).

[41] Piven (2006); Santoro and McGuire (1997).

[42] Some differences in outcome can be attributed in part to the different emphases that civil rights organizations placed upon certain issues to the relative neglect of others (Bonastia 2006).

schools.[43] As suggested above, certain policy attributes affect the political dynamics of the implementation process.[44]

The impact of legislative, administrative, or judicial mandates upon the target behavior can be explained based on the same cost calculations shaping their reactions to movement activities.[45] In a sense, analyses of implementation again point to disruption and concession costs as the principal factors shaping compliance. Regarding disruption costs, public policy analysts routinely describe legislation as being merely symbolic or "toothless" in the absence of substantive enforcement mechanisms to assure compliance. These enforcement mechanisms are often negative inducements (disruption costs) to be imposed upon truculent targets though, in many cases, implementation may entail awarding benefits (positive inducements) to encourage compliance. To the extent that targets have no fear of legal, political, or economic reprisal, then less responsiveness can be anticipated. The effectiveness of the Voting Rights Act of 1965 depended in large measure upon the degree to which local registrars feared federal intervention or displacement if they discriminated against African-American registrants. The singular advantage of governmental provision of disruption costs is their universal scope, such that few targets are insulated from them and their coercive capacities.

At the same time, as argued throughout this investigation, an emphasis upon disruption costs is insufficient without a consideration of concession costs as well. Higher concession costs for target populations furnish them with greater motivation to attempt to evade or circumvent state taking action. For instance, both migration to the suburbs and the formation of private "segregation academies" allowed southern whites to subvert federal mandates to desegregate their urban public schools. Targets thus respond to implementation depending on the convergence of both costs.

In the abstract, successful implementation is most probable when concession costs for the target are low and the implementing agent provides

---

[43] Boger and Orfield (2005).

[44] Insofar as the concession costs are small, diffuse, abstract, or delayed, targets and mass publics may be inattentive and essentially indifferent. In such cases, benefit-seekers will be more likely to obtain compliance and satisfactory implementation. Costly demands stimulate public attentiveness, opposition, and countermobilization. Thus, if the implementation of movement demands diverges from majoritarian preferences, initial victories might be eroded. In between these extremes, the relative electoral significance of competing benefit-seekers within the governing coalition will likely define the pattern of implementation.

[45] As victories are implemented, movement targets shift from presidents and legislators to enforcement agents, other government officials, businesses, and citizens more generally.

significant incentives (either penalties or rewards) to encourage compliance. This general theoretical proposition might be taken further still.[46] As with the explanation of movement outcome, successful implementation depends upon the specification of the targets. Because business interests react based on their calculation of the economic implications of their responses, market incentives can powerfully affect compliance.[47] Legislation will be more effective if it clears a market of an obstruction that had reduced optimum competitiveness or profitability. In the case of the civil rights movement, the degree of compliance in the public accommodation provision of civil rights legislation exemplifies this proposition. As it turned out, most southern whites were much less troubled by the integration of lunch counters and other public facilities than businessmen had anticipated. For those that dropped their Jim Crow barriers, greater business traffic from African-Americans came with economic benefits. Similarly, regarding labor force integration, a combination of activist pressure, government intervention, and tight labor markets fostered greater compliance, as employers sought to expand the pool of prospective workers. As Minchin observes:

The pace of integration was often more rapid in industries where management was pressured simultaneously by government intervention and by the rising demand for labor generated by the booming economy of the mid- and late 1960s. It is this mixture of government pressure and acute labor shortage that explains why African Americans made employment gains in the southern textile industry at a faster pace than in any other American industry.[48]

Likewise in the integration of sports and entertainment, market demand might produce higher profits.[49] Concession costs not only fall to zero, but positive benefits accrue in the absence of public opposition or countermobilization.

Targeted political actors attempt to calculate their disruption and concession costs. For southern registrars, school board members, and elected officials, public opinion, attentiveness, and the electoral leverage

---

[46] Institutional and organizational factors can affect the effectiveness with which state authorities implement the policies they have been tasked to handle. However, from the perspective of the ultimate targets for policy change, these factors manifest as the costs (or benefits) of compliance.

[47] Hochschild (1999) offers a particularly stimulating analysis of variation in civil rights movement outcomes across multiple domains. On market facilitation of policy implementation, see also Rosenberg (1991).

[48] 1999, 44.

[49] Hochschild (1999).

of organized benefit-seekers relative to their opposition continued to matter in the wake of civil rights legislation. With federal government support, positive or negative inducements were provided to facilitate compliance. Attention to both disruption and concession costs points to differences in implementation of voting rights during the postbellum Reconstruction relative to the Second Reconstruction. In the earlier period, due to the centrality of cotton agriculture to the southern economy, plantation elites regarded the concession costs associated with black civil and voting rights to be exorbitantly high and therefore mounted extraordinary resistance to roll them back.[50] In contrast, after decades of black out-migration from the South, in particular the exodus from rural agricultural counties in which African-Americans had often amounted to outright majorities, the electoral threat to white dominance had fallen sharply. Thus, although the federal commitment and administrative capabilities were substantial in both periods, variation in the fervor of white opposition permitted significant and permanent advances only beginning in the 1960s. Less costly concessions and lower attentiveness to black voting permitted significant gains in this domain compared to school desegregation, which whites often vociferously opposed.

A vexing distinction exists between effective implementation and substantive social change. That is, even "tough" legislation might be circumvented and diminished in significance through concerted recalcitrance or determined foot-dragging during the implementation phase. Voter discrimination might be eradicated but, insofar as new white registrants surpass black enrollment, no net change in the real distribution of political leverage will have been achieved.[51] Under federal compulsion, school districts might integrate their facilities, but mass white defections reduce the total share of students in desegregated institutions. In other words, diligent implementation does not guarantee a social transformation, if the targets can thwart the basic purpose behind the legal intervention. Patterns of evasion or compliance, which determine the ultimate impact of legal mandates, can be seen as a final manifestation of the general cost assessment logic. The effectiveness of legislation in bringing about substantive transformation will depend on how costly the changes are deemed to be relative to the costs of evasion. In the case of school desegregation, most effective change was achieved among those whites who

---

[50] Tolnay and Beck (1995), for instance, explain the sharp decline in lynching in the twentieth century as the result of declining elite imperatives.
[51] Levesque (1972).

did not regard integrated schools as threatening, as well as those unable to afford either to move to the suburbs or to flee to private schools.[52] This equilibrium is dynamic, changing with the numbers of those who attempt to evade compliance or with any new enactment modifying the cost of doing so. This discussion underscores the sobering point that the prospects for mass compliance are hardly limitless, but instead are bounded within confines defined by majoritarian preferences, attentiveness, and the extent of countermobilization. Reversals in public opinion, diminished attentiveness, or the escalation in concerted opposition always threaten to undo prior victories.[53]

Implications for Further Research

In calling for greater attention to movement targets and arguing for the inclusion of a fuller ensemble of factors affecting their responses, this perspective questions some of the key methodological choices commonly found in social movement research. Here, I recapitulate only some of the many elements of the critique that has been presented in previous chapters. Specifically, this analysis demands that we think more carefully about what exactly movement activists and their supporters are doing to disrupt the interests of their targets. Too often, movement activities are measured by tallies of protest events, lacking any specification regarding the type of action, overall scale, or other factors that might elucidate the magnitude of the disruption. Of course, an aggregate tally of protest events makes sense as a rough indicator of the overall scale of movement agitation, but, without an explicit consideration of disruption costs, such a measure can be deceptive. The Albany protests, for instance, were substantial and sustained, but their inordinate focus on city hall reduced their full potential. Similarly, the emphasis upon protests or other unconventional actions often leads to the neglect of estimates of a movement's electoral leverage. A complete inventory of disruptive capabilities must include both conventional electoral mobilization and unconventional actions. In brief, further research on political movements must include all of the factors discussed above.

Specific movement demands must be assessed as well in light of their costliness for the targets and relevant third parties. As all movements

---

[52] Andrews (2002).
[53] Reductions in reproductive freedom since the 1973 *Roe* decision, particularly at the state level, exemplify this pattern.

encompass multiple goals, explanations for outcomes must be sensitive to the different cost configurations associated with different ambitions.[54] Presently, studies of movement outcomes either concentrate upon single issues (for example, women's suffrage or the enactment of nondiscrimination legislation, and so on) or aggregate measures of movement success (percentage of pro-movement bills passed by Congress); however, both approaches are problematic because they overlook comparative degrees of success of movement activities across specific domains.[55] The former suffers from tunnel vision in a manner that impairs the development of general explanations while the latter obscures particularistic outcomes using measures that collapse diverse movement goals into broad catchall categories.[56] While doubtless useful for statistical analysis, such all-encompassing measures overlook the vast differences in the concession costs associated with various movement initiatives and the peculiar paths toward outright victory, defeat, or compromises in between.[57] In

[54] From the perspective of the approach presented here, an explanation of, for instance, the outcomes of the environmental struggle would necessarily begin by distinguishing among the movement's many concerns such as clean water, global climate change, hazardous waste disposal, deforestation, air pollution, endangered species, and so on. As with civil rights, it is clear that many different activist factions comprise the environmental movement and these necessarily target different entities with certain characteristic vulnerabilities as well as activate different constellations of third parties. An abbreviated explanation for the greater gains on clean water as compared to global climate change might be derived from a consideration of the relevant disruption and concession costs associated with each. National clean water legislation benefits from strong public support, provides localities with valuable federal funds for water treatment facilities, the costs are hidden in general government revenues, and organized opposition is negligible (Mann 1975). By contrast, bills to reduce the emission of global warming gases threaten to make fossil fuels more costly, which can suddenly and visibly raise the price of gasoline, and home heating, and can negatively impact overall economic activity – all in order to avert a catastrophe that is imperceptible to many at present. Absent strong public support for decisive action on global warming, elected officials might anticipate severe concession costs from affected constituents and organized opponents. Under the latter circumstances, political targets respond with hesitation, and movement actors struggle to accentuate public anxieties about global warming to boost the political costs of inaction.
[55] See Costain and Majstorovic (1994); McCammon and Campbell (2001); Soule, McAdam, McCarthy, and Su (1999).
[56] For instance, legislative outcomes on hazardous wastes, mineral extraction, logging, and the protection of endangered species have previously been lumped together as a single dependent variable (Agnone 2007).
[57] Various studies consider congressional enactments in a particular domain either as the aggregate number of bills or a percentage of all bills passed. The theoretical difficulties of using aggregated quantitative measures are often acknowledged, but justified in various ways. Costain and Majstorovic (1994, 119) explain, "Although numeric categorization of laws minimizes important qualitative differences among them, it is hard to conceive

contrast to these approaches, I suggest that it is crucial to maintain the distinctions among discrete movement demands in order to discern the particular costs associated with them for targets and others.[58] In addition, though many studies neglect how the actions of movement opponents affect target responses, this investigation highlights them.

Along with the political considerations detailed above, this investigation specifies sectoral variations in the vulnerabilities of economic actors to both disruption and concession costs. Since the targets of many social movements are businesses, elucidating these distinctive patterns of cost exposure provides a theoretical basis for predicting a broad range of movement outcomes. As greater attention has been devoted of late to the influence of movements, nongovernmental organizations, and stakeholders on business targets, such an analytical framework can serve to enrich this developing research agenda.

Final Words

Clearly, social movements can and sometimes do bring about momentous social change, but this analysis demonstrates that there is no singular path to movement victory. Whereas the federal legislative success of the civil rights movement depended upon bringing public attentiveness to bear on national legislators, local successes in voting rights before 1965 often resulted from a lack of public attentiveness. Against economic targets, triumph stemmed from the durable imposition of disruption costs upon vulnerable interests and the inability of movement opponents to strike back effectively. Likewise, there are multiple routes toward movement defeat. As variation in outcomes depends upon the differing dynamics identified in this volume, the search for singular causal processes is futile.

of an alternate procedure capable of coding new laws qualitatively over a long time span." They describe how laws "build upon each other" and therefore it is difficult to isolate particular "stand alone" laws. The suggestion here, however, is that the particular types of feminist movement demands need to be distinguished to more accurately model the receptivity of elected officials. Along with the flattening out of differences within the public policy domain, overly aggregated measures are sometimes used to ascertain public opinion as well. Instead of considering public support for *specific* policies, quantitative studies often use exceedingly general questions, such as a willingness to vote for a woman president, to determine mass attitudes about employment discrimination.

[58] Further research might offer greater theoretical specification of the varieties of movement demands and associated costs for targets and others. Public policy studies distinguish, for instance, among distributive, regulatory, and redistributive policies and some research suggests that different political dynamics are associated with these policy types (Lowi 1964; Wilson 1980).

With a fuller appreciation of the diversity inherent in social movement challenges – tactics and demands, the different interests and vulnerabilities of the targets themselves, the activation of third parties, and so on – a more robust explanation for success, or lack thereof, can be offered. While this perspective does not provide an all-encompassing account of all social movement outcomes, it is meant to be provocative and can be extended further still. It is my hope that the historical evidence presented here renders the general argument plausible and that others will take up these analytical tools, refine their theoretical precision, and apply them to other cases and aspects of movement outcome. Ultimately, for those thirsting for social change and turning to movements as vehicles to bring this about, this investigation offers some encouragement and implicit hints at effective strategies to go forward; at the same time, the analysis delineates the real limitations upon movements that aspire to bring about a broader social transformation. Unless the demands are trivial, targets surrender nothing without an interest in doing so; thus, finding their vulnerabilities and giving them a compelling interest in capitulation continues to be an invaluable means for bringing about fundamental social change. The challenges are daunting, but not insurmountable.

References

Abbott, Carl. 1982. The Norfolk Business Community. In E. Jacoway and D. R. Colburn (eds.), *Southern Businessmen and Desegregation*. Baton Rouge: Louisiana State University Press.

Agnone, Jon. 2007. Amplifying Public Opinion: The Policy Impact of the U.S. Environmental Movement. *Social Forces* 85 (4):1593–1620.

Aiken, Charles S. 1998. *The Cotton Plantation South Since the Civil War*. Baltimore: Johns Hopkins University Press.

Amenta, Edwin. 2006. *When Movements Matter: The Townsend Plan and the Rise of Social Security*. Princeton: Princeton University Press.

Anderson, J. W. 1964. *Eisenhower, Brownell, and the Congress: The Tangled Origins of the Civil Rights Bill of 1956–57*. Tuscaloosa: University of Alabama Press.

Andrews, Kenneth T. 1997. The Impacts of Social Movements on the Political Process: The Civil Rights Movement and Black Electoral Politics in Mississippi. *American Sociological Review* 62 (5):800–19.

———. 2001. Social Movements and Policy Implementation: The Mississippi Civil Rights Movement and the War on Poverty, 1965 to 1971. *American Sociological Review* 66(1):71–95.

———. 2002. Movement–Countermovement Dynamics and the Emergence of New Institutions: The Case of "White Flight" Schools in Mississippi. *Social Forces* 80 (3):911–36.

———. 2004. *Freedom Is a Constant Struggle: The Mississippi Civil Rights Movement and Its Legacy*. Chicago: University of Chicago Press.

Arnold, R. Douglas. 1990. *The Logic of Congressional Action*. New Haven: Yale University Press.

Ashmore, Harry S. 1957. *An Epitaph for Dixie: A Southerner Explores a Middle Ground Where Thoughtful Americans Can Come Together*. New York: W. W. Norton and Company.

Aveni, Adrian F. 1978. Organizational Linkages and Resource Mobilization: The Significance of Link Strength and Breadth. *Sociological Quarterly* 19 (2):185–202.

Baker, Liva. 1996. *The Second Battle of New Orleans: The Hundred-Year Struggle to Integrate the Schools*. New York: HarperCollins Publishers.

Banaszak, Lee Ann. 2006. Women's Movements and Women in Movements: Influencing American Democracy from the "Outside"? In *Midwest Political Science Association Annual Meeting*. Chicago.

Barkan, Steven E. 1984. Legal Control of the Southern Civil Rights Movement. *American Sociological Review* 49 (4):552–65.

Bartley, Numan V. 1969 [1997]. *The Rise of Massive Resistance: Race and Politics in the South During the 1950's*. Baton Rouge: Louisiana State University Press.

———. 1995. *The New South, 1945–1980: The Story of the South's Modernization*. Baton Rouge: Louisiana State University Press.

Bartley, Numan V., and Hugh D. Graham. 1975 [1976]. *Southern Politics and the Second Reconstruction*. Baltimore: Johns Hopkins University Press.

Bayor, Ronald. 1996. *Race and the Shaping of Twentieth-Century Atlanta*. Chapel Hill: University of North Carolina Press.

Beck, E. M. 2000. Guess Who's Coming to Town: White Supremacy, Ethnic Competition, and Social Change. *Sociological Focus* 33 (2):153–74.

Belknap, Michal R. 1987. *Federal Law and Southern Order: Racial Violence and Constitutional Conflict in the Post-Brown South*. Athens: University of Georgia Press.

Belknap, Michal R., ed. 1991. *The Drive to Desegregate Places of Public Accommodation*. New York: Routledge.

Benford, Robert D., and David A. Snow. 2000. Framing Processes and Social Movements: An Overview and Assessment. *Annual Review of Sociology* 26:611–39.

Bensel, Richard F. 1984. *Sectionalism and American Political Development, 1880–1980*. Madison: University of Wisconsin Press.

———. 1990. *Yankee Leviathan: The Origins of Central State Authority in America, 1859–1877*. Cambridge: Cambridge University Press.

Bensel, Richard F., and Elizabeth M. Sanders. 1986. The Impact of the Voting Rights Act on Southern Welfare Systems. In B. Ginsberg and Allan Stone (eds.), *Do Elections Matter?* New York: M. E. Sharpe.

Berman, Daniel M. 1962. *A Bill Becomes a Law: The Civil Rights Act of 1960*. New York: Macmillan.

Berman, William C. 1970. *The Politics of Civil Rights in the Truman Administration*. Columbus: Ohio State University Press.

Beschloss, Michael R., ed. 1997. *Taking Charge: The Johnson White House Tapes, 1963–1964*. New York: Simon & Schuster.

Black, Earl. 1973. The Militant Segregationist Vote in the Post-*Brown* South: A Comparative Analysis. *Social Science Quarterly* 54 (1):66–84.

———. 1976. *Southern Governors and Civil Rights: Racial Segregation as a Campaign Issue in the Second Reconstruction*. Cambridge: Harvard University Press.

Black, Earl, and Merle Black. 1987. *Politics and Society in the South*. Cambridge: Harvard University Press.

Black, Merle. 1971. Southern Governors and Political Change: Campaign Stances on Racial Segregation and Economic Development, 1950–1959. *Journal of Southern Politics* 33 (3):703–34.

———. 1978. Racial Composition of Congressional Districts and Support for Federal Voting Rights in the American South. *Social Science Quarterly* 59 (3):435–450.

———. 1979. Regional and Partisan Bases of Congressional Support for the Changing Agenda of Civil Rights Legislation. *Journal of Politics* 41 (2):665–79.

Blalock, Hubert M., Jr. 1967. *Toward a Theory of Minority-Group Relations*. New York: John Wiley and Sons.

Bloom, Jack S. 1987. *Class, Race, and the Civil Rights Movement*. Bloomington: Indiana University Press.

Blumer, Herbert. 1958. Race Prejudice as a Sense of Group Position. *Pacific Sociological Review* 1 (1):3–7.

Bobo, Lawrence D. 1983. Whites' Opposition to Busing: Symbolic Racism or Realistic Group Conflict? *Journal of Personality and Social Psychology* 45 (6):1196–1210.

Bobo, Lawrence D., and Vincent L. Hutchings. 1996. Perceptions of Racial Group Competition: Extending Blumer's Theory of Group Position to a Multiracial Social Context. *American Sociological Review* 61 (6):951–72.

Boger, John Charles, and Gary Orfield, eds. 2005. *School Resegregation: Must the South Turn Back?* Chapel Hill: University of North Carolina Press.

Bolton, Charles C. 2005. *The Hardest Deal of All: The Battle Over School Segregation in Mississippi, 1870–1980*. Jackson: University Press of Mississippi.

Bonacich, Edna. 1972. A Theory of Ethnic Antagonism: The Split Labor Market. *American Sociological Review* 37 (5):547–59.

Bonastia, Christopher. 2006. The Historical Trajectory of Civil Rights Enforcement in Health Care. *Journal of Policy History* 18 (3):362–86.

Branch, Taylor. 1988. *Parting the Waters: America in the King Years, 1954–63*. New York: Simon & Schuster.

———. 1998. *Pillar of Fire: America in the King Years, 1963–65*. New York: Simon & Schuster.

Brauer, Carl M. 1977. *John F. Kennedy and the Second Reconstruction*. New York: Columbia University Press.

Brink, William, and Louis Harris. 1963. *The Negro Revolution in America*. New York: Simon & Schuster.

Burk, Robert F. 1984. *The Eisenhower Administration and Black Civil Rights*. Knoxville: University of Tennessee Press.

Burns, Haywood. 1965. The Federal Government and Civil Rights. In L. Friedman (ed.), *Southern Justice*. New York: Pantheon.

Burstein, Paul. 1979. Public Opinion, Demonstrations, and the Passage of Antidiscrimination Legislation. *Public Opinion Quarterly* 43 (2):157–72.

———. 1985. *Discrimination, Jobs, and Politics: The Struggle for Equal Employment Opportunity in the United States Since the New Deal*. Chicago: University of Chicago Press.

_____. 1999. Social Movements and Public Policy. In M. Giugni, D. McAdam, and C. Tilly (eds.), *How Social Movements Matter*. Minneapolis: University of Minnesota Press.

_____. 2006. Why Estimates of the Impact of Public Opinion on Public Policy Are Too High: Empirical and Theoretical Implications. *Social Forces* 84 (4):2273–89.

Burstein, Paul, Rachel L. Einwohner, and Jocelyn A. Hollander. 1995. The Success of Political Movements: A Bargaining Perspective. In J. C. Jenkins and B. Klandersman (eds.), *The Politics of Social Protest: Comparative Perspectives of States and Social Movements*. Minnesota: University of Minnesota Press.

Burstein, Paul, and April Linton. 2002. The Impact of Political Parties, Interest Groups, and Social Movement Organizations on Public Policy: Some Recent Evidence and Theoretical Concerns. *Social Forces* 81 (2):380–408.

Burstein, Paul, and Sarah Sausner. 2005. The Incidence and Impact of Policy-Oriented Collective Action: Competing Views. *Sociological Forum* 20 (3):403–19.

Button, James W. 1989. *Blacks and Social Change: Impact of the Civil Rights Movement in Southern Communities*. Princeton: Princeton University Press.

Caro, Robert A. 2002. *Master of the Senate*. New York: Alfred A. Knopf.

Carter, Dan T. 1995. *The Politics of Rage: George Wallace, the Origins of the New Conservatism, and the Transformation of American Politics*. New York: Simon & Schuster.

Carter, Hodding III. 1959. *The South Strikes Back*. New York: Doubleday and Company.

Chafe, William H. 1980. *Civilities and Civil Rights: Greensboro, North Carolina, and the Black Struggle for Freedom*. New York: Oxford University Press.

_____. 1986. *The Unfinished Journey: America Since World War II*. New York: Oxford University Press.

Chappell, David. 1994. *Inside Agitators: White Southerners in the Civil Rights Movement*. Baltimore: Johns Hopkins University Press.

_____. 2004. *Stone of Hope: Prophetic Religion and the Death of Jim Crow*. Chapel Hill: University of North Carolina Press.

Chen, Anthony S. 2007. The Party of Lincoln and the Politics of State Fair Employment Practices Legislation in the North, 1945–1964. *American Journal of Sociology* 112 (6):1713–74.

Chen, Anthony S., and Robin Phinney. 2004. Did the Civil Rights Movement Have a Direct Impact on Public Policy? Evidence from the Passage of State Fair Housing Laws, 1959–1965. Ann Arbor: University of Michigan.

Chong, Dennis. 1991. *Collective Action and the Civil Rights Movement*. Chicago: University of Chicago Press.

Cobb, James C. 1984. *Industrialization and Southern Society, 1877–1984*. Lexington: University of Kentucky Press.

_____. 1988. Beyond Planters and Industrialists: A New Perspective on the New South. *Journal of Southern History* 54:45–68.

_____. 1993 [1982]. *The Selling of the South: The Southern Crusade for Industrial Development, 1936–1980*, 2nd ed. Urbana: University of Illinois Press.

———. 1994. *The Most Southern Place on Earth: The Mississippi Delta and the Roots of Regional Identity*. New York: Oxford University Press.

Colburn, David R. 1982. The Saint Augustine Business Community. In E. Jacoway and D. R. Colburn (eds.), *Southern Businessmen and Desegregation*. Baton Rouge: Louisiana State University Press.

Collins, William J. 2003. The Political Economy of State-Level Fair Employment Laws, 1940–1964. *Explorations in Economic History* 40:24–51.

Congressional Quarterly. 1968. *Revolution in Civil Rights*, 4th ed. Washington, D.C.: Congressional Quarterly Service.

Congressional Quarterly. 1987. *Presidential Elections since 1789*, 4th ed. Washington, D.C.: Congressional Quarterly Service.

Cook, James Graham. 1962. *The Segregationists*. New York: Appleton-Century-Crofts.

Cook, Samuel DuBois. 1964. Political Movements and Organizations. *Journal of Politics* 26 (1):130–53.

Corzine, Jay, James Creech, and Lin Corzine. 1983. Black Concentration and Lynchings in the South: Testing Blalock's Power-Threat Hypothesis. *Social Forces* 61:774–96.

Costain, Anne N., and Steven Majstorovic. 1994. Congress, Social Movements and Public Opinion: Multiple Origins of Women's Rights Legislation. *Political Research Quarterly* 47 (1):111–35.

Cox, Maxie Myron, Jr. 1996. 1963 – The Year of Decision: Desegregation in South Carolina. Ph.D. diss., University of South Carolina, Columbia.

Cramer, M. Richard. 1963. School Desegregation and New Industry: The Southern Community Leaders' Viewpoint. *Social Forces* 41 (4):384–89.

Cummings, Scott. 1980. White Ethnics, Racial Prejudice, and Labor Market Segmentation. *American Journal of Sociology* 85 (4):938–50.

Cunningham, David. 2007A. Paths to Participation: A Profile of the Civil Rights–Era Ku Klux Klan. *Research in Social Movements, Conflicts, and Change* 27:283–309.

Cunningham, David, and Benjamin T. Phillips. 2007B. Contexts for Mobilization: Spatial Settings and Klan Presence in North Carolina, 1964–1966. *American Journal of Sociology* 113 (3):781–814.

Dallek, Robert. 1998. *Flawed Giant: Lyndon Johnson and His Times 1961–1973*. New York: Oxford University Press.

Davies, Gareth, and Martha Derthick. 1997. Race and Social Welfare Policy: The Social Security Act of 1935. *Political Science Quarterly* 112 (2):212–35.

Denzau, Arthur T., and Michael C. Munger. 1986. Legislators and Interest Groups: How Unorganized Interests Get Represented. *American Political Science Review* 80 (1):89–106.

Dittmer, John. 1994. *Local People: The Struggle for Civil Rights in Mississippi*. Urbana: University of Illinois Press.

Donovan, Todd, Jim Wenzel, and Shaun Bowler. 2001. Direct Democracy and Gay Rights Initiatives after Romer. In C. A. Rimmerman, K. D. Wald, and C. Wilcox (eds.). *The Politics of Gay Rights*. Chicago: University of Chicago Press.

Downs, Anthony. 1957. *An Economic Theory of Democracy*. New York: Harper and Row.

Dubofsky, Jean Eberhart. 1969. Fair Housing: A Legislative History and a Perspective. *Washburn Law Journal* 8:149–66.

Dudziak, Mary. 2000. *Cold War Civil Rights: Race and the Image of American Democracy*. Princeton: Princeton University Press.

Elazar, Daniel J. 1966. *American Federalism: A View from the States*. New York: Thomas Y. Crowell.

Elliott, Kimberly Ann, and Richard B. Freeman. 2004. White Hats or Don Quixotes? Human Rights Vigilantes in the Global Economy. In R. B. Freeman, J. Hersch, and L. Mishel (eds.). *Emerging Labor Market Institutions for the Twenty-First Century*. Chicago: University of Chicago Press.

Ely, James W., Jr. 1976. *The Crisis of Conservative Virginia: The Byrd Organization and the Politics of Massive Resistance*. Knoxville: University of Tennessee Press.

Eskew, Glenn T. 1997. *But for Birmingham: The Local and National Movements in the Civil Rights Struggle*. Chapel Hill: University of North Carolina Press.

Evers, Charles. 1974. Charles Evers Oral History Interview I. Joe B. Frantz. Johnson Presidential Library (accessed August 4, 2008).

Fairclough, Adam. 1995. *Race and Democracy: The Civil Rights Struggle in Louisiana*, 1915–1972. Athens: University of Georgia Press.

Farhang, Sean. 2007. The Political Development of Job Discrimination Litigation, 1963–1976. Center for the Study of Law and Society Jurisprudence and Social Policy Program Working Paper 59. University of California, Berkeley.

Findlay, James F. 1990. Religion and Politics in the Sixties: The Churches and the Civil Rights Act of 1964. *Journal of American History* 77 (1):66–92.

Fiorina, Morris. 2005. *Culture War? The Myth of a Polarized America*. New York: Pearson Education.

Fleming, Harold C. 1956. Resistance Movements and Racial Desegregation. *Annals of the American Academy of Political and Social Science* 304:44–52.

Flowers, Deidre B. 2005. The Launching of the Sit-In Movement: The Role of Black Women at Bennett College. *Journal of African American History*:52–63.

Forster, Arnold, and Benjamin R. Epstein. 1965. Report on the Ku Klux Klan. New York: Anti-Defamation League of B'nai B'rith.

Fowler, Linda L., and Ronald G. Shaiko. 1987. The Grass Roots Connection: Environmental Activists and Senate Roll Calls. *American Journal of Political Science* 31 (3):484–510.

Freeman, Jo. 1975. *The Politics of Women's Liberation: A Case Study of an Emerging Social Movement and Its Relation to the Policy Process*. New York: Longman.

Friedman, Gerald. 1988. Strike Success and Union Ideology: The United States and France, 1880–1914. *Journal of Economic History* 48:1–25.

Friedman, Monroe. 1985. *Consumer Boycotts: Effecting Change Through the Marketplace and the Media*. New York: Routledge.

Froner, Philip S. 1974. *Organized Labor and the Black Worker, 1619–1981*. New York: Praeger.

Frooman, Jeff. 1999. Stakeholder Influence Strategies. *Academy of Management Review* 14 (4):532–50.

Frymer, Paul. 1999. *Uneasy Alliances: Race and Party Competition in America.* Princeton: Princeton University Press.

Gamson, William A. 1975. *The Strategy of Social Protest.* Homewood: Dorsey Press.

————. 1992. *Talking Politics.* New York: Cambridge University Press.

Gamson, William A., and David S. Meyer. 1996. Framing Political Opportunity. In D. McAdam, J. D. McCarthy, and M. Zald (eds.), *Comparative Perspectives on Social Movements.* New York: Cambridge University Press.

Garrow, David J. 1978. *Protest at Selma: Martin Luther King, Jr., and the Voting Rights Act of 1965.* New Haven: Yale University Press.

————. 1981. *The FBI and Martin Luther King, Jr.: From "Solo" to Memphis.* New York: W. W. Norton and Company.

————. 1986. *Bearing the Cross: Martin Luther King, Jr., and the Southern Christian Leadership Conference.* New York: William Morrow and Company.

————. 1989. Black Civil Rights During the Eisenhower Years. In D. J. Garrow (ed.), *We Shall Overcome: The Civil Rights Movement in the United States in the 1950's and 1960's.* Brooklyn: Carlson Publishing.

Gates, Robbins L. 1964. *The Making of Massive Resistance: Virginia's Politics of Public School Desegregation, 1954–1956.* Chapel Hill: University of North Carolina Press.

Gelb, Joyce, and Marian Leif Palley. 1982. *Women and Public Policies.* Princeton: Princeton University Press.

Giles, Michael W. 1975. Black Concentration and School District Size as Predictors of School Segregation: The Impact of Federal Enforcement. *Sociology of Education* 48 (4):411–19.

Giugni, Marco. 1999. How Social Movements Matter: Past Research, Present Problems, Future Developments. In M. Giugni, D. McAdam, and C. Tilly (eds.), *How Social Movements Matter.* Minneapolis: University of Minnesota Press.

————. 2004. *Social Protest and Policy Change: Ecology, Antinuclear, and Peace Movements in Comparative Perspective.* Lanham, MD: Rowman & Littlefield.

Glaser, James M. 1994. Back to the Black Belt: Racial Environment and White Racial Attitudes in the South. *Journal of Politics* 56 (1):21–41.

Goldstone, Jack A., and Charles Tilly. 2001. Threat (and Opportunity). In R. Aminzade, J. Goldstone, D. McAdam, E. Perry, W. Sewell, S. Tarrow, and C. Tilly (eds.), *Silence and Voice in Contentious Politics.* New York: Cambridge University Press.

Goodwin, Jeff, and James M. Jasper. 1999. Caught in a Winding, Snarling Vine: The Structural Bias of Political Process Theory. *Sociological Forum* 14 (1):27–54.

Graham, Hugh Davis. 1990. *The Civil Rights Era: Origins and Development of National Policy 1960–1972.* New York: Oxford University Press.

Greenberg, Jack. 1994. *Crusaders in the Courts: How a Dedicated Band of Lawyers Fought for the Civil Rights Revolution.* New York: Basic Books.

Greenberg, Stanley B. 1980. *Race and State in Capitalist Development: Comparative Perspectives*. New Haven: Yale University Press.

Gusfield, Joseph. 1966. *Symbolic Crusade: Status Politics and the American Temperance Movement*. Urbana: University of Illinois Press.

Hacker, Jacob S., and Paul Pierson. 2005. *Off Center: The Republican Revolution and the Erosion of American Democracy*. New Haven: Yale University Press.

Haider-Markel, Donald P., and Kenneth J. Meier. 1996. The Politics of Gay and Lesbian Rights: Expanding the Scope of the Conflict. *Journal of Politics* 58 (2):332–49.

Hansen, John Mark. 1985. The Political Economy of Group Membership. *American Political Science Review* 79 (1):79–96.

_____. 1991. *Gaining Access: Congress and the Farm Lobby, 1919–1981*. Chicago: University of Chicago Press.

Harris, Edward E. 1968. Prejudice and Other Social Factors in School Segregation. *Journal of Negro Education* 37 (4):440–3.

Harvey, Anna. 1997. Women, Policy, and Party, 1920–1970: A Rational Choice Approach. *Studies in American Political Development* 11:292–325.

_____. 1998. *Votes Without Leverage: Women in American Electoral Politics, 1920–1968*. New York: Cambridge University Press.

Hayes, Michael T. 1992. *Incrementalism and Public Policy*. New York: Longman.

Heard, Alexander. 1952. *A Two-Party South?* Chapel Hill: University of North Carolina Press.

Heckman, James J., and Brook S. Payner. 1989. Determining the Impact of Federal Antidiscrimination Policy on the Economic Status of Blacks: A Study of South Carolina. *American Economic Review* 79:138–77.

Heer, David M. 1959. The Sentiment of White Supremacy: An Ecological Study. *American Journal of Sociology* 64 (6):592–8.

Hill, Herbert. 1977. The Equal Employment Opportunity Acts of 1964 and 1972: A Critical Analysis of the Legislative History and Administration of the Law. *Industrial Relations Law Journal* 2 (1):1–96.

Hochschild, Jennifer L. 1999. You Win Some, You Lose Some: Explaining the Pattern of Success and Failure in the Second Reconstruction. In M. Keller and R. S. Melnick (eds.), *Taking Stock: American Government in the Twentieth Century*. New York: Cambridge University Press.

Hornsby, Alton, Jr. 1982. A City That Was Too Busy to Hate. In E. Jacoway and D. R. Colburn (eds.), *Southern Businessmen and Desegregation*. Baton Rouge: Louisiana State University Press.

Huckfeldt, Robert, and Carol Weitzel Kohfeld. 1989. *Race and the Decline of Class in American Politics*. Urbana: University of Illinois Press.

Hyman, Herbert H., and Paul B. Sheatsley. 1964. Attitudes toward Desegregation. *Scientific American* (July) 16–23.

Inger, Morton. 1968. *Politics and Reality in an American City: The New Orleans School Crisis in 1960*. New York: Center for Urban Education.

Jackson, Robert Max. 1998. *Destined for Equality: The Inevitable Rise of Women's Status*. Cambridge: Harvard University Press.

Jacobs, Lawrence R., and Robert Y. Shapiro. 2000. *Politicians Don't Pander: Political Manipulation and the Loss of Democratic Responsiveness.* Chicago: University of Chicago Press.

Jacoway, Elizabeth, and David R. Colburn, eds. 1982. *Southern Businessmen and Desegregation.* Baton Rouge: Louisiana State University Press.

James, David R. 1988. The Transformation of the Southern Racial State: Class and Race Determinants of Local-State Structures. *American Sociological Review* 53 (1):191–208.

Jenkins, J. Craig, David Jacobs, and Jon Agnone. 2003. Political Opportunities and African-American Protest, 1948–1997. *American Journal of Sociology* 109 (2):277–303.

Jennings, M. Kent. 1964. *Community Influentials: The Elites of Atlanta.* New York: Free Press of Glencoe.

Jensen, Jane. 1987. Changing Discourse, Changing Agenda: Political Rights and Reproductive Rights in France. In M. F. Katzenstein and C. M. Mueller (eds.), *The Women's Movements of the United States and Western Europe: Consciousness, Political Opportunity, and Public Policy.* Philadelphia: Temple University Press.

Jonas, Gilbert, and Julian Bond. 2004. *Freedom's Sword: The NAACP and the Struggle against Racism in America, 1909–1969.* New York: Routledge.

Jones, Bryan D. 1994. *Reconceiving Decision-Making in Democratic Politics.* Chicago: University of Chicago Press.

Johnson, Lyndon B. Speech before Congress on Voting Rights. March 15, 1965. Miller Center of Public Affairs, University of Virginia, Multimedia Archive. Available online at: http://millercenter.org/scripps/archive/speeches/detail/3386.

Kane, Melinda D. 2007. Timing Matters: Shifts in the Causal Determinants of Sodomy Law Decriminalization, 1961–1998. *Social Problems* 54 (2):211–39.

Katagiri, Yasuhiro. 2001. *The Mississippi State Sovereignty Commission: Civil Rights and States' Rights.* Jackson: University of Mississippi Press.

Katzenbach, Nicholas D. 1964. Administration of Race Relations. Presented at the National Conference on Public Administration, New York.

Katznelson, Ira, Kimberly Geiger, and Daniel Kryder. 1993. Limiting Liberalism: The Southern Veto in Congress, 1933–1950. *Political Science Quarterly* 108 (2):283–306.

Keesing's Research Reports. 1970. *Race Relations in the USA, 1954–1968.* New York: Charles Scribner's Sons.

Kennan, John, and Robert Wilson. 1989. Strategic Bargaining Models and Interpretation of Strike Data. *Journal of Applied Econometrics* 4 (Supplement):S87–S130.

Kennedy, John F. Address on Civil Rights. June 11, 1963. Miller Center of Public Affairs, University of Virginia, Multimedia Archive. Available online at: http://millercenter.org/scripps/archive/speeches/detail/3375.

Key, V. O., Jr. 1949. *Southern Politics in State and Nation.* New York: Alfred A. Knopf.

King, Brayden. 2008. A Social Movement Perspective of Stakeholder Collective Action and Influence. *Business and Society* 47 (1):21–49.

King, Brayden, and Sarah A. Soule. 2007. Social Movements as Extra-Institutional Entrepreneurs: The Effect of Protests on Stock Price Returns. *Administrative Science Quarterly* 52:413–42.

Kingdon, John W. 1973 [1989]. *Congressmen's Voting Decisions*, 3rd ed. Ann Arbor: University of Michigan Press.

Klarman, Michael J. 2006. *Brown v. Board of Education and the Civil Rights Movement*. New York: Oxford University Press.

Klein, Ethel. 1985. *Gender Politics: From Consciousness to Mass Politics*. Cambridge: Harvard University Press.

Klinkner, Phillip, and Rogers Smith. 1999. *The Unsteady March: The Rise and Decline of Racial Equality in America*. Chicago: University of Chicago Press.

Kluger, Richard. 1977. *Simple Justice*. New York: Random House.

Koopmans, Ruud, and Paul Statham. 1999. Ethnic and Civic Conceptions of Nationhood and Differential Success of the Extreme Right in Germany and Italy. In M. Guigni, D. McAdam, and C. Tilly (eds.), *How Social Movements Matter*. Minneapolis: University of Minnesota Press.

Kotz, Nick. 2005. *Judgment Days: Lyndon Baines Johnson, Martin Luther King Jr., and the Laws That Changed America*. New York: Houghton Mifflin Company.

Kousser, Morgan. 1974. *The Shaping of Southern Politics: Suffrage Restriction and the Establishment of the One-Party South*. New Haven: Yale University Press.

Kraft, Michael E. 2000. U.S. Environmental Policy and Politics: From the 1960s to the 1990s. *Journal of Policy History* 12 (1):17–42.

Krehbiel, Keith. 1998. *Pivotal Politics: A Theory of US Lawmaking*. Chicago: University of Chicago Press.

Kryder, Daniel. 2001. *Divided Arsenal: Race and the American State During World War II*. New York: Cambridge University Press.

Laue, James H. 1965 [1989]. *Direct Action and Desegregation, 1960–1962: Toward a Theory of the Rationalization of Protest*. Brooklyn: Carlson Publishing.

Lawson, Steven F. 1991. From Boycotts to Ballots: The Reshaping of National Politics. In A. L. Robinson and P. Sullivan (eds.), *New Directions in Civil Rights Studies*. Charlottesville: University Press of Virginia.

Lee, Taeku. 2002. *Mobilizing Public Opinion: Black Insurgency and Racial Attitudes in the Civil Rights Era*. Chicago: University of Chicago Press.

Levesque, Russell J. 1972. White Response to Nonwhite Voter Registration in Southern States. *Pacific Sociological Review* 15 (2):245–55.

Lewis, David L. 1970. *King: A Critical Biography*. Baltimore: Praeger.

Lewis, George. 2006. *Massive Resistance: The White Response to the Civil Rights Movement*. New York: Hodder Arnold.

Lieberman, Robert C. 1995. Race and the Organization of Welfare Policy. In P. E. Peterson (ed.), *Classifying by Race*. Princeton:. Princeton University Press.

———. 2001. *Shifting the Color Line: Race and the American Welfare State*. Cambridge: Harvard University Press.

Lincoln, C. Eric. 1989. The Strategy of a Sit-In. In D. J. Garrow (ed.), *Atlanta, Georgia,1960–1961: Sit-Ins and Student Activism*. Brooklyn: Carlson Publishing.

Lipsky, Michael. 1968. Protest as a Political Resource. *American Political Science Review* 62 (4):1144–58.

Lo, Clarence Y. H. 1982. Countermovements and Conservative Movements in the Contemporary U.S. *Annual Review of Sociology* 8:107–34.

Loevy, Robert D. 1990. *To End All Segregation: The Politics of the Passage of the Civil Rights Act of 1964*. Lanham, MD: University Press of America.

Logan, Rayford W. 1965. *The Betrayal of the Negro from Rutherford B. Hayes to Woodrow Wilson*. New York: Collier Books.

Lohmann, Susanne. 1993. A Signaling Model of Informative and Manipulative Political Action. *American Political Science Review* 87 (2):319–33.

———. 1998. An Information Rationale for the Power of Special Interests. *American Political Science Review* 92 (4):809–27.

Lowi, Theodore. 1964. American Business, Public Policy, Case-Studies, and Political Theory. *World Politics* 16 (4):677–715.

Luders, Joseph E. 2000. The Politics of Exclusion: The Political Economy of Civil Rights in the American South, 1954–65. Ph.D. diss., New School for Social Research.

———. 2003. Countermovements, the State, and the Intensity of Racial Contention in the American South. In J. Goldstone (ed.), *States, Parties, and Social Movements: Protest and the Dynamics of Institutional Change*. New York: Cambridge University Press.

———. 2005. Civil Rights Success and the Politics of Racial Violence. *Polity* 37 (1):108–29.

———. 2006. The Economics of Movement Sucess: Business Responses to Civil Rights Mobilization. *American Journal of Sociology* 111 (4):963–98.

Luebke, Paul. 1990. *Tar Heel Politics: Myths and Realities*. Chapel Hill: University of North Carolina Press.

Lytle, Clifford M. 1966. The History of the Civil Rights Bill of 1964. *Journal of Negro History* 51 (4):275–96.

MacNeil, Neil. 1970. *Dirksen: Portrait of a Public Man*. New York: World Publishing Company.

Man, Albon P., Jr. 1951. Labor Competition and the New York Draft Riot of 1863. *Journal of Negro History* 36 (4):375–405.

Mann, Dean E. 1975. Political Incentives in U.S. Water Policy: Relationship between Distributive and Regulatory Politics. In M. Holden, Jr., and D. L. Dresang (eds.), *What Government Does*. Beverly Hills, CA: Sage Publications.

March, James G., and Johan P. Olsen. 1989. *Rediscovering Institutions: The Organizational Basis of Politics*. New York: Free Press.

Marger, Martin N. 1984. Social Movement Organizations and Response to Environmental Change: The NAACP, 1960–1973. *Social Problems* 32 (1):16–30.

Martin, Louis. 1969. Louis Martin Oral History Interview I. David G. McComb. Johnson Presidential Library (cited August 4, 2008).

Mathias, Charles McC., Jr. 1999. Fair Housing Legislation: Not an Easy Row to Hoe. *Cityscape: A Journal of Policy Development and Research* 4 (3):21–33.

Matthews, Donald R., and James W. Prothro. 1962. Southern Racial Attitudes: Conflict, Awareness, and Political Change. *Annals of the American Academy of Political and Social Science* 344:108–21.

———. 1963. Social and Economic Factors and Negro Voter Registration in the South. *American Political Science Review* 57 (1):24–44.

———. 1966. *Negroes and the New Southern Politics.* New York: Harcourt, Brace and World.

Mayhew, David R. 1974. *Congress: The Electoral Connection.* New Haven: Yale University Press.

McAdam, Doug. 1982. *Political Process and the Development of Black Insurgency, 1930–1970.* Chicago: University of Chicago Press.

———. 1983. Tactical Innovation and the Pace of Insurgency. *American Sociological Review* 48 (6):735–54.

———. 1986. Recruitment to High-Risk Activism: The Case of Freedom Summer. *American Journal of Sociology* 92 (1):64–90.

———. 1996. The Framing Function of Movement Tactics: Strategic Dramaturgy in the American Civil Rights Movement. In D. McAdam, J. D. McCarthy, and M. N. Zald (eds.), *Comparative Perspectives on Social Movements: Political Opportunities, Mobilizing Structures and Cultural Framings.* Cambridge: Cambridge University Press.

McCammon, Holly J., and Karen E. Campbell. 2001. Winning the Vote in the West: The Political Successes of the Women's Suffrage Movement, 1866–1919. *Gender and Society* 15 (1):55–82.

McCarrick, Earlean Mary. 1964. Louisiana's Official Resistance to Desegregation. Ph.D. diss., Vanderbilt University.

McCarthy, John D., and Mayer N. Zald. 1977. Resource Mobilization and Social Movements: A Partial Theory. *American Journal of Sociology* 82 (6):1212–41.

McCullough, David. 1992. *Truman.* New York: Simon & Schuster.

McKiven, Henry M., Jr. 1995. *Iron and Steel: Class, Race, and Community in Birmingham, Alabama, 1875–1920.* Chapel Hill: University of North Carolina Press.

McMillen, Neil R. 1971 [1994]. *The Citizens' Council: Organized Resistance to the Second Reconstruction.* Urbana: University of Illinois Press.

———. 1977. Black Enfranchisement in Mississippi: Federal Enforcement and Black Protest in the 1960s. *Journal of Southern History* 43 (3):351–72.

McVeigh, Rory. 1999. Structural Incentives for Conservative Mobilization: Power Devaluation and the Rise of the Ku Klux Klan, 1915–1925. *Social Forces* 77 (4):1461–96.

McWhorter, Diane. 2001. *Carry Me Home: Birmingham, Alabama: The Climactic Battle of the Civil Rights Revolution.* New York: Simon and Schuster.

Mettler, Suzanne. 1998. *Dividing Citizens: Gender and Federalism in New Deal Public Policy.* Ithaca: Cornell University Press.

Meyer, David S., and Debra Minkoff. 2004. Conceptualizing Political Opportunity. *Social Forces* 82 (4):1457–91.

Meyer, David S., and Suzanne Staggenborg. 1996. Movements, Countermovements, and the Structure of Political Opportunity. *American Journal of Sociology* 101 (6):1628–60.

Miller, Helen Hill. 1960. Private Business and Public Education in the South. *Harvard Business Review* 38 (4):75–88.

Miller, Warren E., and Donald E. Stokes. 1963. Constituency Influence in Congress. *American Political Science Review* 57: 45–57.

Minchin, Timothy J. 1999. *Hiring the Black Worker: The Racial Integration of the Southern Textile Industry, 1960–1980.* Chapel Hill: University of North Carolina Press.

Montgomery, David. 1979. *Workers' Control in America: Studies in the History of Work, Technology, and Labor Struggles.* Cambridge: Cambrige University Press.

Moon, Henry Lee. 1948. *Balance of Power: The Negro Vote.* Garden City, NY: Doubleday.

Morris, Aldon D. 1984. *The Origins of the Civil Rights Movement: Black Communities Organizing for Change.* New York: Free Press.

———. 1993. Birmingham Confrontation Reconsidered: An Analysis of the Dynamics and Tactics of Mobilization. *American Sociological Review* 58 (5):621–36.

Mottl, Tahi. 1980. The Analysis of Countermovements. *Social Problems* 27 (5):620–35.

Moye, J. Todd. 2004. *Let the People Decide: Black Freedom and White Resistance Movements in Sunflower County, Mississippi, 1945–1986.* Chapel Hill: University of North Carolina Press.

Murphy, Walter F. 1959. The South Counterattacks: The Anti-NAACP Laws. *Western Political Quarterly* 12 (2):371–90.

Muse, Benjamin. 1961. *Virginia's Massive Resistance.* Bloomington: Indiana University Press.

———. 1964. *Ten Years of Prelude: The Story of Integration since the Supreme Court's 1954 Decision.* New York: Viking Press.

Myrdal, Gunnar, with the assistance of Richard Sterner and Arnold Rose. 1944. *An American Dilemma: The Negro Problem and Modern Democracy.* New York: Harper and Row.

Nicholls, William H. 1960. *Southern Tradition and Regional Progress.* Chapel Hill: University of North Carolina Press.

Northrup, Herbert R., and Richard L. Rowan. 1970. *Negro Employment in Southern Industry: A Study of Racial Policies in Five Industries.* Philadelphia: Industrial Research Unit of Wharton School of Finance and Commerce.

Nunnelly, William A. 1991. *Bull Connor.* Tuscaloosa: University of Alabama Press.

Odegard, Peter. 1928. *Pressure Politics: The Story of the Anti-Saloon League.* New York: Columbia University Press.

Oldfield, Duane M. 1996. *The Right and the Righteous: The Christian Right Confronts the Republican Party.* Lanham, MD: Rowman & Littlefield.

Olson, Mancur. 1965. *The Logic of Collective Action.* Cambridge: Harvard University Press.

Olzak, Susan. 1992. *The Dynamics of Ethnic Competition and Conflict.* Palo Alto: Stanford University Press.

Olzak, Susan, and Joane Nagel. 1986. *Competitive Ethnic Relations*. New York: Academic Press.

Oppenheimer, Martin. 1963 [1989]. *The Sit-In Movement of 1960*. Brooklyn: Carlson Publishing.

O'Reilly, Kenneth. 1989. *"Racial Matters": The FBI's Secret File on Black America, 1960–1972*. New York: Free Press.

———. 1995. *Nixon's Piano: Presidents and Racial Politics from Washington to Clinton*. New York: The Free Press.

Orfield, Gary. 1969. *The Reconstruction of Southern Education: The Schools and the 1964 Civil Rights Act*. New York: Wiley-Interscience.

Overby, L. Marvin, and Sarah Ritchie. 1991. Mobilized Masses and Strategic Opponents: A Resource Mobilization Analysis of the Clean Air and Nuclear Freeze Movements. *Western Political Quarterly* 44 (2):329–51.

Page, Benjamin, and Robert Y. Shapiro. 1983. Effects of Public Opinion on Policy. *American Political Science Review* 77:175–90.

———. 2000. *Politicians Don't Pander: Political Manipulation and the Loss of Democratic Responsiveness*. Chicago: University of Chicago Press.

Patterson, Barbara. 1964. The Price We Pay. Atlanta: Southern Regional Council and the Anti-Defamation League.

Patterson, Jack. 1966. Business Response to the Negro Movement. *New South* (Winter):67–74.

Payne, Charles M. 1995. *I've Got the Light of Freedom: The Organizing Tradition and the Mississippi Freedom Struggle*. Berkeley: University of California Press.

Permaloff, Anne, and Carl Grafton. 1995. *Political Power in Alabama: The More Things Change*. Athens: University of Georgia Press.

Pettigrew, Thomas F. 1957. Demographic Correlates of Border-State Desegregation. *American Sociological Review* 22 (6):683–9.

Piven, Frances Fox. 2006. *Challenging Authority: How Ordinary People Change America*. Lanham, MD: Rowman & Littlefield.

Piven, Frances Fox and Richard A. Cloward. 1977. *Poor People's Movements: Why They Succeed, How They Fail*. New York: Vintage Books.

Plotke, David. *Democratic Breakup: From the Civil Rights Act to the End of the Democratic Order*. New York: Cambridge University Press (in press).

Pruitt, Dean G., and Peter J. Carnevale. 1993. *Negotiation in Social Conflict*. Buckingham: Open University Press.

Pruitt, Stephen W., and Monroe Friedman. 1986. Determining the Effectiveness of Consumer Boycotts: A Stock Price Analysis of Their Impact on Corporate Targets. *Journal of Consumer Policy* 9:375–87.

Raper, Arthur. 1968. *Preface to Peasantry: A Tale of Two Black Belt Counties*. New York: Atheneum.

Ripley, Randall B., and Grace A. Franklin. 1976. *Congress, the Bureaucracy, and Public Policy*. Homewood: Dorsey Press.

Robinson, Plater. 1995. *A House Divided: A Teaching Guide on the History of Civil Rights in Louisiana*. Southern Institute for Education and Research at Tulane University. New Orleans, Louisiana.

Roche, Jeff. 1998. *Restructured Resistance: The Sibley Commission and the Politics of Desegregation in Georgia*. Athens: University of Georgia Press.

Rochon, Thomas R., and Daniel A. Mazmanian. 1993. Social Movements and the Policy Process. *Annals of the American Academy of Political and Social Science* 528 (Citizens, Protest, and Democracy): 75–87.

Rodgers, Harrell R., Jr., and Charles S. Bullock III. 1972. *Law and Social Change: Civil Rights Laws and Their Consequences*. New York: McGraw-Hill Book Company.

Rodriguez, Daniel B., and Barry R. Weingast. 2003. The Positive Political Theory of Legislative History: New Perspectives on the 1964 Civil Rights Act and Its Interpretation. *University of Pennsylvania Law Review* 151 (4):1417–1542.

Roediger, David. 1999. *The Wages of Whiteness: Race and the Making of the American Working Class*. New York: Verso.

Rogers, Kim Lacy. 1993. *Righteous Lives: Narratives of the New Orleans Civil Rights Movement*. New York: New York University Press.

Rosenberg, Gerald N. 1991. *The Hollow Hope: Can Courts Bring About Social Change*. Chicago: University of Chicago Press.

Rosenberg, Jonathan, and Zachary Karabell. 2003. *Kennedy, Johnson, and the Quest for Justice*. New York: W. W. Norton and Company.

Rosenstone, Steven J., and John Mark Hansen. 1993. *Mobilization, Participation, and Democracy in America*. New York: Macmillan.

Ross, J., and B. M. Shaw. 1993. Organizational Escalation and Exit: Lessons from the Shoreham Nuclear Power Plant. *Academy of Management Journal* 36:701–32.

Routh, Frederick B., and Paul Anthony. 1957. Southern Resistance Forces. *Phylon Quarterly* 18 (1):50–8.

Rucht, Dieter. 2004. Movement Allies, Adversaries, and Third Parties. In D. A. Snow, S. A. Soule and H. Kriesi (eds.), *The Blackwell Companion to Social Movements*. Malden: Blackwell Publishing.

Rueschemeyer, Dietrich, Evelyne Huber Stephens, and John D. Stephens. 1992. *Capitalist Development and Democracy*. Chicago: University of Chicago Press.

Rustin, Bayard. 1965. From Protest to Politics: The Future of the Civil Rights Movement. *Commentary* (February):25–31.

Salamon, Lester M., and Stephen Van Evera. 1973. Fear, Apathy, and Discrimination: A Test of Three Explanations of Political Participation. *American Political Science Review* 67 (4):1288–1306.

Sale, Kirkpatrick. 1993. *The Green Revolution: The American Environmental Movement, 1962–1992*. New York: Hill and Wang.

Sanders, Elizabeth. 1999. *Roots of Reform: Farmers, Workers, and the American State, 1877–1917*. Chicago: University of Chicago Press.

Sanders, Francine. 1997. Civil Rights Roll-Call Voting in the House of Representatives, 1957–1991: A Systematic Analysis. *Political Research Quarterly* 50 (3):483–502.

Santoro, Wayne A. 2002. The Civil Rights Movement's Struggle for Fair Employment: A "Dramatic Events–Conventional Politics" Model. *Social Forces* 81 (1):177–206.

Santoro, Wayne A. and Gail M. McGuire. 1997. Social Movement Insiders: The Impact of Institutional Activists on Affirmative Action and Comparable Worth Policies. *Social Problems* 44 (4):503–19.

Schaefer, Richard T. 1971. The Ku Klux Klan: Continuity and Change. *Phylon* 32 (2):143–57.

Schattschneider, E. E. 1960. *The Semisovereign People: A Realist's View of Democracy in America*. New York: Holt, Rinehart, and Winston.

Schlesinger, Arthur M., Jr. 1965. *A Thousand Days: John F. Kennedy in the White House*. Boston: Houghton Mifflin Company.

Schneider, Anne, and Helen Ingram. 1993. Social Construction of Target Populations: Implications for Politics and Policy. *American Political Science Review* 87 (2):334–47.

Schuman, Howard, Charlotte Steeh, and Lawrence Bobo. 1985. *Racial Attitudes in America: Trends and Interpretations*. Cambridge: Harvard University Press.

Schurman, Rachel. 2004. Fighting "Frankenfood": Industry Opportunity Structures and the Efficacy of the Anti-Biotech Movement in Western Europe. *Social Forces* 51 (2):243–68.

Schwartz, Michael. 1976. *Radical Protest and Social Structure: The Southern Farmers' Alliance and Cotton Tenancy, 1880–1890*. New York: Academic Press.

Sheatsley, Paul B. 1966. White Attitudes Toward the Negro. In T. Parsons and K. B. Clark (eds.), *The Negro American*. Boston: Houghton Mifflin.

Silver, James W. 1964. *Mississippi: The Closed Society*. New York: Harcourt, Brace and World.

Sitkoff, Harvard. 1981. *The Struggle for Black Equality, 1954–1980*. New York: Hill and Wang.

Smith, Miriam. 2005. The Politics of Same-Sex Marriage in Canada and the United States. *PS: Political Science and Politics* 38 (2):225–8.

Smith, N. Craig. 1990. *Morality and the Market: Consumer Pressure for Corporate Accountability*. London: Routledge.

Smith, Richard A. 1995. Interest Group Influence in the U.S. Congress. *Legislative Studies Quarterly* 20 (1):89–139.

Smith, Tom W. 1980. America's Most Important Problem – A Trend Analysis, 1946–1976. *Public Opinion Quarterly* 44 (2):164–80.

Snow, David A. 2004. Framing Processes, Ideology, and Discursive Fields. In D. A. Snow, S. A. Soule, and H. Kriesi (eds.), *The Blackwell Companion to Social Movements*. Malden, MA: Blackwell Publishing.

Sokol, Jason. 2006. *There Goes My Everything: White Southerners in the Age of Civil Rights, 1945–1975*. New York: Alfred A. Knopf.

Soule, Sarah A. 2004. Going to the Chapel? Same-Sex Marriage Bans in the United States, 1973–2000. *Social Problems* 51 (4):453–77.

Soule, Sarah A., Doug McAdam, John McCarthy, and Yang Su. 1999. Protest Events: Cause or Consequence of State Action? The U.S. Women's Movement and Federal Congressional Activities, 1956–1979. *Mobilization* 4 (2):239–56.

Soule, Sarah A., and Jennifer Earl. 2001. The Enactment of State-Level Hate Crime Law in the United States: Intrastate and Interstate Factors. *Sociological Perspectives* 44 (3):281–305.

Soule, Sarah A., and Susan Olzak. 2004. When Do Movements Matter? The Politics of Contingency and the Equal Rights Amendment. *American Sociological Review* 69 (4):473–97.

Soule, Sarah A., and Nella Van Dyke. 1999. Black Church Arson in the United States, 1989–1996. *Ethnic and Racial Studies* 22 (4):724–42.

Southern Education Reporting Service. 1964. Statistical Summary of School Segregation–Desegregation in the Southern and Border States. Nashville.

Southern Regional Council. 1960. Intimidation, Reprisal, and Violence in the South's Racial Crisis. Atlanta: Southern Regional Council.

———. 1961. The Student Protest Movement: A Recapitulation. Atlanta: Southern Regional Council.

Spar, Debora, and Lane Le Mure. 2003. The Power of Activism: Assessing the Impact of NGOs on Global Business. *California Management Review* 45 (3):78–101.

Stampp, Kenneth M. 1965. *The Era of Reconstruction*. New York: Vintage Books.

Stein, Lana, and Stephen E. Condrey. 1987. Integrating Municipal Workforces: A Comparative Study of Six Southern Cities. *Publius* 17 (2):93–103.

Steinmo, Sven, and Jon Watts. 1995. It's the Institutions, Stupid! Why Comprehensive National Health Insurance Always Fails in America. *Journal of Health Politics, Policy and Law* 20 (2):329–72.

Stern, Mark. 1987. The Democratic Presidency and Voting Rights in the Second Reconstruction. In L. W. Moreland, R. P. Steed and T. Bakers (eds.), *Blacks in Southern Politics*. New York: Praeger.

———. 1992. *Calculating Visions: Kennedy, Johnson and Civil Rights*. New Brunswick: Rutgers University Press.

Stimson, James A., Michael B. MacKuen, and Robert S. Erikson. 1995. *Dynamic Representation. American Political Science Review* 89:543–65.

Stone, Chuck. 1968. *Black Political Power in America*. New York: Dell Publishing.

Stone, Deborah. 2002. *Policy Paradox: The Art of Political Decision Making*. New York: W. W. Norton and Company.

Stratmann, Thomas. 1991. What Do Campaign Contributions Buy? Deciphering Causal Effects of Money and Votes. *Southern Economic Journal* 57:606–20.

Sundquist, James L. 1968. *Politics and Policy: The Eisenhower, Kennedy, and Johnson Years*. Washington, D.C.: Brookings Institution.

Sutherland, Elizabeth, ed. 1965. *Letters from Mississippi*. New York: McGraw-Hill Book Company.

Szymanski, Ann-Marie E. 2003. *Pathways to Prohibition: Radicals, Moderates, and Social Movement Outcomes*. Durham: Duke University Press.

Terchek, Ronald J. 1974. Protest and Bargaining. *Journal of Peace Research* 11 (2):133–44.

Thernstrom, Abigail M. 1987. *Whose Votes Count? Affirmative Action and Minority Voting Rights*. Cambridge: Harvard University Press.

Thornton, J. Mills III. 1991. Municipal Politics and the Course of the Movement. In A. L. Robinson and P. Sullivan (eds.), *New Directions in Civil Rights Studies*. Charlottesville: University Press of Virginia.

———. 2002. *Dividing Lines: Municipal Politics and the Struggle for Civil Rights in Montgomery, Birmingham, and Selma*. Tuscaloosa: University of Alabama Press.

Tilly, Charles. 1978. *From Mobilization to Revolution*. Reading, PA: Addison-Wesley.

———. 1995. *Popular Contention in Great Britain, 1758–1834*. Cambridge: Harvard University Press.

Timpone, Richard J. 1995. Mass Mobilization or Government Intervention? The Growth of Black Registration in the South. *Journal of Politics* 57 (2):425–42.

Tolnay, Stewart E., and E. M. Beck. 1995. *A Festival of Violence: An Analysis of Southern Lynching, 1882–1930*. Urbana: University of Illinois Press.

Tuck, Stephen G. N. 2001. *Beyond Atlanta: The Struggle for Racial Equality in Georgia, 1940–1980*. Atlanta: University of Georgia Press.

Tumin, Melvin M. 1958. *Desegregation: Resistance and Readiness*. Princeton: Princeton University Press.

Turner, Ralph H. 1970. Determinants of Social Movement Strategies. In S. Tamotsu (ed.), *Human Nature and Collective Behavior: Papers in Honor of Herbert Blumer*. Englewood Cliffs, NJ: Prentice-Hall.

Tversky, Amos, and Daniel Kahneman. 1991. Loss Aversion in Riskless Choice: A Reference-Dependent Model. *Quarterly Journal of Economics* 106:1039–61.

Valelly, Richard. 2004. *The Two Reconstructions: The Struggle for Black Enfranchisement*. Chicago: University of Chicago Press.

Vander Zanden, James W. 1965. *Race Relations in Transition*. New York: Random House.

Van Dyke, Nella, and Sarah A. Soule. 2002. Structural Social Change and the Mobilizing Effect of Threat: Explaining Levels of Patriot and Militia Organizing in the United States. *Social Problems* 49 (4):497–520.

Vanfossen, Beth E. 1968. Variables Related to Resistance to Desegregation in the South. *Social Forces* 47 (1):39–44.

Vogel, David. 1996. *Kindred Strangers: The Uneasy Relationship Between Business and Politics in America*. Princeton: Princeton University Press.

Wald, Kenneth D., Dennis E. Owen, and Samuel S. Hill, Jr. 1988. Churches as Political Communities. *American Political Science Review* 82 (2):531–48.

Walker, Jack L. 1963. Protest and Negotiation: A Case Study of Negro Leadership in Atlanta, Georgia. *Midwest Journal of Political Science* 7 (2):99–124.

———. 1989A. Sit-Ins in Atlanta. In D. J. Garrow (ed.), *Atlanta, Georgia, 1960–1961: Sit-Ins and Student Activism*. Brooklyn: Carlson Publishing.

———. 1989B. The Functions of Disunity: Negro Leadership in a Southern City. In D. J. Garrow (ed.), *Atlanta, Georgia, 1960–1961: Sit-Ins and Student Activism*. Brooklyn: Carlson Publishing.

Walton, Hanes, Jr. 1988. *When the Marching Stopped: The Politics of Civil Rights Regulatory Agencies*. Albany: State University of New York Press.

Watters, Pat, and Reese Cleghorn. 1967. *Climbing Jacob's Ladder*. New York: Harcourt, Brace, and World.

Webb, Clive, ed. 2005. *Massive Resistance: Southern Opposition to the Second Reconstruction*. New York: Oxford University Press.

Whalen, Charles, and Barbara Whalen. 1985. *The Longest Debate: A Legislative History of the 1964 Civil Rights Act*. Washington, D.C.: Seven Locks Press.

Wilhoit, Francis M. 1973. *The Politics of Massive Resistance*. New York: George Braziller.

Wilkins, Roy. 1969. Roy Wilkins Oral History Interview. Thomas H. Baker. Johnson Presidential Library (accessed August 5, 2008).

Williams, Juan. 1988. *Eyes on the Prize: America's Civil Rights Years, 1954–1965*. New York: Penguin.

Wilson, James Q. 1961. The Strategy of Protest: Problems of Negro Civic Action. *Journal of Conflict Resolution* 3:291–303.

———. 1980. *The Politics of Regulation*. New York: Basic Books.

Wolff, Miles. 1970. *Lunch at the Five and Ten*. New York: Stein and Day.

Wolk, Allan. 1970. Implementation of Southern Negro Civil Rights: The Federal Executive Branch. Ph.D. diss., New York University.

———. 1971. *The Presidency and Black Civil Rights: Eisenhower to Nixon*. Rutherford, NJ: Fairleigh Dickinson University Press.

Woodward, C. Vann. 1951. *Origins of the New South, 1877–1913*. Baton Rouge: Louisiana State University Press.

———. 1955 [1979 3rd. rev. ed.]. *The Strange Career of Jim Crow*. New York: Oxford University Press.

Wright, Gavin. 1986. *Old South, New South: Revolutions in the Southern Economy since the Civil War*. Baton Rouge: Louisiana University Press.

———. 2003. The Economics of Civil Rights. Citidel Conference on the Civil Rights Movement in South Carolina. Charleston, South Carolina.

Wright, John R. 1996. *Interest Groups and Congress: Lobbying, Contributions, and Influence*. Boston: Allyn and Bacon.

Zald, Mayer N., and Bert Useem. 1987. Movement and Countermovement Interaction: Mobilization, Tactics, and State Involvement. In M. N. Zald and J. D. McCarthy (eds.), *Social Movements in an Organizational Society*. New Brunswick, NJ: Transaction Books.

Zartman, I. William. 1978. *The Negotiation Process*. Beverly Hills, CA: Sage Publications.

Index

accommodators. *See* movement
    targets; third parties
African-Americans
    in Atlanta politics, 87
    discrimination against, 24–25, 133
    electoral significance of, 18, 24,
        150
    electoral support for Kennedy
        among, 162
    electoral support for Truman
        among, 151
    electoral weakness in southern
        politics, 55, 74, 123, 137
    instability in voting behavior
        among, 152, 154–155, 188
    as institutional activists, 186n153,
        188n157
    as organized voting bloc, 144
    as political threat to southern
        officials, 21, 26, 28
    political weakness during
        Reconstruction among, 150
    Republican interest in votes of, 155,
        157n55
    as threat to white advantages, 22,
        26, 39
Aid to Dependent Children (ADC),
    149
Alabama, 31, 37, 42, 47, 54,
    128–130, 139

Albany, Georgia, 17, 23, 79, 109,
    110, 197, 211
    explanation for defeat in, 96, 197
    movement campaign in, 92–96
    SCLC joins local struggle, 93
Allen, Ivan, Jr., 87
Almond, J. Lindsay, 65
Amenta, Edwin, 14
Americans for the Preservation of the
    White Race (APWR), 43, 68. *See
    also* segregationist organizations
Andrews, Kenneth, 131, 206
animal rights movement, 3
Anniston, Alabama, 165
Anti-Defamation League, 42, 47
anti-lynching legislation, 73, 148
Anti-Saloon League, 3
Atlanta, Georgia, 47, 84, 87–92, 113,
    120, 139, 197
    political alignments in, 88
    segregationists in, 87–89
    vulnerable economic elites in, 109
Atlanta Negro Voters League, 88
attentiveness, 175, 207, 209
    to civil rights, 170, 175
    and civil rights movement
        outcomes, 18, 175, 192, 198–199
    general lack of, 201
    movement actions to stimulate, 18,
        34, 143n2, 183, 188, 200

235